SŪQ

GEERTZ ON THE MARKET

HAU
Books

HAU Books are published by the
Society for Ethnographic Theory (SET)

www.haubooks.org

SŪQ

GEERTZ ON THE MARKET

Clifford Geertz

Edited and introduced by Lawrence Rosen

HAU Books
Chicago

Cover: Detail from Figure 5, "Sūq: The Bazaar Economy in Sefrou" by Clifford Geertz.

Cover design: Daniele Meucci
Layout design: Deepak Sharma, Prepress Plus
Typesetting: Prepress Plus (www.prepressplus.in)

ISBN: 978-1-912808-98-4 [paperback]
ISBN: 978-1-914363-00-9 [PDF]
LCCN: 2022944233

Hau Books
Chicago Distribution Center
11030 S. Langley Ave.
Chicago, Il 60628
www.haubooks.org

Hau Books publications are printed, marketed, and distributed by The University of Chicago Press.
www.press.uchicago.edu

Printed in the United States of America on acid-free paper.

Contents

Introduction

Lawrence Rosen

Sefrou, Morocco, 1965: In his search for an appropriate venue for his anthropological fieldwork, Clifford Geertz arrived in Sefrou, Morocco, and proceeded to the office of the local pasha to inquire as to the possibility of doing his research in that small city. The pasha's secretary said that the mayor was busy. Professor Geertz responded that he understood and that he would be happy to wait until the pasha was free. He then sat down and waited patiently.[1]

Sefrou, Morocco, 1987: The town of Sefrou organized a symposium celebrating the work of Clifford Geertz. A banner announcing the event was strung over the main street of the Ville Nouvelle, lectures were delivered in the riad *(small palace), which had been built by a ruler in the late nineteenth century, and festive meals and performances took place in various locations over several days. The town administration later published two books with the lectures delivered during the event.*

Two vignettes about Clifford Geertz and his work in Morocco. The first may seem rather anodyne, but I have heard it told and retold by many in Sefrou with wonder and approval. Why? Because, knowing that Geertz was an important American professor, they are amazed that he simply waited for the pasha to be free to receive him. Any Frenchman, they

1. Si Bekkai Lahbil was the pasha of Sefrou and the first minister of the interior of an independent Morocco. His biography is recounted in Lahbil (1999).

say, would have insisted on seeing the official immediately. The story of Geertz's deferential behavior is of a piece with stories that used to be told of Prince Muhammad VI (now king) who, so it goes, once pulled into a gas station and actually paid for his fuel (rather than demanding it for free, in line with his status as a royal personage) or who allowed a woman driver to pass ahead even when he had the right of way and could have asserted his noble prerogative. For both prince and professor, humility and respect were taken as signs of admirable character.

The second vignette is equally striking, albeit in a different way. Anthropologists have been honored by nations depicting their portraits on postage stamps — Bronislaw Malinowski (New Guinea), Franz Boas (Chad), Paul Rivet (Ecuador), Margaret Mead and Ruth Benedict (USA) — while David Aberle was honored by Navajo elders participating at his funeral and Keith Basso by Apache chiefs. But where else has a small town allocated resources for a public event and several publications relating to an anthropologist's work among them? Where else have they brought the king's close advisor and other high-ranking officials to participate in the seminars? It is a mark of both the town's respect for Geertz's work and the way in which he engaged people in the region that his modesty and his accomplishment should have received such notice.[2]

Clifford Geertz first arrived in Morocco in the early 1960s. Following years of research in several parts of Indonesia, he and his wife, anthropologist Hildred Geertz, had sought a field site somewhere in the Muslim world as the basis for a comparative study. They had considered Pakistan, but with two young children they needed a place that was both safe and accessible. After a survey of various sites, they settled on the small city of Sefrou, located fifteen miles south of Fez on the edge of the Middle Atlas Mountains, a town of some 25,000–30,000 inhabitants that also served as central market and administrative hub for a large, mainly Berber tribal hinterland.[3] The work stretched over a number of years, included the independent studies of several students working in the region and elsewhere in Morocco, and came to embrace

2. The celebration of Geertz's work by the city of Sefrou resulted in several publications by the municipality (*Développement local et aménagement* 1989; Association Marocaine pour la Recherche Historique 1999; Jennan and Zerhouni 2000).

3. Sefrou has been the subject of several studies by geographers, including Guibbert and Benhalima (1982) and Benhalima (1987).

a wide range of topics with which both Geertzes had already established their reputations.[4]

Clifford Geertz had focused his Indonesian work on two substantive domains and a broad theoretical arc. His research in Java concentrated on religion, particularly the ways in which nominally Muslim believers divided into three groups representing varying degrees and forms of syncretism. He also studied the Javanese marketplace at a time when American development theory was asking why certain countries (e.g., Japan) were able to "take off" while others seemed to be held back. Together with his book *Agricultural Involution* on the agricultural history of the archipelago, Geertz suggested that the intensification of Dutch colonial extractive demands allowed for absorption into the rural labor force of ever-increasing numbers of people and the subdivision of tasks that resulted in a form of shared poverty. The marketplace not only reflected the economic aspects of relative stasis but, from the perspective of a cultural anthropologist, enfolded and animated a wide array of concepts about persons, relationships, and the symbolic meaning of their presentation.[5]

It was on the basis of these highly detailed studies that Geertz constructed his more extended theoretical work. Arguing that our species developed the capacity to generate symbols that serve both as "models of and models for" our relationships and worldview, Geertz showed that through intensive on-site studies it is possible to unpack the ways in which people grasp both the mundane and the ineffable. By the time he arrived in Morocco these more theoretical essays, later collected in *The Interpretation of Cultures* (Geertz 1973), had already marked him as a major figure in and beyond the discipline of anthropology.

As with his Indonesian studies, in Morocco Geertz took a very wide view of the social and cultural life arrayed before him. In his extensive fieldnotes, his letters to friends and colleagues, and the recollections of his students and interlocutors, Geertz's belief in the interconnections among all aspects of a culture showed him eager to study everything

---

4. Writings of the saint whose shrine is located in a nearby Middle Atlas village to which Geertz refers have recently been translated in Yusi (2019).
5. Geertz's study of the Indonesian market was the subject of *Peddlers and Princes* (Geertz 1963) and figured as well in *The Social History of an Indonesian Town* (Geertz 1965). His response to critics of the Indonesian market studies can be found in Geertz (1978). His book on the agricultural history of Indonesia is *Agricultural Involution* (Geertz 1969).

from kinship and marriage patterns to demographic changes, political history, and the impact of local poets, Jewish traders, and saintly lineages. Thus when Geertz began a detailed examination of the marketplace (souk, Ar. *sūq*), after years of intensive study of colloquial Arabic and with numerous connections to informants from very diverse backgrounds, it was with the broadest of cultural knowledge and curiosity that he approached his subject.[6]

Fairly early on in his fieldwork Geertz had sought out an elderly man named Moulay Rachid al-Adluni, himself a descendant of the Prophet, scion of an old Sefroui family, and, as head of the café owners in town, the man to whom disputants in that market arena turned for counsel and mediation. Through him Geertz not only began to study the structure of the marketplace but to sort through, in extraordinary detail, the players and relationships that marked this critical public domain. Combining similarly meticulous work on the charitable mortmain system (*ḥabus*) that controlled numerous marketplace structures and resources as well as spending many weeks transcribing land records at the central registry in Fez, Geertz was prepared, on his return to Sefrou in the fall of 1968, to undertake a full-scale survey of the souk. In a letter to me dated October 27, 1968, he wrote:

> As far as projects go, the main one has been a store-by-store mapping of all the stores and craft ateliers (as well as major institutions — mosques, *zawias* [Sufi brotherhoods], *hammams* [Moorish baths], *ferrans* [public ovens], etc.) in town with their type, owner's name, and his origins, which I have been doing with a literate Sussi storekeeper [people from the southern part of Morocco, noted for their entrepreneurship] who goes around and asks, and then we work it out together. … [A]side for [sic] the hard data on shops and shopkeepers, it is giving me a detailed physical knowledge of the Medina [old walled portion of the city] such as I have never had before (I also go around after we've mapped with Sussi to see what we've been doing concretely). After I finish it — I'm almost done — five or six hundred

6. Geertz's souk essay was translated into French (Geertz 2003) and preceded by an introduction by Daniel Cefaï (2003). In addition to *Islam Observed* (Geertz 1968), Geertz wrote a number of pieces that elaborated on the findings contained in his souk essay (see, especially, Geertz 1983, 1995, 2012). Market studies in Morocco that are valuable additions to the subject include Kapchan (1996) and Waterbury (1972).

> stores or so, so far — I want to choose representatives on the basis of it and get occupational histories, organization of the trade, etc.[7]

Two points stand out from this brief passage. First, Geertz was assiduous in collecting detailed information from numerous sources. Indeed, given his preferred form of writing — the extended essay — he had, on occasion, been questioned as to the extent of the data upon which he based his ethnographic interpretations. Thus, when the time came to prepare the volume in which his work on the market first appeared, *Meaning and Order in Moroccan Society* (co-authored with Hildred Geertz and myself), one reason for the book's very detailed content was to demonstrate the high level of minutiae on which he based all of his work and to free each of us to write more interpretive pieces later while pointing to the mass of data contained in the collective volume (Geertz, Geertz, and Rosen 1979).[8]

Unlike in the study of the Indonesian marketplace, in his Moroccan work Geertz was not bound by a dominant theory of the day (e.g., "take-off" theory), even though he was attentive to a variety of economists' theories. Nevertheless, many of the themes he struck have profound implications for economic theorists. A key feature of the market study was what Geertz called the search for information. Where prices are not fixed, where multiple systems of weights and measures operate simultaneously, and where the ordinary buyer is constantly challenged to learn about the quality and timing of the goods on offer, it is essential for Moroccans to cast a wide net in their quest for relevant data. But

7. This letter is part of the Clifford Geertz Papers, Hanna Holborn Gray Special Collections Research Center, Regenstein Library, University of Chicago. The Geertz papers housed at the Institute for Advanced Study, Princeton University, contain mostly internal documents, though a few entries relate to seminars touching on Geertz's work in Morocco.
8. *Meaning and Order in Moroccan Society* was aptly subtitled *Three Essays in Cultural Analysis* (Geertz 1979). It contained a general chapter on social identity, which, like the volume's introduction, was written by Lawrence Rosen, and Hildred Geertz's essay on family ties, together with her detailed analysis of the 1960 Sefrou census for which all of the original census forms, like the land records for the region, were collected by all three authors. A photo essay by Paul Hyman also graced the volume. Sefrou forms the basis for much of the work by the present editor, Lawrence Rosen (see, for example, Rosen 1984, 1989, 2000, 2002, 2008, 2016, 2018, 2023).

where economists may have focused solely on a narrow band of market information, Geertz, having already learned so much about other facets of Sefrou society, appreciated that a similar quest for information also informed each Moroccan's search for reliable persons with whom to establish a wide range of relationships. He wrote:

> The very difficult of [obtaining reasonably reliable information] in a diffuse, highly personal, highly fractionated setting without the aid of settled standards, unambiguous signals, or believable statistics raises the natural enough desire not to operate in the dark to the level of a ruling passion and heightens enormously the utility of even partially succeeding. … [S]earch is the paramount economic activity, the one upon which virtually everything else turns, and much of the apparatus of the marketplace is concerned with making it practicable. (Geertz 1979: 215–16)

In the constant negotiation of their social ties, Moroccans thus give evidence of the proposition uttered by a Muslim figure in a Joseph Conrad novel: "In the variety of knowledge lies safety."

While the market may, in certain respects, look (as Geertz says) like "an unbroken confusion," a place characterized by the "promiscuous tumbling in the public realm of varieties of men kept carefully partitioned in the private one," the ever-present search for information finds meaning not only in the quest for secure socioeconomic ties but for consonance with the broader sphere of morality and religion. The point of entry for Geertz into these connections resides in language. Combining his own intellectual heritage in the works of the American pragmatists, Wittgensteinian linguistics, and a personal penchant for creating a world of meaning through the terms by which we seek to capture it, Geertz focused on the concepts that inform the search for information in social and economic life. He sought not a simple vocabulary of marketplace concepts but what he called "a communication model of the bazaar economy," whether in his quest for the implications of the root term for truthfulness (*ṣ-d-q*); in the overtones attendant on *klam*, the concept of control through language ("not just an attribute people have; it is a force they wield" [Geertz 1979: 202]); or in the multiple terms used to appraise another's credibility and reliability. And it is through the tangle of such concepts that he saw the marketplace as a sphere of enacted beliefs, moral propositions, and social evaluations that extend beyond and are themselves rendered comprehensible by the multiple domains they conjoin.

Thus, for Geertz the boundaries of a cultural system — like our means for trying to grasp it — are necessarily blurred yet brought into greater focus precisely by their socially pervasive overtones. He could, therefore, argue that the Muslim *umma* (Community of Believers) *is* the bazaar, that by stabilizing occupational groupings the *zawia* (religious brotherhood) and the souk "were separated only by a doorsill," or that, in the larger cultural system, the *zeṭṭāṭ* (protection) afforded a rural trader so condensed the personas of big men as to constitute a veritable "fusion of their public selves." Like those he was studying, Geertz did not concentrate on such concepts as abstract propositions but as the very tools through which, in the hustle-bustle of everyday engagement, act and word give meaning to one another.

In his comparative work, Geertz observed the strengths and the vulnerabilities of both Morocco and Indonesia — whether the repressive Days of Lead occasioned by the king in the former or the massacre of political/ethnic opponents in the latter.[9] In his self-reflective Frazer Lecture he could therefore write:

> Such, indeed, are the perils of trying to write history as it happens, as I was, in part, attempting to do. The world will not stand still till you complete your paragraph, and the most you can do with the future is sense its imminence. What comes, comes: the important thing is whether, when it comes, it makes any sense as an outgrowth of the directive processes you think you have seen. History, it has been said, may not repeat itself but it does rhyme. And from that point of view, looking back from what I see now to what I saw then, though I am both worried and disheartened (I had hoped for better), I don't feel particularly embarrassed, chastened, defensive, or apologetic. Sensing rain, I may have gotten a flood; but it was, at least, a corroborative one. However unformed and gathering the clouds where then, and however uncertain I was about what to make of them, they were real. And so, it now turns out, was the storm they portended. (Geertz 2005: 10)

Nearly sixty years have passed since Geertz arrived in Sefrou, but while much has changed, much has remained familiar. A city that

9. Among the useful accounts of Geertz's overall work, including discussions of his Moroccan studies, are Inglis (2000), Shweder and Good (2005), and Slyomovics (2010).

numbered 25,000–30,000 upon his arrival now numbers over 80,000; a countryside that was beginning to be depopulated has now become strikingly so. Sefrou is now a larger administrative center and, emptied of its substantial Jewish population, somewhat less diverse.[10] But it is also still the market center for its people and their hinterland, and a key source of urban experience for those who enter and exit it with great ease. More to the point, the conceptual apparatus to which Geertz directed our attention continues to inform the perceptions and relationships he so elegantly analyzed. His words still have resonance, as when he noted: "Nothing if not diverse, Middle Eastern society, and Moroccan society as a frontier variant … copes with diversity by distinguishing with elaborate precision the contexts (marriage, diet, worship, education) within which men are separated by their dissimilitude and those (work, friendship, politics, trade) where, however warily and however conditionally, men are connected by their differences" (Geertz 1979: 141). And it is in those differences — within Sefrou and the reader's grasp of it — that the fascination we share with Clifford Geertz and the people he so deeply respected continues to reverberate.

Acknowledgements

Particular thanks for assistance in preparing this volume go to Karen Blu and Hylton White for all their help in making this seminal work available to a new generation of readers.

References

Assaraf, Robert. 2005. *Une certaine histoire des Juifs du Maroc, 1860–1999*. Paris: Brodard & Taupin.

10. A number of scholars, Moroccan Muslims among them, have focused attention on interfaith relations, referring at times to the Jewish community of Sefrou. Among them are Kenbib (2016), Boum (2013), Assaraf (2005), Assaraf and Abitbol (1998), and Stillman (1973, 1988). For the life and works of the former chief rabbi of Sefrou, Rabbi David Ovadia, see Shalom Bar-Asher (2010). An online source for conversations and remembrances of the Sefrou Jewish community can be found at Dafina.net.

Assaraf, Robert, and Michel Abitbol, eds. 1998. *Perception et réalités au Maroc: Rélations Judéo-Musulmanes*. Casablanca: Crim.

Association Marocaine pour la Recherche Historique (Rabat). 2000. *Archives et écriture de l'histoire du Maroc: XIème Colloque de Sefrou (19–21 Mars 1999)*. Publication du Conseil Municipal de Sefrou 10. Sefrou: Association Marocaine pour la Recherche Historique.

Bar-Asher, Shalom. 2010. "Ovadia, David," In *Encyclopedia of Jews of the Islamic World*, edited by Norman A. Stillman. Leiden: Brill, 2010.

Benhalima, Hassan. 1987. *Petites villes traditionnelles et mutation socio-économiques au Maroc, le cas de Sefrou: Étude de géographie urbane*. Publications de la Faculté des lettres et des sciences humaines de Rabat, Série thèses et mémoires 14. Rabat: Imprimerie de Fédala.

Boum, Aomar. 2013. *Memories of absence: How Muslims remember Jews in Morocco*. Stanford: Stanford University Press.

Cefaï, Daniel. 2003. "Le souk de Sefrou: Analyse culturelle d'une forme sociale." In *Le souk de Sefrou: Sur l'économie du bazar*, by Clifford Geertz, 1–58. Paris: Editions Bouchène.

Développement local et aménagement de l'espace au Maroc: Le cas de Sefrou et de sa région, organisé des 17, 18, 19, 20 mars 1988. 1989. Fez: Imprimerie al-Balabil.

Geertz, Clifford. 1963. *Peddlers and princes: Social change and economic modernization in two Indonesian towns*. Chicago: University of Chicago Press.

Geertz, Clifford. 1965. *The social history of an Indonesian town*. Cambridge, MA: MIT Press.

Geertz, Clifford. 1968. *Islam observed*. New Haven: Yale University Press.

Geertz, Clifford. 1969. *Agricultural involution: The processes of ecological change in Indonesia*. Chicago: University of Chicago Press.

Geertz, Clifford. 1973. *The interpretation of cultures*. New York: Basic Books.

Geertz, Clifford. 1978. "The bazaar economy: Information and search in peasant marketing." *American Economic Review* 68 (2): 28–32.

Geertz, Clifford. 1979. "Suq: The bazaar economy in Sefrou." In *Meaning and order in Moroccan society: Three essays in cultural analysis*, edited by Clifford Geertz, Hildred Geertz, and Lawrence Rosen, 123–313. Cambridge: Cambridge University Press.

Geertz, Clifford. 1983. *Local knowledge: further essays in interpretive anthropology*. New York: Basic Books.

Geertz, Clifford. 1995. *After the fact: Two countries, Four decades, One anthropologist*. Cambridge, MA: Harvard University Press.

Geertz, Clifford. 2003. *Le souk de Sefrou: Sur l'économie du bazar*. Paris: Editions Bouchène.

Geertz, Clifford. 2005. "Shifting aims, moving targets: On the anthropology of religion." *Journal of the Royal Anthropological Institute* 11 (1): 1–15.

Geertz, Clifford. 2012. *Life among the anthros and other essays*. Princeton: Princeton University Press.

Geertz, Clifford, Hildred Geertz, and Lawrence Rosen. 1979. *Meaning and order in Moroccan society: Three essays in cultural analysis*. Cambridge: Cambridge University Press.

Guibbert, Jean-Jacques, and Hassan Benhalima. 1982. *Sefrou de desserte locale au relais pour le drainage*. Dakar: Enda.

Inglis, Fred. 2000. *Clifford Geertz*. Cambridge: Polity Press.

Jennan, Lahsen, and Mohammed Zerhouni, eds. 2000. *Sefrou: Mémoire, territoires et terroirs, des moments, des lieux et des hommes: récits et témoignages: hommage à Clifford Geertz*. Fez: Commission Culturelle.

Kapchan, Deborah. 1996. *Gender on the market: Moroccan women and the revoicing of tradition*. Philadelphia: University of Pennsylvania Press.

Kenbib, Mohammed. 2016. *Juifs et musulmans au Maroc: Des origines à nos jours*. Paris: Tallendier.

Lahbil, Achour Bekkaï. 1999. *Si Bekkai: Rendez-vous avec l'histoire*. Rabat: Imprimeries Mithaq al-Maghrib.

Rosen, Lawrence. 1984. *Bargaining for reality: The construction of social relations in a Muslim community*. Chicago: University of Chicago Press.

Rosen, Lawrence. 1989. *The anthropology of justice: Law as culture in Islamic society*. New York: Cambridge University Press.

Rosen, Lawrence. 2000. *The justice of Islam: Comparative perspectives on Islamic law and society*. Oxford: Oxford University Press.

Rosen, Lawrence. 2002. *The culture of Islam: Changing aspects of contemporary Muslim life*. Chicago: University of Chicago Press.

Rosen, Lawrence. 2008. *Varieties of Muslim experience: Encounters with Arab cultural and political life*. Chicago: University of Chicago Press.

Rosen, Lawrence. 2016. *Two Arabs, a Berber, and a Jew: Entangled lives in Morocco*. Chicago: University of Chicago Press.

Rosen, Lawrence. 2018. *Islam and the rule of justice: Image and reality in Muslim law and culture*. Chicago: University of Chicago Press.

Rosen, Lawrence. 2023. *Encounters with Islam: Studies in the anthropology of Muslim cultures*. Cambridge: Cambridge University Press.

Shweder, Richard A., and Byron Good, eds. 2005. *Clifford Geertz by his colleagues*. Chicago: University of Chicago Press.

Slyomovics, Susan, ed. 2010. *Clifford Geertz in Morocco*. London: Routledge.

Stillman, Norman A. 1973. "The Sefrou remnant." *Jewish Social Studies* 35 (3/4): 255–63.

Stillman, Norman A. 1988. *The language and culture of the Jews of Sefrou, Morocco: An ethnolinguistic study*. Manchester: University of Manchester.

Waterbury, John. 1972. *North for the trade: The life and times of a Berber merchant*. Berkeley: University of California Press.

Yusi, Al-Hasan ibn Masʿūd. 2019. *The discourses*. Vol. 1, *Reflections on history, sufism, theology, and literature*. Translated by Justin Stearns. New York: New York University Press.

On Sefrou: the market in context*

The study

The movement of anthropologists toward a concern with complex agrarian societies has accelerated over the past quarter century until now it probably accounts for the bulk of the work in the field. Yet many problems of method, theory, and data presentation remain, and the sense that the classical monograph forms of anthropology - the "people" study (Nuer, Tikopia, Trobriand, Navajo) and the "community" study (Chan Kom, Amazon Town, Ramah, Lesu) - are awkward and ungainly in this context grows steadily deeper. Studies of "the Chinese," "the Brazilians," or "the Arabs," though suggestive, seem to claim too much for local findings; studies of this or that village, town, or settlement as such, though informative, seem caught in a kind of data parochialism. Committed by training and heritage, and in most cases by conviction, to microsociological investigation, anthropologists working in places like India, Mexico, or (the case at hand) North Africa find themselves faced with what looks like a Hobson's choice between dissipating the circumstantiality their narrowed focus provides in order to escape a sense of inconsequence and resigning themselves to adding a few footnotes to broader streams of scholarship in which they play no central role.

---

* This brief account of Sefrou has been adapted by Lawrence Rosen for this volume, from the original introduction, co-authored by Clifford Geertz and Lawrence Rosen, to *Meaning and Order in Moroccan Society*. The present tense should be read as referring to 1979.

Matters are not, perhaps, all that desperate. Not only do important contributions continue to be made within the older formats that are neither provincial nor globalistic - as witness, so far as Morocco is concerned, David Hart's "people" study of the Aith Waryaghar and Kenneth Brown's "community" study of Salé - but a growing number of problem-oriented works - Dale Eickelman's on maraboutism, Vincent Crapanzano's on popular psychiatry, for example - manage to connect local findings with general considerations with great effectiveness.[1] Yet, the search for more adequate ways to render the special contribution of nook-and-cranny anthropological work to the wider, multidisciplinary effort to comprehend ... Morocco ... the Maghreb ... the Middle East ... the Third World ... the Modern World Order ... continues, because new approaches to new issues in new settings demand them. As in any other field, genres evolve as intentions do.

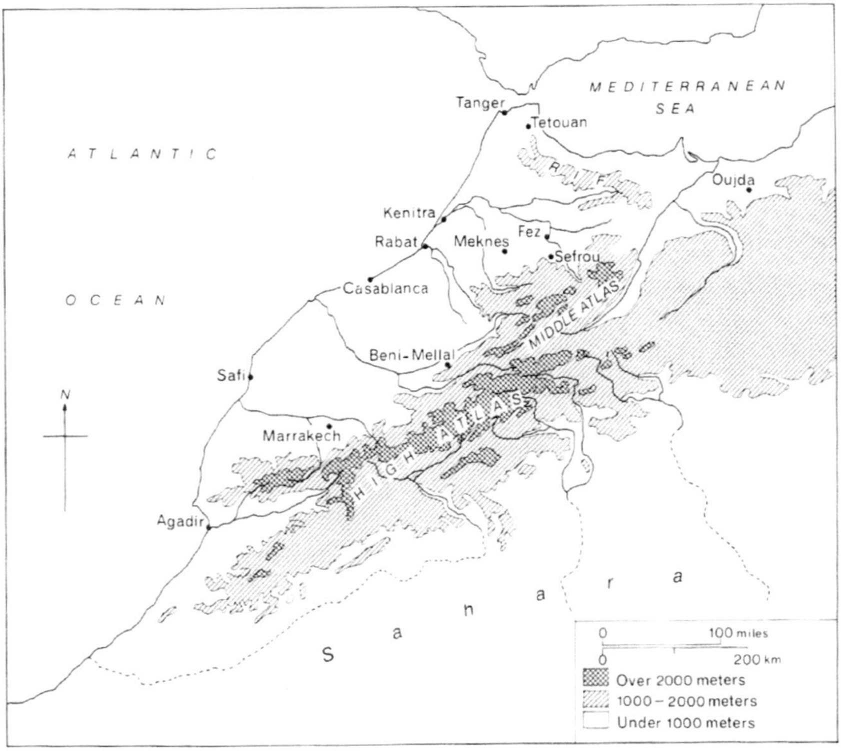

Map 1. Morocco

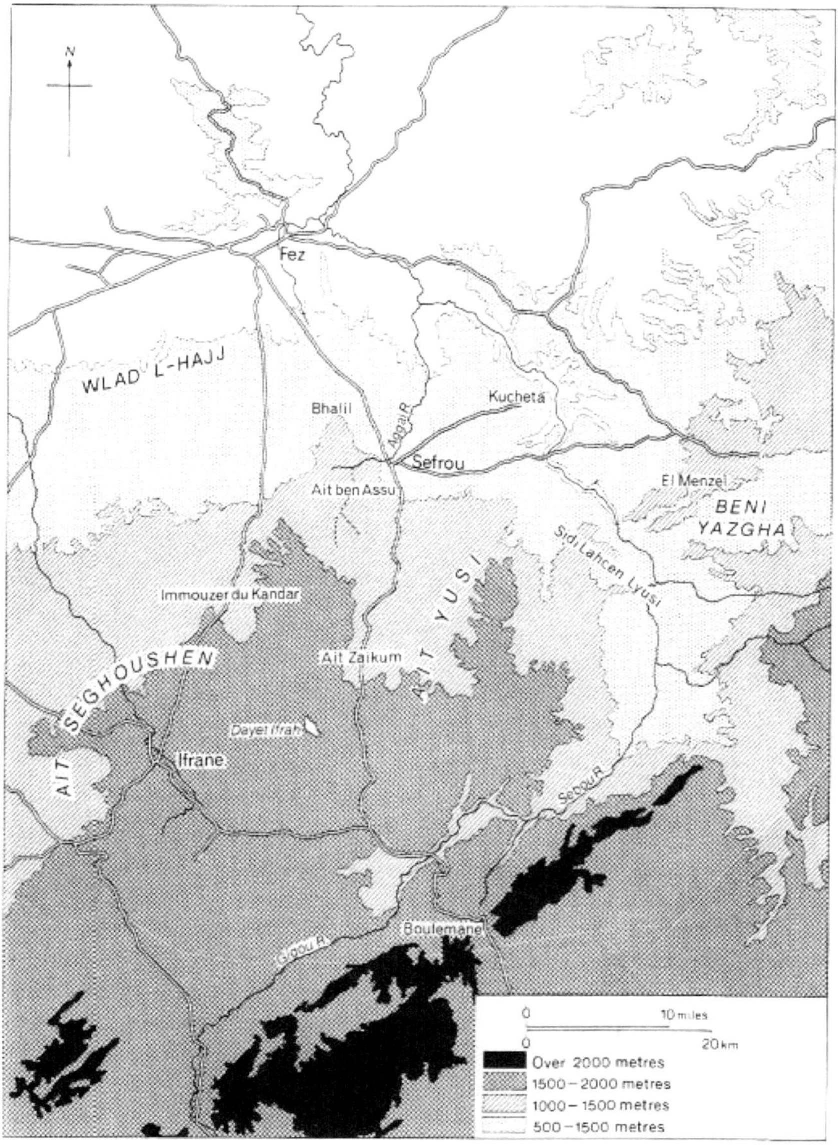

Map 2. The region of Sefrou

In such terms, the present work, in its organization and in the assemblage of ideas that in an overall way animates it, is but another attempt, hardly final and in no way ideal, to find a form in which particular facts can be made to speak to general concerns. The research on which it was based was mostly conducted between 1965 and 1971 in a single small-city-and-dependent-environs of north central Morocco: Sefrou (see Maps 1-4).

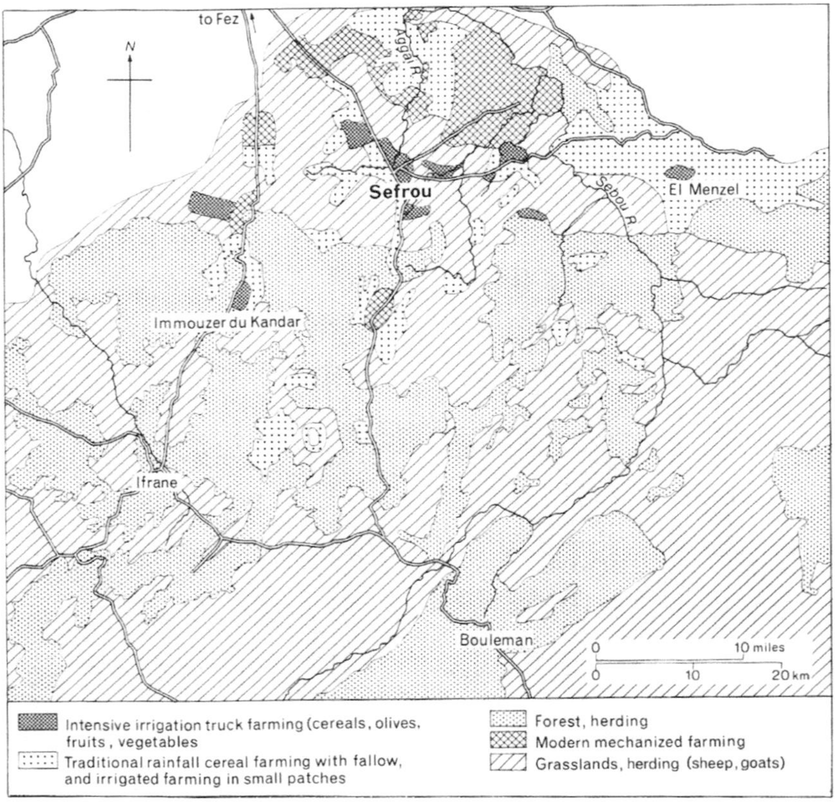

Map 3. The region of Sefrou: the economy

The place

Sefrou is the name for both the city and the countryside that surrounds it. Although finer discriminations, geographical and social, are

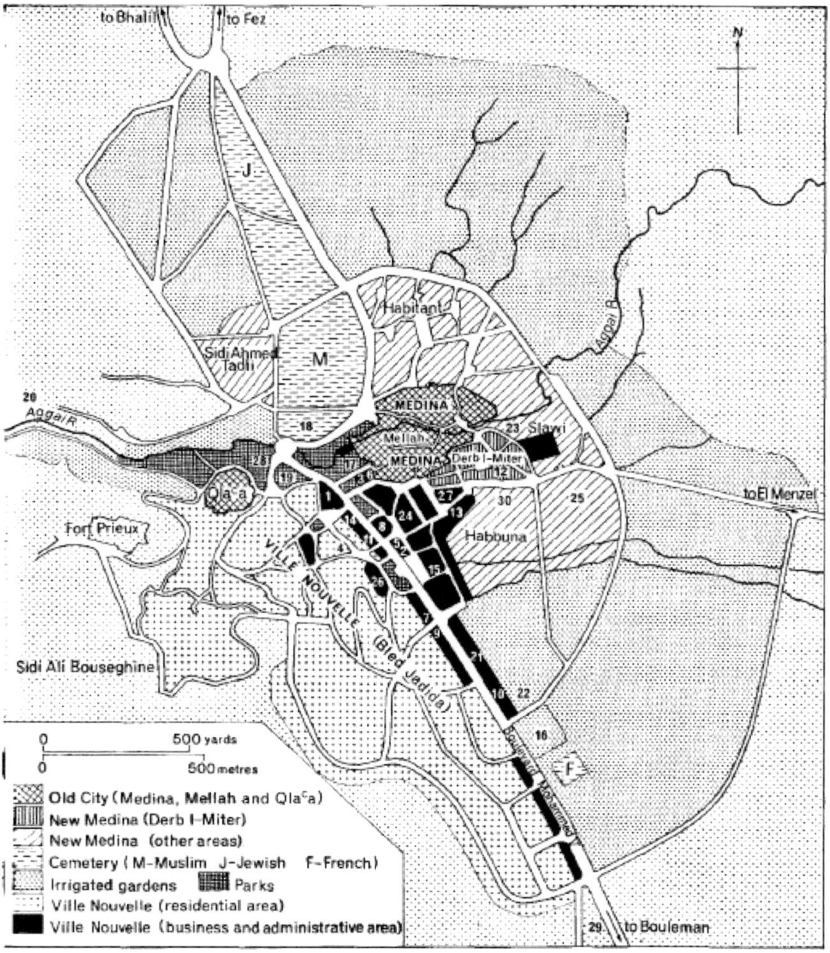

Map 4. The town of Sefrou: major areas. *Key:* 1. Super-Qaid's office; 2. Qaid's office; 3. Pasha's office; 4. Police station; 5. Civil court; 6. Qadi's court; 7. Gendarmerie; 8. Rural tax office; 9. Forestry and irrigation office; 10. Fire house; 11. Post office; 12. Nadir's office; 13. Hospital; 14. Bank; 15. Movie house; 16. Soccer field; 17. Swimming pool; 18. Bus and taxi station; 19. Tennis club; 20. Power station; 21. Livestock market; 22. Vegetable market; 23. Dry-goods and rug market; 24. College; 25. Lycée; 26. Former Jewish school; 27. Jewish school; 28. Public prayer ground (mṣellā); 29. Military barracks; 30. Prison.

constantly employed in this extremely variegated region, residents usually apply the generic term *bled* to embrace the whole of it. Ideally, the term means "region" or "locality," and insofar as a locality can refer to a wide range of entities bled can, depending on the context, mean "city" and "country," "town" and "village." But the term bled projects a deeper sense of place than the merely locational: It also conveys a sense of relation between men and the landscape they inhabit. It is the region from which a particular individual or group draws its nurture, its sustenance, its most distinctive traits and ties. To identify someone as being from bled Sefrou - to say he is a "Sefroui"- is to imply those characteristics of manner, knowledge, relationships, and modes of interaction that have come to be associated with it, to connect a "who" with a "where."

This sense of place as an index or source of social identity is more directly implied in the idiom *mūl l-bled* (pl. *mwālīn l-bled*). Mul means "owner," and to speak of someone as mul l-bled, when referring to a given parcel of land, is simply to mean that he has possession or control of that property. But the phrase is also used to refer to the natives of a particular region, the people who characterize - and are characterized by - that place. Virtually every plot of land in the Sefrou region - each garden, field, and irrigation ditch - has a name, and every part of the region has one or more specific designations. To speak of particular individuals or families as mwalin l-bled, however, is to imply that they are the true embodiments of that which is distinctive to the locale, the people who carry its distinguishing qualities with them even when they leave the place or become a minority among the hosts of newcomers. To know a man's origins, the place in which his people are mwalin l-bled, is to know something of the ways he may think, act, and form relationships with others.

Physically, bled Sefrou refers both to the city proper and to the territory for which it constitutes the urban hub. The city of Sefrou is situated near the northern edge of the region just at the point where the foothills of the Middle Atlas Mountains meet the western plain of Morocco. Although the 30,000 inhabitants of the city have important ties to the large metropolis of Fez, which can be reached by a half hour's bus ride to the north, it is toward the south that most of the city's activities have long been directed. Here, in a 30-kilometer-wide strip that cuts through the foothills and plateaus of the Middle Atlas Mountains, lies the territory of the Ait Yusi Berbers. Nearer to the city are found several larger settlements, among them the saintly complex of Sidi Lahcen Lyusi and the Arab-speaking village of Bhalil.

But to see bled Sefrou as a place on the cartographer's map - a roughly bounded area containing various populations and settlement types - is to miss its true character. Bled Sefrou is really a social space - a network of relationships mediated by markets, public institutions, local identities, and densely interwoven bonds of kinship and alliance. No less importantly, it is a conceptual domain - a perceived set of populations, territories, pathways, and meeting places that are intimately, if not always harmoniously, linked to the nurturance and identity of those who live there. As an indigenous conceptual category, bled Sefrou underlines the interdependency, as well as the interaction, of its component parts. It stresses the conceptualization of the region as an arena within which social life is played out through institutions that crosscut internal divisions of geography and society, even as the substance and course of social life are deeply influenced by the contexts in which its various manifestations are found. So conceived, bled Sefrou also presents itself as an appropriate unit for analysis. It establishes, as the subject of study, a cultural field comprising a number of domains and frameworks within which Sefrouis' own concepts of selfhood and social relationship can be explored for their bearing on the organization of collective life.

The landscape

The interplay of environment and culture is one of the basic themes to which anthropologists have devoted themselves. If their studies have established anything, it is that the environment is no mere given, no neutral constant, no passively endured condition. Rather, it is an integral part of man's life-world, as deeply shaped by social conditions as social conditions are mediated by it. The natural setting is more than a context to adapt to, a store of resources to draw on, or a stage on which the drama of social life is played out; the ways in which a civilization works out its relation to its setting over a long period of time makes the environment a vital aspect of that civilization itself. To explore the irrigation or land use patterns of people in the bled Sefrou is to explore how its inhabitants use the available resources, how they make the resources a part of their own social drama, and how their ecological adaptations relate to other aspects of their culture.

The Sefrou region, like most of Morocco, is characterized by a highly irregular and uncertain set of climatic conditions and a wide variety of microenvironments capable of responding quite differently to the alterations of the weather. The French, in grand colonial fashion, simply divided the country into "useful" and "useless" Morocco, a distinction that embraced in the former the wheat lands of the nation's western plain and foothill oases and included in the latter the mountains and deserts surrounding them. But Sefrouis themselves draw a finer distinction among three main ecological zones: the plains (*weṭya*), the mountains (*jabel*), and the piedmont (*dir*).

Extending back from the Atlantic coast almost to the edge of the Middle Atlas Mountains, the Moroccan plains embrace most of the western part of the nation. As the main wheat-growing section of the country it was the area in which colonial farming was most actively pursued, and the foothills lying at its edge were used as winter pasturage by highland tribes until the French began limiting access to these sites. Although subject to wide climatic variations, the plains afford comparatively good conditions for the intensive cultivation of wheat and barley.

The Middle Atlas Mountains begin immediately south of the city of Sefrou. Although they rise in places to peaks of 3,000 meters, the Middle Atlas are mainly composed of a series of forested hills broken in spots by highland plateaus and small protected valleys. Herds of sheep and goats are grazed throughout the zone, and small-scale farming on the more accessible hills and plateaus is interspersed with irrigated cultivation in many of the valleys. The area is less densely populated than the plains, but pockets of more concentrated settlement exist around available sources of water. Of the 55,000 hectares of mountainous terrain in the Sefrou region, only about 10,000 hectares is cultivable land, and much of this must be left fallow in any given year. Overgrazing and extensive wood cutting have sharply reduced the forests near Sefrou, and erosion has become a serious problem.

Lying between the mountains and the plains is the dir, or piedmont zone. The dir - an Arabic term related to *darra* ("to flow copiously, be abundant") and *dirra* ("breast") - is a zone some 10 to 15 kilometers wide that runs along the foot of the mountains just before they join the plains. Here, springs bubble up from beneath the surface to supply a relatively stable source of water for irrigation and larger concentrations of population. It is within this oasis-like zone that all the larger settlements of the area - most notably, the city of Sefrou - are found.

The interaction of these three ecological zones is intimately related to the overall climatic features of the region. The climate of the area is characterized mainly by its variability and unpredictability. For any given feature - temperature, rainfall, hours of sunlight, wind - the range of variation over a series of years is quite extreme. More importantly, perhaps, the variation within each year can be enormous. The response to this situation - by farmers, herdsmen, and merchants alike - takes the cultural form of a complicated set of strategies affecting all domains of life. Diverse crops are planted within a single garden or field to hedge against uncertain weather and markets; rights to fields or pastures are distributed in various micro-ecological niches to spread the risk of changing circumstances; social ties are formed beyond the bounds of kinship or locality to cope with the whole range of environmental and social uncertainties, religious rituals are employed to coerce supernatural aid against the fluctuation of the elements. All these strategies intertwine and have mutual effects extending far beyond the confines of any simply adaptive solution.

The environmental uncertainties themselves are very real. Take, for example, the variation in temperature for a given month over several years. In June of 1958 the mean temperature varied from 87 to 48 degrees Fahrenheit, a range of 39 degrees in a single month. The following year the range was only 7 degrees (66 to 59); the third year, 19 degrees (85 to 66). Equally large fluctuations could be cited for any other month of the year. Indeed, no significantly predictable pattern emerges over longer spans of time. This is not to say that there is no regularity whatsoever, but only that changes of a magnitude that can seriously affect agricultural productivity occur as a matter of course, and the Moroccan farmer must arrange his affairs to compensate for this unpredictability.

The variation in temperature, which has an impact on growing cycles and evaporation rates, is matched by the more serious variation in rainfall. Because most of the plains and mountain regions are unirrigated, crops are dependent not only on the sheer quantity of rain that falls but, more importantly, on when it comes. Both these factors are extraordinarily erratic. For example, over one five-year period the total rainfall in the Sefrou region varied from 379 to 728 millimeters. In October 1956 there was 7 millimeters of rain; the following October there was 105; and in October of the third year, 55 millimeters. The variation is equally great within and among other seasons of the year. It is no comfort to the Moroccan farmer to say that the average rainfall in October of 1956-58 was

55.6 millimeters because the actual distribution of rainfall could never be even roughly guessed in advance.

The consequences of this environmental variation are diverse. Harvests, naturally, fluctuate considerably as the weather shifts. Between 1952 and 1962 the national output of cereals, measured in millions of quintals, was as follows: 22, 32, 36, 28, 30, 18, 25, 26, 21, 10, 22. For a country in which a year's harvest of the staple crop can vary over a range of 26 million quintals (roughly 3 million tons), and where the change from one year to the next may be of the order of 100 percent, this is indeed a precarious situation. True, severe droughts and floods occur infrequently, and the availability of foreign aid has eased some of the insecurity. Most important for our present purposes, however, is the fact that the success or failure of crops is itself unevenly and uncertainly distributed over a given region. Adjoining hillsides in the bled Sefrou may have very different yields in a single year, and people have, therefore, arranged their ties and their concepts of the social world in which they live to account for these events.

To say that the environment suffuses social and cultural life is not to reduce the one to a function of the other or to conceive of the natural setting as a thing apart from social life. Tracing the relationships that surround the approach taken by the Sefrou people to their environment, one can see the importance of a town like Sefrou, which is set in the intermediate dir zone and whose steady supply of water and interstitial position makes it a natural entrepôt for the region. Similarly, one can see how the uncertainties of the environment have influenced the interdependence of all three zones, rendering the bled Sefrou an interacting entity in which simple dichotomies of urban and rural possess little explanatory force. Moreover, one can see that although there is no necessary reason why people of the area have adapted as they have, the environment and their view of it are as much a characteristic part of the social being of the Sefrou people as their kinship, their politics, or their religion. Indeed, the relationship of each of these domains and the commonality of many of their defining features are particularly striking.

Situated in the piedmont, between mountain and plain, and surrounded by a wide expanse of irrigated gardens, the city of Sefrou has often been referred to by travelers as an oasis. In many respects its physical design and setting convey an almost storybook vision of a Middle Eastern city. The old city, or *medina,* is surrounded by a high, crenelated wall pierced in a number of places by gates that were formerly used to seal the city off nightly from the gardens and countryside beyond. Within, the city is further subdivided by a number of quarters and byways. Rows of small shops, specialized trade areas, narrow streets lined by the characterless facades of dwelling places, and all those features - mosques, baths, fountains, ovens - that give to this Islamic city its distinctive urban character are found within the walls. With the exception of a small urban sector, the Qla^{c}a, located just to the west of the medina, Sefrou was, until the beginning of the colonial period, wholely contained within its ramparts.

With the advent of the Protectorate, the design of the city began to change. It was the policy of the Protectorate's first resident general, Lyautey, that the structure of indigenous cities be supplemented, rather than fundamentally altered, by the French presence. Accordingly, a new area, the Ville Nouvelle, was constructed along the southeastern edge of the oasis' gardens. This sector now comprises a long street with cinemas, shops, cafés, and government buildings, as well as a number of residential streets lined by Western-style villas. After World War II, several new residential areas were constructed just outside the walls of the old city. These "new medina" areas contain houses of more traditional design, but the streets, laid out in rectangular pattern, are wide enough to carry the automobiles and trucks that are unable to traverse the narrow streets of the medina proper. Many of the residents of these new medina areas are better off financially than those who continue to live in the old city proper, although some of the oldest and most important families of the city still occupy sections of the medina.

The postwar years also saw a substantial influx of rural people to the city. The poorest of these immigrants tend to reside in the mellah, the former Jewish quarter. Those who can afford to often move later into other sections of the city, including a barracks-like set of structures, called Slawi, originally built to house victims of a flood that occurred in 1950.

Physically, then, the city of Sefrou has long been characterized by the presence of those institutions - economic, cultural, and administrative - that could serve as an urban focus for the surrounding region. The waters of the Aggai River and its network of irrigation canals gave to the city a reliable agricultural baseline that contrasts with the more uncertain supply of rainfall available in the countryside. Far from being a totally self-contained unit closed off from the surrounding hinterland, the city of Sefrou is, and probably always has been, thoroughy intertwined with the ecology and the history of the whole region.

The past

Just as their working of the environment becomes an integral part of the culture and organization of a people's distinctive existence, so too their history - seen not solely as a succession of people, places, and events, but as a gradual alteration of patterns, associations, and concepts - is a vital aspect of their characteristic nature. The history of Sefrou and its region - at least as it bears on an analysis of contemporary social life - situates and indeed serves to explain how the concepts and institutions distinctive to this place in this setting inform the actions of its residents.

The city of Sefrou was probably established in the ninth century, when the founder of Fez, Idris II, is said to have settled there briefly. Not, however, until the latter part of the seventeenth century, with tribal movements and the restructuring of governmental legitimacy, did the Sefrou region begin to crystallize in a still recognizable form. The great Berber dynasties of the eleventh to fifteenth centuries - the Almoravids, the Almohads, and the Merinids - arose from the mountain and desert fringes of the country and, fueled by religious zeal, successively established themselves as the primary forces. Moreover, they helped to establish the pattern of a central government, or *maḵzen,* that was focused on a few major families and that sought - through alliance and military foray, intrigue and negotiation - to maintain solidity at the center and control over the tribes on the periphery. Regions of governmental control and local independence - *bled l- maḵzen* and *bled s-sība* - were not, however, geographically defined because constellations of power were numerous, shifting, and not organized along simply territorial lines. Even when makhzen dominance was amenable to actual enforcement - especially in the major cities - it was constantly subject to internal and external pressures. Rather than hierarchical, the pattern of political organization, from this formative period, became horizontal, and the bases of recruitment, alliance, and power were fractionated and multiple.

The period from the mid-fifteenth to the mid-seventeenth centuries was one of great disequilibrium throughout Morocco. European intrusion and the decline of the last Berber dynasty led to the dissolution of the country into a host of competitive, independent centers of power. Partly in reaction to the Christian intrusion on the coast, partly as a result of the threat to Moroccan civilization posed by the Christian recovery of Spain, and partly owing to intellectual influences from the Middle East, there developed throughout Morocco a number of mystical sects, headed by men (called *murābtīn*) conceived to be divinely inspired and divinely propelled. Although the most important of these maraboutic centers were defeated in the latter part of the seventeenth century, the emergent dynastic regimes sought to reestablish the makhzen on a more solid foundation by fusing the moral intensity of the Berber dynasties and the maraboutic centers with claims of legitimacy based on descent from the Prophet Mohammed. Founded in 1668, the still-ruling Alawite dynasty thus incorporated features of genealogical and charismatic legitimacy while nevertheless constituting a regime that, like its predecessors, was confronted with multiple sources and centers of power and itself only as good as its powers of intrigue and enforcement.

In the early period of the Alawite dynasty, local marabouts continued to threaten the existence of the regime even as they sought to associate themselves with the sources of legitimacy now mobilized around it. In the Sefrou area, for example, a scholar and saint, Sidi Lahcen Lyusi, whose descendants still constitute the main saintly focus of the tribal region surrounding the city, sought to have his own legitimacy as a descendant of the Prophet underwritten by the Alawite sultan.

The seventeenth century was also a period of great movement of the Berber tribes in central Morocco. Propelled, in part, by drought in the Sahara, segments of a loosely organized Berber confederation pushed into the Middle Atlas Mountains and down onto the plains beyond. Separate groupings, hiving off all along the way, settled in the area and engaged the Alawite sultans in battle and alliance as each group sought to establish itself in the area. In the Sefrou region the Ait Yusi tribe predominated, and, like other loosely organized groupings throughout the Middle Atlas, lived in agonistic symbiosis with one another and the settled, mainly Arabic-speaking townsmen of Sefrou and other urban centers.

Contemporary residents of the bled Sefrou are not unmindful of this history, and because many of its institutional features - the sherifian dynasty of the Alawites, the spiritual force of saints, the aggressive individualism of each nodal point in the body politic - are very much a part of their present-day lives, this history is, whether or not they are conscious of its details, very much a part of what they now are. But it is in more recent and more localized events, persons, and periods that the consciousness of the people described in this book was formed, and their delineation of that history points up the contexts in which their own historically based perceptions have been forged.

The decade from 1894 to 1904 is notable to the Sefrou people as the period dominated by Qaid Umar al-Yusi, A Berber from high up in the mountain reaches of the Ait Yusi territory, Umar was one of those rural figures who created a network of alliances of such significance that the makhzen, by officially appointing him as *qaid* ("administrator") of the region, hoped to contain or coopt his power. Umar's appointment followed an all-out fight with a rival Berber contender, after which - in a highly unusual move - he was appointed not only qaid of the region but its urban analogue, *pasha* of the town, as well. His days were those in which caravans still moved through Sefrou to the Sahara, when almost all the Arab townsmen were engaged in some form of agricultural activity, and when a powerful local figure ratified by a weak central government could control the entire region so long as he was able to keep one step ahead of his ever-present rivals.

The assassination of Umar in 1904 came at a time when the Moroccan government, headed by the ineffectual sultan Mulay Abdel Aziz, was under constant pressure from European intrusion. Beginning with the direct incursion of the French in the Casablanca area in 1907 and continuing until the actual formation of the French Protectorate in 1912, the disarray of the makhzen was reinforced, was part of, the widespread political disorder on the local level. The little makhzen of Qaid Umar and the interlocking relations between tradesmen, agriculturalists, and tribesmen that characterized the economy and social organization of his time, were replaced, in this disorderly period, by a weak form of collegial rule by notable families in the city and the oscillation of rural figures competing for the role Umar had formerly played.

But the arrival of the French had unalterably changed such roles. Establishing a kind of colonial police rule through the pasha Lamouri, the French consolidated their control of Sefrou and the Ait Yusi territory and, after World War I, gradually began to obtain the best areas on the plains for colonial farms. A separate European quarter was also constructed alongside the old walled city of Sefrou. The early colonial period saw a greater distinction drawn by the French between the city and the countryside and among various sectors of the population than had characterized the area in earlier times. Later, during the high colonial period of the interwar decades, when the technological and economic impact of the French was more significant, the institutional differentiation of city and countryside, Arab and Berber, became even more important. New marketplaces were constructed in the countryside, new administrative boundaries were drawn throughout the region, the population of the city grew as rural people came in search of jobs and education, and an elaborate infrastructure of roads and communications accelerated the contacts of people within and beyond the city and its surroundings.

Already in the 1930s the first elements of modern Moroccan nationalism were clearly in evidence. The attempt to split Berbers and Arabs by means of the Berber Dahir of 1930, which sought to place the Berbers under customary Berber and French rather than Islamic legal jurisdiction, actually reinforced the ties between city and countryside, and the deposition and exile by the French of the sultan Mohammed V in 1953 coalesced sentiment around the nationalist movement. Some rural people worked with the irregular Army of Liberation, and many of the urban people contributed to the activities of the nationalist political party, Istiqlal. The importance of the Sefrou region to the newly independent government was demonstrated by the fact that, following the return of the exiled sultan Mohammed V and the acquisition of national independence in 1956, the pasha of the city, Si M'barek Bekkai, was appointed the nation's first prime minister, and the qaid of the Ait Yusi, Qaid Lahcen Lyusi, was designated the country's first minister of interior.

In the years since Independence the city has grown at an accelerated pace, as rural migrants have sought what schooling and employment are available in the city. Most of the Jews of Sefrou, once a major presence there, have departed since Independence, seeking in the cities of the Atlantic coast and abroad the opportunities Berber immigrants now seek in Sefrou.

Through these periods of rapid but clearly distinguishable change the present inhabitants of the Sefrou region have come to receive and work with the categories and conventions, political forms and cultural concepts that inform their view of their social world. It is not just that the aged remember a time when rival Berber tribesmen shot at one another from the city's rooftops or that today's youths focus their ambitions on obtaining jobs in the national bureaucracy. It is, rather, that the concerns with which the institutions of kinship, marriage, trade, and the like are approached vary with the historical career of the groupings involved, and hence the means by which culture is shared and interpreted within these groupings are linked to the changing circumstances of experience and perception. But for all that, the institutions of social life and the categories of persons and relationships employed remain common among the various generations and segments of the Sefrou population, and it is in the flexible application of these concepts and institutions that the shared distinctiveness of the region is to be found.

Together, the co-authors of the original version the book of which this essay formed a part caught a particular society in a particular place at a particular time. From that encounter, as unique to us as to those we confronted, we have tried to construct a picture - or, more accurately, a related set of pictures - of what that society is like, how it got to be that way, and, so far as we can figure it out, why. To this last question - unanswerable, unavoidable, and the one by which such enterprises as this are justified - our response has been to conceive of social order as meaningful form and to conceive of meaningful form as embedded in the life, from one angle deeply singular, from another deeply familiar, the Sefrouis live.

Transcription note*

The problem of transcribing spoken Arabic remains a vexed one. The orthographies that exist are designed for classical Arabic, which, for the most part, exists only in literary form. One is caught between what one hears said and what one sees written, and thus - a worse fate yet - between the passions of linguists and those of philologists. Here, we have sought to render what we have heard, with the exception that minor regional dialectical variations - rather pronounced in Sefrou - have been ignored for a Moroccan standard that, though it does not yet entirely exist, is rapidly coming to do so.

The transcription is that used in the most generally accessible Arabic-English dictionary, H. Wehr's fine *Dictionary of Modem Written Arabic* (edited by J. M. Cowan, Ithaca, 1976), with some adjustments to the special demands of Moroccan colloquial. The most important of these are the introduction of a *g* where necessary; the use of *e* for the short vowel represented in Wehr as *a* in cases where, as is common in Moroccan, that vowel is even further shortened so as to become a neutral midvowel, rather like the *e* in "glasses," the *u* in "butter," or the *e* in "bet"; and the omission of *ṯ*, *ḏ*, and *ẓ*, which do not appear in Moroccan speech. Definite articles are transcribed as *l-*, *š-*, *b-l-*, *d-*, *j-*, *r-*, and *ṭ-*.

In order not to clutter the text with italics and diacritics, Arabic words are strictly transcribed in each essay only the first time they appear, except when their appearances are widely separated. Otherwise they are rendered unitalicized in the most common English orthography for Arabic, in which neither vowel length nor consonant strength (e.g., *s*

* Reproduced from *Meaning and Order in Moroccan Society.*

against *ṣ, h* against *ḥ)* is indicated, and *k* is *kh, s* is *sh, ḡ* is *gh.* As the strict transcriptions are indicated in the index, this system should make it possible for the Arabist to determine what the word in fact "really" is, while leaving the non-Arabist free from distracting technicalities.

Neither place names nor personal names are strictly transcribed; the former are rendered as one is likely to find them represented on maps. Berber words are indicated by a preceding *Br.*; classical Arabic forms by a *cl.*; Hebrew words, by an *Heb.*

We are indebted to a number of our Arabist colleagues for generous help in these matters, but leave them unnamed for fear of implicating them in the errors that remain.

Suq: the bazaar economy in Sefrou

Clifford Geertz

The bazaar as an object of study

Characterizing whole civilizations in terms of one or another of their leading institutions is a dubious procedure, but if one is going to indulge in it for the Middle East and North Africa the bazaar is surely a prime candidate. Generations of observers, native and foreign, historical and ethnological, have seen in the bazaar's fat grocers and bent tailors, ingratiating rug sellers and elusive moneylenders, the image of life as it is lived in that part of the world. Goitein discerns a "large and powerful merchant class" rising "all over the Middle East" as early as the eighth and ninth centuries, a class that, by the tenth through twelfth "was the main bearer of Muslim civilization, including its Jewish and (Oriental) Christian enclaves."[1] What the mandarin bureaucracy was for classical China and the caste system for classical India – the part most evocative of the whole – the bazaar was for the more pragmatic societies of the classical Middle East.

Yet for all that, the intensity of scholarly attention directed toward the mandarin bureaucracy or the caste system, running to hundreds of titles in both cases, has not been even remotely approached with respect to the Middle Eastern bazaar. There are a few data-collection-type reports, usually brief, on this or that market; some discussion, usually general, on the role of the merchant class in this or that Islamic society; and a lot of travel literature, complete nowadays with color photographs, romanticizing about smells and sharp practices. But there is only a handful of extended analyses – such as Goitein's – seriously concerned to characterize the bazaar as a cultural form, a social institution, and an economic type.[2] Whatever the reason for this neglect (the fascination of Middle Eastern scholars with the phenomenon of Islam is surely one of them), the result has been that the revisions forced on our concept of status by Indian studies, or of power by Chinese, have not, as they should have, been forced on our concept of exchange by Middle Eastern.

The bazaar is more than a place set aside where people are permitted to come each day to deceive one another, and more, too, than one more demonstration of the truth that, under whatever skies, men prefer to buy cheap and sell dear. It is a distinctive system of social relationships centering around the production and consumption of goods and services (i.e., a particular kind of economy), and it deserves analysis as such. Like an "industrial economy" or a "primitive economy," from both of which it markedly differs, a "bazaar economy" shows whatever general processes it shows in a particular and concrete form, and in so doing it reveals an aspect of those processes that alters, or should, our conception of their nature. *Bazaar*, that Persian word of uncertain origins which has come to stand in English for the oriental market, thus becomes, like the word *market* itself, as much an analytic idea as the name of an institution, and the study of it, like that of the market, as much a theoretical as a descriptive enterprise.

The search for information

Considered as a variety of economic system, the bazaar shows a number of distinctive characteristics, characteristics that center less around the processes that operate there than around the way those processes are shaped into a coherent form. The usual tautologies apply here as elsewhere, perhaps even more here than elsewhere: Sellers seek maximum profit, consumers maximum utility; price relates supply and demand; and factor proportions reflect factor costs. But the principles governing the organization of commercial life are less derivative from such truisms than one might imagine from reading standard economics textbooks, where the passage from axioms to actualities tends to be rather nonchalantly traversed. And those principles, matters less of utility balances than of information flows, give the bazaar both its particular character and its general interest.

To start with a dictum, in the bazaar information is generally poor, scarce, maldistributed, inefficiently communicated, and intensely valued. Neither the rich concreteness or reliable knowledge that the ritualized character of nonmarket economies makes possible, nor the elaborate mechanisms for information generation and transfer upon which industrial ones depend, are found in the bazaar – neither ceremonial distribution nor advertising; neither prescribed exchange partners nor product standardization.[3] The level of ignorance about everything from product quality and going prices to market possibilities and production costs is very high, and a great deal of the way in which the bazaar is organized and functions (and within it, the ways its various sorts of participants behave) can be interpreted as either an attempt to reduce such ignorance for someone, increase it for someone, or defend someone against it.

That is, these ignorances are *known* (or known about) ignorances, not simply matters concerning which information is lacking. Bazaar participants realize how difficult it is to know if the cow is sound or the price is right, and they realize also that it is impossible to prosper without knowing. The search for information one lacks and the protection of information one has is the name of the game. Capital, skill, and industriousness play, along with luck and privilege, as important a role in the bazaar as they do in any economic system. But they do so less by increasing efficiency or improving products than by securing for their possessor an advantaged place in an enormously complicated, poorly articulated, and extremely noisy communication network.

Looked at in this way, the institutional peculiarities of the bazaar seem less like mere accidents of custom and more like connected elements in a coherent system. A finely drawn division of labor and a sharp localization of markets, inhomogeneity of products and intensive price bargaining, extreme fractionalization of transactions and stable clientship ties between buyers and sellers, itinerant trading and extensive traditionalization of occupation in ascriptive terms do not just co-occur: They imply one another. The same is true for the personal nature of reputation and the preference for partnership arrangements over employer–employee ones; for the diversity of weights and measures and the primacy of buying skills over selling ones; and for item-by-item accountancy and the tendency to investigate possibilities in depth with single partners serially rather than to survey them broadly with several concurrently. The search for information – laborious, uncertain, complex, and irregular – is the central experience of life in the bazaar, an enfolding reality its institutions at once create and respond to. Virtually every aspect of the bazaar economy reflects the fact that the primary problem facing the farmer, artisan, merchant, or consumer is not balancing options but finding out what they are.

The bazaar of Sefrou

The term for both market and marketplace in Sefrou is, of course, the same as it is generally in the Arab world – *sūq*. The term can be applied to a market center as a whole, as in *sūq Ṣ-Sefrū* ("the Sefrou market"); to a specialized marketplace, as in *sūq l-behāyim* ("the animal market"); to the part of a quarter that is commercial as opposed to residential (i.e., as a place name), as in Bistna Suq, Bistna being the name of a quarter; to a commodity market considered analytically, as in *sūq l-fūl* ("the bean trade"); for a market day, as in *sūq l-ḵemīs* ("the Thursday market"). *Kaysūwweq* is to sell in the marketplace, *kaytsūwweq* is to go to market (or, of a girl, to have loose morals), a *sūwwāq* (or *suwwāq*) is a market seller, a *taswīqa* is something bought in the market, *meswāq* is the act of marketing, *sūwwāqī* is something "marketlike" (i.e., cheap, commercial, manufactured, vulgar), and so on.

At the most general level, however, Sefrouis divide the bazaar into three main sectors or, as we might better call them, realms: (1) the permanent trading quarters of the old town and its recent extensions; (2) the network of periodic markets, centered on the town but spreading out through the neighboring countryside; (3) the more Westernized business district of the so-called new town. Each of these realms is vaguely bounded. Not only is it not always possible to place a particular activity, much less a particular trader, firmly within one or another of them, but the interconnections between them are multiple, deep, and intricate. Yet, for all that, they do represent, in the eyes of the Sefrouis and in actual fact, distinguishable spheres of commercial activity, trading systems with somewhat different functions and somewhat different modes of operation.

The permanent bazaar in the old city and the newer quarters adjoining it consists, first, of more than 600 shops, representing about forty well-defined commercial trades, each specifically named in terms of the product handled. Second, in addition to the shops, there are nearly 300 craft ateliers, representing about thirty distinct crafts. And third, there is a significant number of people whose activities seem to fall mainly within the realm of the permanent bazaar, but who are not housed in a shop or an atelier: auctioneers, brokers of various sorts, "footloose" craftsmen such as masons or tile layers, curers, scribes, musicians, porters, keepers of caravanserais, bath attendants, prostitutes, street peddlers, buttonmakers. Taken together these three categories of permanent bazaar occupations probably account for 40 to 50 percent of the town's employed labor force.[4]

The periodic market system consists of a cloud of open-air markets scattered more or less continuously across the whole of Morocco, each of which meets once a week.[5] Some of these markets are in towns; more are spread out on open plains or strung along narrow valleys. Some are rooted and have been in place for centuries; more are recent and responses to increasing commercialization. Some are large and focus the trading activities of extensive regions; more are small and focus the trade of ten or fifteen surrounding settlements.

The ties between these markets are loose and irregular, the product of the activities of those who move from one of them to the next. But within any general area market days tend to be arranged in such a way that locality-focusing markets do not conflict with one another, locality-focusing markets do not conflict with region-focusing ones, and region-focusing markets do not conflict with their equivalents in adjoining regions.[6] Sefrou town, whose market day is Thursday, is the region-focusing market for some 2,000 square kilometers and 90,000 or 100,000 people. Some 19 kilometers to the south, 10 kilometers to the north, 26 kilometers to the southeast, 27 kilometers to the east, and 21 kilometers to the southwest, five locality-focusing markets meet, respectively, on Tuesday, Wednesday, Saturday, Sunday, and Monday. Immediately adjoining the Sefrou region, large region-focusing markets meet on Sunday, Monday, Tuesday, and Wednesday. And 40 kilometers along the highroad north lies Fez, the premier bazaar of central Morocco (Figure 1).

The participants in the periodic market system are of three main sorts: (1) itinerant traders, who move through it in various routes, hardly any two the same, seeking a living from the difference something can be bought for in one place and sold for in another; (2) local traders, who are also usually part-time cultivators and/or pastoralists; (3) farmers and herdsmen, who come habitually into one or another market to offer their grains and animals and purchase what they need. On Thursday, the whole of the Sefrou countryside (or rather, this being the Arab world, the male half of it) seems to descend upon the town to buy and sell grain, wool, animals, rugs, fruits and vegetables, wickerwork, household equipment, and various sorts of secondhand objects in the locations specialized for trade in these commodities established at various points around the perimeter of the town, while from all directions of the compass (including, of course, from Sefrou itself) professional traders come to meet them there. Exact estimates of the number of people coming into Sefrou town for market day are impossible to make in the absence of extended survey research dedicated precisely to that question, but some idea of the scale is given by the fact that in 1965 about 50,000 animals (i.e., an average of almost 1,000 a week) changed hands in the Thursday market. Were comparable figures for the other major commodities available, the impression of intense, even feverish, activity would only be reinforced.[7]

Finally, the more Westernized business district is the Sefrou extension, slight as it is, of the French-built industrial economy of Morocco, whose center of gravity is in Casablanca and the other half-developed cities – Tangiers, Safi, Rabat, Kenitra – of the Atlantic coast. In Sefrou, whose only proper factories are a couple of machine-driven olive-oil mills, a small cannery, and a building in which ten or fifteen people stuff mattresses with hassock grass, this sector consists of various glass-fronted stores selling electrical appliances, auto parts, packaged groceries, plumbing fixtures, bicycles, European furniture, and Bata shoes; some garages, several gas stations, a half dozen bars and French-style sidewalk cafés, a few seedy hotels, and a couple of photo studios; a pharmacy, a bank, a bus depot, a pinball parlor, and a, cinema. Interspersed with the main government offices of the town – the city hall, the court, the tax bureau, the post office, the gendarmerie, the hospital – and strung ribbonlike along the Fez highroad as it passes west of the old city, these poor fragments of European capitalism constitute commercial modernity as it exists in Sefrou.

In any case, the boundaries of the *sūq l-medīna* ("the old city bazaar"), the *sūq l-k̲emīs* ("the Thursday bazaar"), and the *sūq l-betrīna* ("the show-window bazaar", from the French *vitrine*), though visible and recognized, are readily crossable. Tribesmen come to town on Thursday, haggle in the shops and ateliers of the old city, and sit gossiping in the cafés along the highroad. An old city cloth merchant deals in the wool market. A man who sells European furniture out of a highroad show window manufactures it (or has it manufactured) in a medina atelier. An itinerant grain buyer owns a taxi, a bath, and a business district garage. Structurally, the Sefrou bazaar is a partitioned system; behaviorally, it is an unbroken confusion.

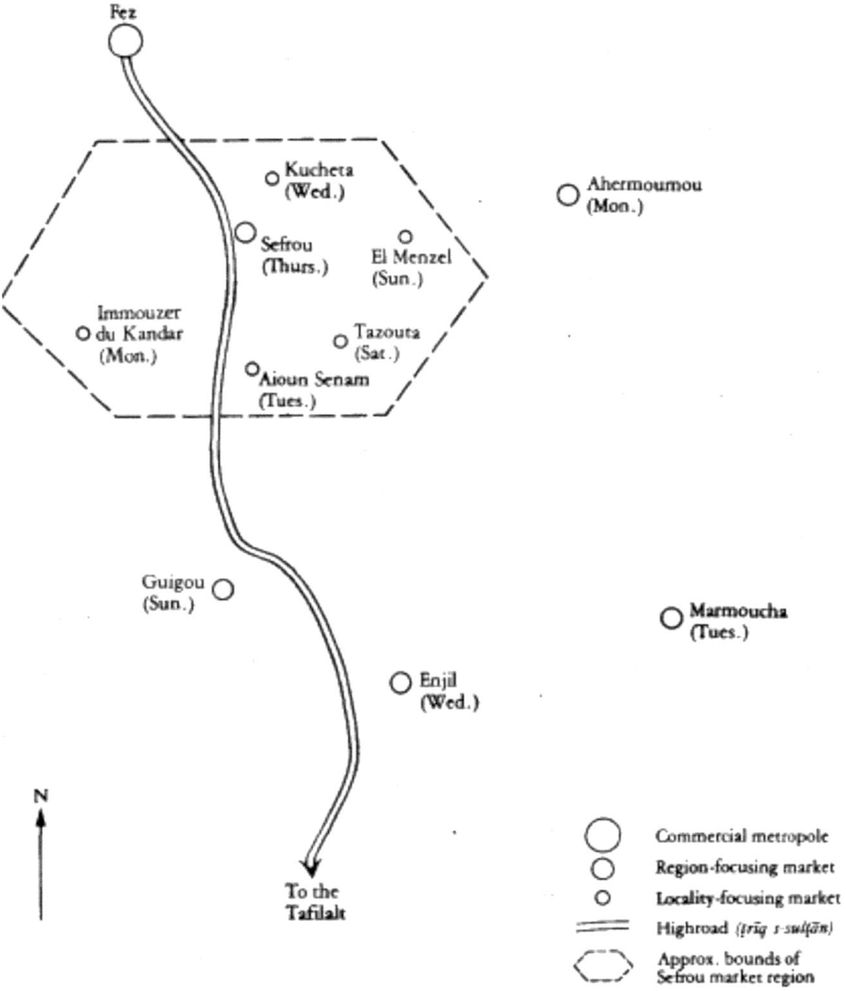

Figure 1. The Sefrou market system. Note that locality-focusing markets are shown only for Sefrou region.

The formation of the Sefrou bazaar

Though Sefrou is today essentially a regional market, a place where half-commercialized tribesmen meet supercommercialized shopkeepers on free if somewhat less than equal ground, it has not always been thus. Prior to the Protectorate (and especially prior to the French incursion into the Algerian Sahara around the turn of the century), the town's role in short-distance trade was distinctly secondary to its role in long-distance trade. It was out of the caravan traffic – south toward the Sahara and black Africa and north toward the Mediterranean and Latin Europe – that the Sefrou bazaar arose. For about the first millennium (900 to 1900) of its existence, the town was less a hub than a way station, a link between remote economies rather than a focus for adjacent ones. Its function was to connect.

Probably the most important, and certainly the most elaborately developed, of such connectings was that between Fez, then the political and cultural as well as the commercial capital of the country, and the Tafilalt, the great desert port of southeastern Morocco.[8] The first stopover (and the last town) on the way out, and the last stopover (and the first town) on the way in, Sefrou was both the jumping-off place and the landfall of this trade – the passage gate to 480 kilometers of winding mule trail, as accidented politically as it was physically.

This trail, the famous *ṭrīq s-sulṭān* ("The Royal Way," so-called because it linked the dynasty's capital with its ancestral shrine) ran from Fez across the Sais Plain into Sefrou, from which it climbed up into the Middle Atlas, then down to cross the blank Mulwiya Plateau, then up again, this time to 2,000 meters, through the High Atlas, finally descending into the palm groves and camel tracts of the north Sahara – an eleven- or twelve-day trek (Figure 2). Little circumstantial can be said about Sefrou's involvement in the trade that passed along this route prior to 1900. Except for the fact that the volume of trade was not what it must once have been and that, by 1900, European guns and cottons were beginning to appear in it, though the amber, slaves, and civet cats of black Africa no longer did, there is no reason to believe that the essential form of the trade itself, and thus of the town's relationship to it, had changed for centuries.[9] Certainly the main institutions regulating the trade – the caravanserai (*funduq*), the commenda (*qirāḍ*), and the passage toll (*zeṭṭaṭa*) – had not.

The funduq

A combination depot, hostelry, emporium, artisinat, animal pen, whorehouse, and ecclesiastical benefice, the funduq was the social heart of the caravan economy. Its physical form was invariant: a narrow, two-story building constructed rectangularly around a broad open court, with a large gated passage cut into one end and an open gallery stretched along

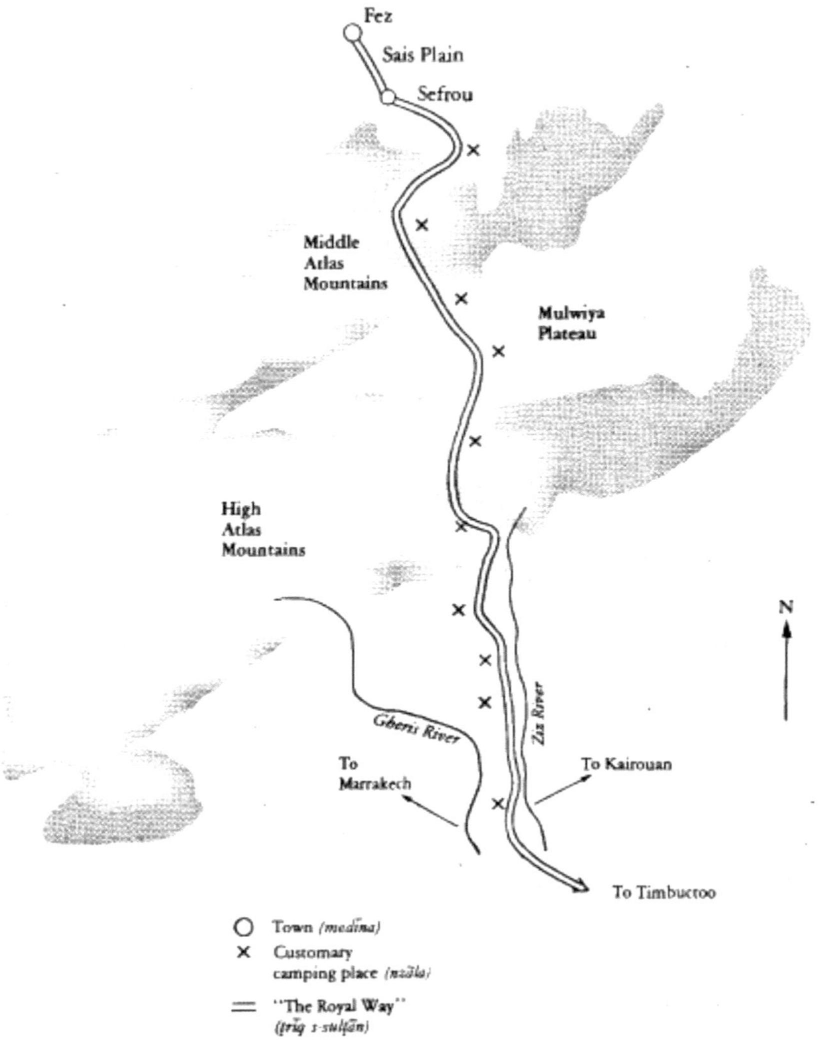

Figure 2. The Royal Way. (Based on J. Brignon et al., *Histoire du Maroc*, Paris, 1967.)

the whole length of the second floor. A series of extremely small, airless cubicles opened off this gallery, and beneath it, along the arcade it formed on the ground floor, were ranged a number of storerooms, workshops, and countinghouses. The passing caravaners picketed their mules and donkeys in the courtyard, bolted their merchandise inside the storerooms, and slept (as noted, not usually unattended) in the second-floor cubicles. There were eleven such funduqs, of varying size and significance, in the Sefrou of 1900; and in and immediately around them virtually the whole of the city's commercial life, then much more highly concentrated and much less various than it is now, was centered (Figure 3).

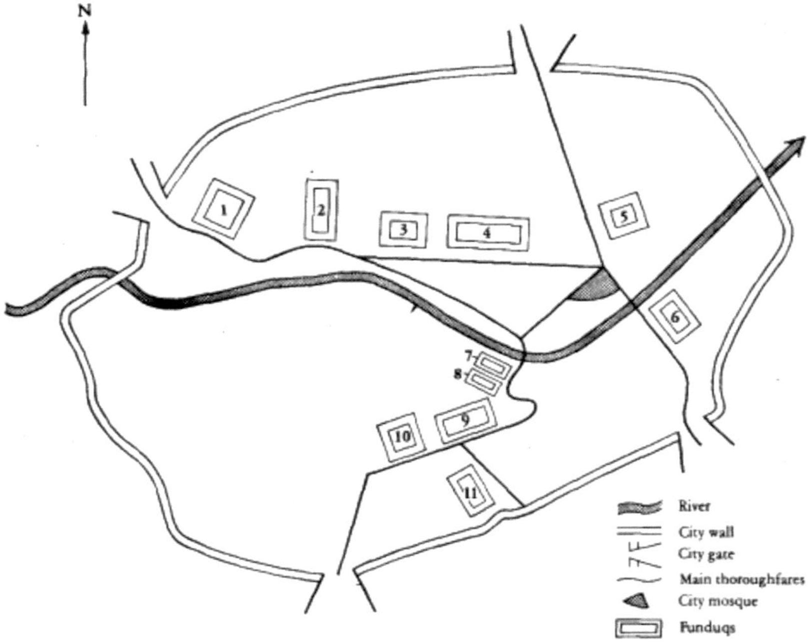

Figure 3. Location of the funduqs in Sefrou, ca. 1900.

The funduqs were not privately owned, but were, insofar as one may use the term in a Muslim context, church holdings. More exactly, they were what Moroccans call *ḥabus* – properties deeded by their original owners (pious traders of the seventeenth and eighteenth, in one case apparently the sixteenth, centuries) to God's community of believing Muslims, the *umma*. Entrusted to the stewardship of a religious official known as a *nāḍir* (cl. *nāẓir*), they were auctioned by him to private merchants, usually several of them in partnership, to operate in their own way and for their own profit, the rents thus collected being distributed by the nadir for the construction and operation of mosques, the support of Quranic education, and so on.[10] They were, in short, pious foundations given wholly over to commercial activities themselves untrammeled by any sort of pious scruples. And, as we shall see, this curious symbiosis between the most headlong sort of merchant capitalism – business is business, and may God take pity on the both of us – and the established institutions of public Islam has remained, through all sorts of detailed changes, a central characteristic of the Sefrou economy to this day.

This odd circumstance is all the more odd because, although, as Islamic law demands, the funduq holders themselves were inevitably Muslims, most of the Sefrouis involved in the funduq world – a quite restricted group in any case – were Jews. There has been an untypically large number of Jews in Sefrou for as long as we have record, and between about 1880 and 1948 (the year Israel was born), they seem consistently to have composed about 40 percent of the town's population and 80 percent of its commercial labor force. Of the perhaps 600 or 700 men involved in the swirl of activity around the funduqs in turn-of-the-century Sefrou, not more than 100 were Muslims; the rest were Jews. (For the general picture ca. 1900 compared with the strikingly different one in 1960, see Table 1.)[11]

Table 1. *Muslims and Jews in Sefrou commerce, ca. 1900 and in 1960 (1960 figures in parentheses)*

			Employed in bazaar occupations		
	Total population	Employed labor force	Number	% of group's employed labor force	% of total bazaar labor force
Muslims	3,000 (17,583)	1,000 (3,249)	100 (1,966)	10 (61)	14 (79)
Jews	2,000 (3,041)	700 (634)	600 (526)	86 (83)	86 (21)
Total	5,000 (20,624)	1,700 (3,883)	700 (2,492)	41 (64)	100 (100)

Note: Totals for 1960 exclude 337 foreigners, mostly French and Algerian. Unemployed and "inactive" men over fifteen composed 19% of the population in 1960; only 9% of the employed labor force was female, and that mostly in schools and government offices.

Source: Based on historical population figures for the town assembled from various sources in L. Rosen, "The Structure of Social Groups in a Moroccan City," doctoral dissertation, Department of Anthropology, University of Chicago, 1968, p. 40; a detailed computer analysis of the 1960 census data for Sefrou; and extensive interviews with aged informants concerning the social composition of the town during the decades immediately preceding the Protectorate.

In any case, Jewish or Muslim, large or small, the relationship of the funduq class to the Saharan trade is both critical to an understanding of the development of the bazaar economy and quite difficult to characterize. The funduq class was surely not the driving force of that trade: The grand merchants of Fez, seldom stirring from their countinghouses, but linked to agents in the Tafilalt (and indeed all over Morocco and into Europe) through a developed letter-of-credit system, financed and organized virtually the whole of the trade. Nor did the funduq class have anything to do with the transport side of things: The caravaners were pre-Saharan Berber nomads whose sheikhs assembled them into companies, found them cargoes, and then piloted them through the tangle of tribal jealousies that separated the capital from the oasis. The Sefrou involvement was mostly ancillary, limited to providing the passing services of the funduq – food, lodging, women, various sorts of craftwork (blacksmithing, saddlemaking, tinsmithing, shoemaking, weaving) – and a certain amount of petty trading of sugar, tea, and cannabis with the caravaners. Yet, beyond this undynamic roadside commerce, there was a handful of men – around 1900, perhaps a dozen Muslims and twice that many Jews – who did contrive to buy into the caravan trade as such, to become what Moroccans call, still today with a touch of awe, *tājir*.[12] They, employing the second of the organizing institutions upon which that trade depended, the *qirāḍ*, laid the real foundations of the bazaar economy and turned the town from a mere service station or doorsill to Fez into a commercial center, minor but vigorous, in its own right.[13]

The qirad

The qirad, or what is called in the Western tradition, the commenda, combines, as Udovitch has remarked, the advantages of the loan with those of the partnership, without quite managing to be either one.[14] Indeed, unless pressed, Sefrouis still refer to it, as they do to almost any persisting commercial relationship, as a "partnership" (*šerka*). The qirad is not precisely that because instead of risks being shared between the contracting parties they are borne wholly by the supplier of the capital, who provides money or (despite some juridical opinions opposing it) goods to a trader, who then trades on his own, in his own way, and without answering to anyone but himself. If there is a profit, the investor shares in it in some preagreed proportion; if there is not, then not, and no debt remains to haunt the relationship. The trader's liability (anyway, his financial liability) is not only limited, it is for all intents and purposes nonexistent. And, contrariwise, the investor has no responsibility for anything the trader does or says and is expected, indeed, not to meddle. The qirad is a curious sort of contract, one that so isolates the participants' commercial activities from one another as to maximize the need for a personal bond between them.[15]

In turn-of-the-century Sefrou, the few merchants with resources enough to launch qirad arrangements were, again, mostly Jews. They made the arrangements with both Muslims and Jews, but the latter formed the core of their operations.[16]

There was a large Jewish community, at least as ancient if not so urbane as Sefrou's, in the Tafilalt, and small knots of Jews, also originating mainly from the Tafilalt, could be found huddled around most of the camp stops along the route, doing a little selling here, a little buying there.[17] It was between the urban *maḡārba* ("Moroccan," but more generally "northern town-dwelling") Jews of Sefrou and the *filālī* ("Tafilalt," but more generally "rural of the south and east") Jews that quite extensive and usually highly stable investor-agent qirad relationships crystallized. And again, as we shall see, this not uninvidious intracommunity contrast between the prosperous, settled, civilized "sitting" (*gles*) merchant and the impoverished, itinerant, unlearned "riding" (*rkeb*) peddler became, like the habus-funduq pattern, an enduring feature of the bazaar economy. It was across this city Jew–country Jew synapse of class that the shopkeeper and artisan world of the permanent bazaar was first linked with the shepherd and traveling-man world of the periodic bazaar.

Yet, for all the prominence of Jewish qirad givers in Sefrou's penetration of the caravan trade – and their activities surely accounted for vastly the greater part of it – the two most considerable of such buyers into the passing traffic were Muslims: a kinetic Berber chieftain and a descendant-of-the-Prophet munitions maker. What the Jews had in volume, these men had in scale; and what the Jews had in skill, they had in power.[18]

The Berber, Umar al-Yusi Buhadiwi, was the dominant political figure both in the town and in the countryside immediately around it from 1894 to 1904. A tribesman from the great Ait Yusi confederation that ranged the countryside south and east of town, he was recognized by the then sultan, Mulay Abdel Aziz, as the local *qā'id* ("chief," "commander," "governor," "administrator"). Unlike previous qaids, however, he installed himself, his family, and his entourage inside the town (the only Berbers then living there) to become, until lured to an ambush assassination by tribal rivals, a small sultan of the place.

So far as the caravan trade is concerned, he was, of course, himself neither a merchant nor possessed of extensive contacts with merchants. He was, as well, illiterate, and so he operated through two or three Sefrou Jews as his personal agents. The depth of his involvement in the caravan trade is now difficult to measure with any precision, but his investments, based on his ability to appropriate wool and hides from Berber herds and, as his grip grew tighter, on a similar ability with respect to the wheat and olives of the town itself, were clearly both large and far-flung. As he muscled into Sefrou's political life, he thrust himself (and, indirectly, his tribal followers) into its economic.

The munitions maker, Mulay Ali b-l-Hashimi Bu Bnitat l-Alawi, was something rather different: a classic urban type. He was, as noted, a descendant of Mohammed, what Muslims refer to as a *šerīf*. But, more than that, he was an Alawi sherif, which meant he was, in theory anyway, a distant relative of the sultan and the closest thing to a local patrician (what the French later called a "notable" and, even later, and more misleadingly, a "bourgeois") that the intensely plebian, most ungenteel Sefrou society was capable of producing.

His Alawi ancestors had come to Sefrou from the Tafilalt, probably shortly after the dynasty's capture of Fez in 1667, and his contacts with the large (Dunn says "several thousand") Alawi community still living and trading there at the end of the nineteenth century provided the social foundation for his activities. The economic foundation lay, as indicated, in the gun trade – after the 1890s, a very rapidly expanding affair.[19] In the funduq, of which first his father and then he held the lease (number 4 in Figure 3), Mulay Ali organized a fair-sized craft industry, some twelve or fifteen workers, in ammunition manufacture (i.e., cartridge stuffing). This industry not only projected him into the midst of the local traffic but gave him something of a monopoly hold on it and proved immensely profitable.

In time, Qaid Umar, jealous of the growing power of Mulay Ali and of the emerging class of funduq entrepreneurs, of which he was in a sense the doyen, persuaded the sultan to remove the sherif from this particular line of work. (The sultan's predecessor had given him the right to drive arms in the first place.) This was done. The workers were imprisoned and the funduq ransacked; Mulay Ali escaped, as such men will, with a ransom. But by then he had built up an extensive network of qirad relations with Tafilalt sherifs and other traders, Muslim and Jewish alike, to become a large-scale operator – almost of Fez proportions – in the tea, sugar, wool, cloth, and olive trades, and disentanglement from the not altogether healthy arms business may have come as something of a relief. Himself literate in only a quran-school sense, Mulay Ali had four secretaries, all Sefroui Muslims, in his funduq, which was the most substantial commercial institution in the town until about 1915, when rural security, calico tastes, and the gasoline engine put an end to the caravan trade forever. No longer a mere pause point for trade headed elsewhere, Mulay Ali's funduq had become what Moroccans call a "commodity house" (*ḍār s-silʿa*), a domicile of trade in itself.

It was not, however, the only one. By the turn of the century, almost all the funduq lessees were qirad givers, some of them on a fair scale, and their funduqs had become commodity houses too, each specialized in one or another trade. Funduq number 6 in Figure 3, headed by a pair of wealthy Meccan pilgrims, one of whom became the dominant political figure in Sefrou after Umar's death, was the center of the grain trade. The wool and lumber trades, separated in different parts of the building, were concentrated in number 11, whose director was another Alawi, but no immediate relation of Ali's. Yet a third Alawi, unrelated to either of the other two, leased number 9 in partnership with an Arab-speaking migrant from northwest Morocco, the so-called Jbala, and made it the focus of the hide and leather trade. The tea and sugar trade was centered in Mulay Ali's funduq, number 4, after its munition days were over; the cloth trade in the Fez-launched one, number 2; the olive and olive-oil trade, under two wealthy local farmers (about the only example at this time of significant trade involvement by large landowners) in number 7. And so on.[20] All sorts of people – financiers, traders, millers, weavers, tanners, blacksmiths, shoemakers, caravaners, Jews, Arabs, Berbers – crowded in and around these miniemporiums (which were, of course, public places not private firms). Shops, ateliers, and even small ad hoc in-the-street markets in old clothes, bread, vegetables, and mats sprang up around them. Mule stops transformed into markets, they provided the nucleus around which the developed region-focused bazaar economy that emerged in full force after World War I crystallized.[21]

The zettata

For that to happen, however, the hub had to be joined to its rim: The Sefrou-centered trade swirl the qirad induced had to be integrated with the local economy, and most especially with the rural economy of transhumant shepherds and olive grove farmers surrounding the town. And for this, the third of the caravan trade's enabling institutions, the *zeṭṭāṭa*, provided, suitably reworked, at once the means and the model.

In the narrow sense, a zettata (from the Berber *tazettat*, "a small piece of cloth") is a passage toll, a sum paid to a local power (the *zeṭṭāṭ*, Br. *azettat*) for protection when crossing localities where he is such a power. But in fact it is, or more properly was, rather more than a mere payment. It was part of a whole complex of moral rituals, customs with the force of law and the weight of sanctity – centering around guest-host, client-patron, petitioner-petitioned, exile-protector, suppliant-divinity relations – all of which are somehow of a package in rural Morocco.[22] Entering the tribal world physically, the out-reaching trader (or at least his agents) had also to enter it culturally.

Despite the vast variety of particular forms through which they manifest themselves, the characteristics of protection in the Berber societies of the High and Middle Atlas are clear and constant. Protection is personal, unqualified, explicit, and conceived of as the dressing of one man in the reputation of another. The reputation may be political, moral, spiritual, or even idiosyncratic, or, often enough, all four at once. But the essential transaction is that a man who counts "stands up and says" (*qām wa qāl*, as the classical tag has it) to those to whom he counts: "This man is mine; harm him and you insult me; insult me and you will answer for it." Benediction (the famous *baraka*), hospitality, sanctuary, and safe passage are alike in this: They rest on the perhaps somewhat paradoxical notion that though personal identity is radically individual in both its roots and its expressions, it is not incapable of being stamped onto the self of someone else.

The zettata proper involved the establishment by the caravan sheikh of such a protective covering of borrowed personality at point after point along his route. The sheikh on the one side and the zettat on the other solemnly exchanged turbans, cloaks, saddle covers, or sections of tent material – "the little piece of cloth" – to create a symbolic fusion of their public selves. The basis thus laid (the rite usually took place in the local market with every man of local standing in attendance), each time the sheikh came through thereafter, his zettat provided him with a small band of men, again more as a symbolic indication of the fact of protection than as a literal guard. Meeting his caravan at one limit of the zettat's influence, this band conducted it, via a grand meal in the zettat's camp at which the toll (paid in currency and adjusted to the size and value of the caravan) was negotiated, to the other limit, where the next escort of the next protector waited to begin the process anew. From the Tafilalt to Fez there were long chains of such relationships, enclosing the caravan sheikh in a series of local identities – Moha's or Rahu's or Lahcen's – as he led his train through the turbulent countryside.[23]

When the Sefrou-centered economy moved, after around 1890, to reach out with some definitiveness to join its immediate hinterland to itself, to become, eventually, a region-focusing bazaar rather than an emporium-linking caravan stop, the zettata type of protection pattern provided the mechanism by which the connection was made.[24]

In the first instance the connection was made, as mentioned earlier, by the Jews, who for months at a time, located themselves in the villages, camps, and markets of the countryside under the protection of one or another tribal strong man. Here, the protection pact was signalized by a sheep sacrifice – again public, with all the local men assembled for a meal in the protector's tent – rather than a turban exchange (perhaps because *that* intimate a mingling of identity with a Jew was too much for a Berber to tolerate) and was called a *mezrāg* (literally, "a spear").[25]

It was as solemn an undertaking, and based on the same complex of ideas about hospitality, personal reputation, the bindingness of oral contract, and divine human retribution, as the zettata relation between two Berbers, and it was at least as resolutely observed.[26] Except for its focus and its cross-ethnic, indeed cross-religious, quality, it was the same institution.

The mezrag made, the protector, the *mūl l-mezrāg*, would send a small group of his men down to Sefrou town to pick up the Jew and escort him and his goods to their locality. There, usually by the side of a small market or set off a few hundred meters outside a settlement, the Jew would trade for several months and, his stock exhausted, be escorted back home with his wool, hides, grain, or whatever. By the early 1900s, the countryside behind Sefrou was laced with Jewish-Berber mezrag relations of this sort. There was hardly a tribesman who, through the courtesy of his local strong man, did not have a riding Jewish trader reasonably nearby, and hardly a sitting Sefroui Jew, whose agents these riding Jews were, who did not have extensive mezrag-based interests in the countryside.

Change and continuity

A caravanserai transformed into a commercial house, a passage trade transformed into an investment business, and a protection pattern transformed into a market channel – these were the elements out of which the bazaar economy was built. In time, the commercial house dissolved into the hundreds of stores and ateliers of the permanent bazaar, the qirad disappeared in favor of the more familiar financial arrangements of central place hierarchies, and the mezrag gave way to the free market higgling of the cycling suq. But the general character, the cultural ground plan, of the commercial network in Sefrou was established by then. The sort of system it is, the way in which information gets around it (or does not get around it), the manner in which trade is conducted, and the assumptions in terms of which it is conducted are not only outcomes of the world of Umar, Mulay Ali, and the riding Jew; they are, for all the differences in scale, products, and personnel, continuations of it. A lot has changed in Sefrou since 1900, a time at least two epochs away. But the cultural framework within which the homely business of buying and selling proceeds, the conceptual structure that gives it point and form, has altered but in detail.

Once fairly launched, the metamorphosis of long-distance trade into short-distance trade rapidly accelerated. In place of the extended lines of commercial connection, twisting across large tracts of merely intervenient social structure, came a dense field of immediate exchanges gathered around Sefrou and centered directly on it. The world of the Sefroui merchant at once contracted and expanded. Contracted, for now the range of his operations was drawn in toward the symmetrical hexagon shown in Figure 1. Expanded, because, within that hexagon, the variety of his activities multiplied, their volume increased, and their social importance grew. By the onset of the Protectorate, the penetration of Sefroui Jews into the surrounding countryside, the linking, through them, of the isolated Berber markets to the town and to each other in an organized pattern, and the transformation of the town's Muslims from a population overwhelmingly agricultural to one overwhelmingly commercial had wrought an economic revolution that the French establishment of security and improvement of transport merely consolidated.[27]

This revolution had begun at least three decades earlier and had emerged out of a complex of ideas and institutions as old as, or older than, Sefrou itself. Stimulated by outside forces, imitative of outside forms, and integrated first into a colonial system and now into that curious combination of capitalism and sultanism that has succeeded it, the bazaar economy is, nevertheless, neither an import nor an enclave. Its shape is as indigenous as its origins.[28]

The bazaar as a cultural form

There are bazaar economies all over the so-called underdeveloped world, as there were not so long ago over much of that now supposedly developed, and, in some difficult to articulate sense, they clearly form a coherent class. There are important similarities among them, as there are important differences between them taken as a group and the sorts of economies one finds in, say, Germany or New Zealand, New Guinea or the Kalahari desert. Yet, in another sense, one even more difficult to articulate, they all partake as well of the place where they are and the time in which they exist. And this is as true of the Moroccan bazaar as of any other. As a social institution, and even more as an economic type, it shares fundamental similarities with the Chinese, the Haitian, the Indonesian, the Yoruban, the Indian, the Guatemalan, the Mexican, and the Egyptian – to choose only some of the better described cases. But as a cultural expression, it has a character properly its own. And one of the advantages of looking in depth at so particular a case as Sefrou is that it is possible thereby to discern something of what that character is: what is Moroccan about Moroccan commerce, and what difference it makes.[29]

In these terms, terms at least implicitly comparative, three aspects of the Sefrou bazaar are worth more extended attention: (1) its enmeshment in a vast arabesque of what, lacking an English word that genuinely applies, one can only call ethnic-like distinctions; (2) its integration – interfusion, even – with some of the major institutions of popular Islam; and (3) the role of the Jewish community in its development and functioning.

Nisba: trade and cultural identity

The discussion of the formation of the bazaar economy has already demonstrated that the class, if it can properly be called that, which was formed with it was not religiously, linguistically, or culturally homogeneous. For all the prominence of the Jews in the bazaar economy and for all their tendency to concentrate in it, not only was the bazaar an all-sorts affair, but the interrelations among the various kinds of people within it – sitting Jews, riding Jews, Berber chiefs, Arab notables, Saharan mule skinners, and a number of other types not yet mentioned – were intricate, crosscutting, and anything but distant. The bazaar economy was particolored from the start: Different varieties of people entered it in differing degrees, in different ways, and with not altogether complimentary views of one another. But the crystallization of a culturally encysted trading class, half intruder and half pariah, so common in other parts of the world (Southeast Asian Chinese, East African Indians, Medieval European Jews) never occurred in Sefrou.[30] Between those in commerce and those not, there has been, and is, essentially no line save that.

This promiscuous tumbling in the public realm of varieties of men kept carefully partitioned in the private one, cosmopolitanism in the streets and communalism in the home, is, of course, a general feature of Middle Eastern civilization. Often called a mosaic pattern of social organization – differently shaped and colored chips jammed in irregularly together to generate an overall design within which their distinctiveness remains nonetheless intact – it is made possible by a number of characteristic ideas: that religious truth is so little subject to argument and so little responsive to temporal concerns that it ought not to hinder practical activities; that non-Muslim groups are not outside Muslim society but have a scripturally allocated place within it; that law is personal and determined by who one is, not territorial and determined by where one is; and that, though usually cruel and always capricious, the state is a machine less for the governing of men, who are anyway more or less ungovernable, than for the amassment and consumption of the material rewards of power. Nothing if not diverse, Middle Eastern society, and Moroccan society as a frontier variant of Middle Eastern society, does not cope with diversity by sealing it into castes, isolating it into tribes, or covering it over with some common denominator concept of nationality – though, fitfully, all have occasionally been tried. It copes with diversity by distinguishing with elaborate precision the contexts (marriage, diet, worship, education) within which men are separated by their dissimilitudes and those (work, friendship, politics, trade) where, however warily and however conditionally, men are connected by their differences.

In contemporary Sefrou, though the contrast between Jew and Muslim is perhaps the most vivid and obvious example of the way this concern for fitting differences together operates within the bazaar economy, it is hardly the only such contrast of importance.[31] Ascriptive distinctions – generated out of language, religion, residence, race, kinship, birthplace, ancestry – run through the whole of the bazaar, partitioning the Muslim community into literally dozens of categories. In 1968–9, there were 1,013 shops and ateliers in Sefrou's permanent bazaar; among the "owners" of these establishments there were represented no less than sixty-six different locally recognized "ethnic-like" categories.[32] Were a similar analysis of the periodic bazaar possible, the number of different sorts of men – again different sorts in the eyes of the Sefrouis themselves – would quite possibly double.[33]

This collective habit, not to say obsession, of classifying man into a large number of essentialist categories – categories resting on the general premise that a person's provenance pervades his identity – is practically effected by the extensive use of a morphological process of the Arabic language known as *nisba*. Deriving from the root (*n-s-b*) for "ascription," "attribution," "imputation," "relationship," "affinity," "correlation," "connection," "kinship" (*nsīb* means "in-law"; *nsab* means "to attribute or impute to"; *munāsaba* means "a relation," "an analogy," "a correspondence"; and so on), nisba as a linguistic device consists of changing a noun into what we would call a relative adjective, but what for Arabs is just another noun, by adding *ī* (fem. *īya*). Examples are: *Ṣefrū*/Sefrou – *Ṣefrūwī*/native son of Sefrou; *Sūs*/region of southwest Morocco – *Sūsī*/man coming from that region; *Beni Yazḡa*/a tribal group near Sefrou – *Yazḡī*/a member of that group; *Yahūd*/the Jews as a people, Jewry – *Yahūdī*/a Jew; *Adlūn*/surname of a prominent Sefrou family – *Adlūnū*/a member of that family. As, once formed, nisbas tend to be incorporated into personal names (Umar al-Yusi Buhadiwi – Umar of the Buhadu fraction of the Ait Yusi confederation; Mulay Ali b-l-Hashimi Bu Bnitat al-Alawi – the sherif Ali, son of the Hashim family, father of little girls [a sobriquet], of the Alawite line), the ethnic-like classification is publicly stamped onto a man's identity.[34] A few newcomers and marginal figures aside, there is not a single case in the bazaar survey where an individual's nisba type (if, dropping approximate glosses, we may now call it that) was not generally known. Indeed, people, in the bazaar and out, are far more likely to be ignorant of what a man does, how long he has been around, what his personal character is, or where exactly he lives than they are of where he fits – Sussi or Sefroui, Buhadiwi or Alawi, Yazghi or Yahudi – in the perduring mosaic.

All this is important not only because the bazaar is extravagantly heterogeneous with respect to nisba types, a profusion of peoples, but because such types are correlated with trades and occupations within it. This correlation is, of course, a statistical, not an absolute, matter; but it is pronounced enough to be clear to the naked (and native) eye, and to affect profoundly the organization of commercial life. The distinct nonrandomness of the classification of individuals according to background vis-à-vis their classification according to vocation leads to the partial assimilation of the two ways of sorting men and thus to the view that there is an immanent, transaccidental connection between social origins and lines of work.[35] The mosaic quality of Moroccan society, and beyond it Middle Eastern civilization, not only penetrates the bazaar but finds there perhaps its most articulate and powerful expression, its paradigmatic form.

To gain a clearer picture of that form, of what, in concrete terms the mosaic principle comes to in the bazaar, we can begin with Table 2. In fact, the table does not deal with nisba types, which are cultural categorizations applied by the Moroccans themselves to themselves, but with externally invented sociological categorizations that are here called socioethnic.[36] Though notions like Sefrou Arab, rural Arab, Berber, and, of course, Jew have a certain general currency and application among Sefrouis, especially when they are regretting one another's existence, the effective everyday categorizations in terms of which people are actually perceived and reacted to are Adluni, Meghrawi, Yazghi or Bhaluli, Zaikumi or Zgani, Tobali or Robini; that is, nisbas.[37] Table 2 indicates few of the general sociological forces – rural-to-urban migration, linguistic integration (i.e., Arabization), and religious contrast – that engendered the particular mosaic found in Sefrou and that continue to maintain it. It does not reach, save indirectly, to the mosaic itself. Yet, for all that, some important aspects of the cultural shape of the bazaar are discernible in the pattern of its entries.

The first is that the traditional sector of the bazaar, still the heart of it, is the particular bailiwick of the two old urban groups, the town-born Arabs and the Jews. This is especially true for the crafts – the largest single occupational sector in the town, approached only by agriculture – but it extends to traditional commerce too. Until 1960 anyway, old Sefrouis, both Arab and Jewish, were not only heavily concentrated in the traditional bazaar, they clearly dominated it.

The second matter visible from the table is the formation by the immigrant Arabs and, to a lesser extent, the Berbers of a kind of bazaar rabble of marketplace peons – the flunkies, menials, and hangers-on of commercial life. Even the relatively high participation figures in traditional craft and, for the Berbers, traditional commerce categories do not modify this seriously. The line between being a casual laborer in the bazaar and a lowly assistant or apprentice (or, indeed, between being a casual laborer and outright unemployed) is far from sharp, and most of the rural Arabs and Berbers in these categories are in fact at the bottom edge o them.[38]

In short, there are at least two main clusters of socioethnic/occupation association: (1) the Jews and the "real Sefrouis" (as they sometimes

Table 2. *Percent of Sefrou town employed labor force of various socioethnic categories in different occupational categories, 1960*

	Traditional commerce[a]	Traditional craft[b]	Bazaar worker[c]	Nontraditional commerce and craft[d]	Total bazaar	"New middle-class" occupations?[e]	Agriculture[f]
Sefrou-born Arabs[g]	18	39	6	7	70	10	20
Rural-born Arabs[h]	14	26	24	1	65	10	25
Arabs born in other towns[i]	10	21	3	8	35	46	19
Berbers[j]	17	17	17	8	59	21	20
Jews[k]	35	37	6	5	83	16	1
Overall[l]	19	30	8	7	64	16	20

[a] Arab-type shopkeepers, market peddlers, auctioneers, etc. dealing in food, clothing, craft goods, hardware, agricultural products. N = 738.

[b] Weavers, tailors, masons, butchers, saddlemakers, carpenters, blacksmiths, millers, potters, etc. N = 1,166.

[c] Manual workers in the bazaar, porters, bath employees, watchmen, etc. N = 311.

[d] Large- or medium-scale extralocal merchants, managers of commercial firms, Western-type storekeepers, bus and taxi owners, auto mechanics, plumbers, electricians, photographers, radio repairmen, etc. N = 272.

[e] Public officials, clerks, professionals, policemen, soldiers, schoolteachers, etc. N = 621.

[f] Farmers, sharecroppers, farm laborers. N = 777.

[g] Persons whose first language is Arabic and who were born in Sefrou town. N = 1,397.

[h] Persons whose first language is Arabic, who were born in a village and have moved to Sefrou town. N = 981.

[i] Persons whose first language is Arabic, who were born in another town and have moved to Sefrou town. N = 580.

[j] Persons whose first language is Berber (virtually all urban-dwelling Berber men are bilingual in Arabic). As the vast majority of Berbers living in Sefrou town are immigrant from the surrounding countryside, the category is not subdivided. N = 580.

[k] As almost all Jews living in Sefrou town were bom there, the category is not subdivided. N = 634.

[l] N = 3,883.

Source: Data from official 1960 Census of Sefrou.

call themselves) in the traditional commercial trades and the crafts, the heart of the classical bazaar; and (2) Arab and Berber ex-tribesmen in the ancillary, marginal, and, as population grows, outright redundant jobs that surround this heart. But though this is a stratificatory difference and a systematic one, it is not, in the proper sense, a class one. Neither old Sefroui Arabs and Jews, nor rural-born Arabs and Berbers, form any group at all, or even a category, either in their own eyes or in those of others. Because they do not have any effective reality as collective social actors (the Jews are a partial exception, but only partial), they do not form units in the bazaar's stratification system. To explain that system and, in fact, the social organization of the bazaar generally, it is necessary to talk in terms, not of groups, classes, and other sociological constructions of the outside observer, but of trades and nisba types – the chips in the mosaic.

We can begin with Table 3, which summarizes what the bazaar survey has to say about the degree to which traditional trades pattern out in nisba terms. The table is arranged in accordance with a measure of *nisba compactness*, running from blacksmiths at the compact (i.e., nisba-homogeneous) end to grocers at the diffuse (i.e., nisba-heterogeneous) end. The measure consists essentially of the degree to which the membership of the trade diverges from an equal-nisba percentage distribution, and thus can be read with zero as the nisba random, perfectly diffuse, base point.[39]

As is readily apparent, the established primary crafts are the most compact; the everyday consumption goods trades, the least; and various secondary crafts, less generalized trades, and service occupations spread out in between. (The anomalies – bakers, who should on this reasoning be somewhat higher; hardware and spice sellers, who should be somewhat lower, etc. – have as usual, special explanations.) About half the blacksmiths come, indeed, from a single old Sefroui family, and at least one of every sort of man found in Sefrou is engaged, if only in some marginal way, in the grocery business. But all the trades are reasonably well defined in nisba terms, as Table 4, in which concentration is measured by percent of the total membership in a given occupation accounted for by the four most numerously represented nisbas in it, makes even more clear. Not only is there no trade in which the top four nisba types do not account for a majority of the occupants, but in about 80 percent of the trades, these four nisba types account for more than three-quarters of the occupants.

Table 3. *Traditional trades ranked (high to low) according to degree of compactness in nisba terms*

Trade[a]	Nisba compactness index[b]	Number of workers	Number of nisbas
High			
1. Blacksmith	43.0	15	2
2. Carpenter	36.7	18	3
3. Weaver	30.3	22	4
4. Butcher	21.4	22	5
5. Mason	20.4	31	5
Medium			
6. Hardware/spice seller	17.0	10	5
7. Silk merchant/spinner	16.4	22	6
8. Prepared-food seller	15.6	15	5
9. Cloth merchant	15.2	35	9
10. Coffee shop keeper	14.7	29	6
11. Baker	12.6	19	7
12. Tinsmith	12.5	10	4
13. Miller	10.5	12	7
14. Tobacconist	10.2	16	7
15. Barber/cupper	10.1	42	10
16. Wool/hide trader	10.0	11	5
Low			
17. Tailor	6.6	83	17
18. Shoemaker	6.5	31	13
19. Odds-and-ends seller	6.2	17	8
20. Ready-made clothes seller	5.4	36	11
21. Wheat/bean trader	4.0	13	9
22. Vegetable and fruit seller	3.4	90	25
23. Grocer	3.3	211	34

[a] Occupations with less than ten members or whose main locus is the periodic bazaar have been ignored. For a full list of bazaar occupations in Sefrou, see Annex A.

[b] Nisba compactness index:

$$X = \frac{\mathring{a}\ (P_E - P_1) + (P_E - P_2) + \ldots (P_E - P_n)}{N_{\text{nsb}}}$$

where P_E = expected percentage of workers with a particular nisba = 100/N_{nsb}
$P_1 \ldots P_n$ = actual percentage of workers with a given nisba = $N_1/N_{nsb} \ldots N_n/N_{nsb}$
$N_1 \ldots N_n$ = number of workers with a given nisba in the trade
N_{nsb} = number of nisbas in the trade
All signs positive

Table 4. *Percent of total members of trade accounted for by top four nisbas*

Trade	Percent	Trade	Percent
Weaver	100	Cafe keeper	89
Carpenter	100	Cloth seller	86
Blacksmith	100	Baker	85
Tinsmith	100	Barber	84
Bathhouse keeper	100	Tobacconist	82
Saddlemaker	100	Tailor	79
Goldsmith	100	Odds-and-ends seller	77
Mason	97	Miller	66
Butcher	95	Wheat/bean trader	62
Silk merchant/spinner	95	Grocer	62
Prepared-food seller	93	Shoemaker	60
Hard ware/spice seller	91	Vegetable and fruit seller	57
Wool/hide trader	91	Ready-to-wear clothes seller	55

Approaching the problem from the other direction, in terms of the degree to which a given nisba type is concentrated as to trade, poses more difficulties technically. First, the multiplicity of nisba types means that most nisbas embrace too small a number of persons for meaningful statistical treatment. Second, as already noted, nisba classification is fundamentally a relative matter. At one level, everyone in Sefrou has the same nisba: Sefroui. At another level, Sefrouis, Yazghis, Bhalulis, Zganis form a coordinate set; at another, Sefrouis, as one member of this set, divide into Alawis, Adlunis, Meghrawis, Ngadis, and similarly, with other divisions, do the other types. And so on. There are twelve different sorts of

Alawis in Sefrou, and some of the larger of these groups further subdivide. The whole matter is far from regular: What level or sort of nisba is used and seems relevant and appropriate (relevant and appropriate, that is, to the users) strongly depends on the situation. A man who is a Sefroui to his acquaintances in Fez may be a Yazghi to his acquaintances in Sefrou town, and a Ydiri to other members of the Beni Yazgha tribe, a Taghuti to other members of the Wulad Ben Ydir fraction of the Beni Yazgha, a Himiwi to other members of the Taghut subfraction, and so on, if not ad infinitum, at least to quite striking lengths.[40] (Should he happen to journey to Egypt, he would, of course, become a Maghrebi.)

Looking at the matter from the trade end, one can operate at the "Sefrou" level of differentiation without excessive distortion, and this is what has been done in Tables 3 and 4. But this procedure has some consequences when one turns the matrix over, as in Table 5, and looks at the situation from the nisba end. The most important consequence is that a very large number of cases falls into the Sefroui (as opposed to Yazghi, Jebli, Fassi, etc.) category. That category can be further differentiated, of course, but at this next level down, the numbers tend to get quite small.[41] Nor can one simply aggregate these "lower level," or "finer grain" nisbas, because then the occupational concentrations cancel one another out. If the eight Bushamawi are, with one exception, blacksmiths, three of the four Busharebi are carpenters, and half of the eight Adluni are in weaving, then lumping them merely produces the false appearance of a scatter, as the wildly misleading figure of 0.13 in Table 5 for "other Sefroui" shows. In Table 5, then, those ten nisbas with more than ten representatives in the traditional trades are merely ranked, by the same sum-of-the-de- viations index applied earlier to the trades as such, and the conglomerate Sefroui are left unranked. This is not entirely satisfactory. But even from such a procedure the fact that nisba types are markedly concentrated in certain trades as opposed to others is clear, as is the fact that this concentration varies in far from random ways.

The nisba system not only provides a classification scheme in whose terms men perceive one another and themselves, but a framework within which they organize certain of their transactions with one another-in the immediate case, certain economic ones. The mosaic is more than merely a Moroccan representation of what persons are and how society is composed, a specific conception *of* social reality, though it is that. It is also a set of principles by means of which to order the interaction of persons – in the bazaar, in politics, in the casual intercourse of everyday life – a guide *for* the construction of social reality.

Table 5. *Nisba types ranked (high to low) according to degree of traditional trade concentration*

Nisba type	Nisba compactness index	Number of workers in nisba in trade	Number of occupations represented in nisba
High			
1. Fassi[a]	12.53	12	6
2. Alawi[b]	9.66	43	13
3. Sussi[c]	6.21	23	7
4. Announceur[d]	5.71	25	6
5. Bhaluli[e]	5.08	30	12
6. L-Weta[f]	4.85	30	8
7. Jew[g]	3.47	30	14
Low			
8. Jebli[h]	1.63	71	15
9. Qlawi[i]	1.60	34	14
10. Yazghi[j]	1.54	69	14
Unranked (see text)			
11. Other Sefroui	0.13	297	24

[a] Fez-born. Very few of the Fassis in Sefrou (about 10% of their total employed labor force) are in traditional trade; most are white-collar workers and administrators. Of those in traditional trades, near half are grocers, and the only other trades represented, by a man or two each, are tailor, shoemaker, silk merchant/spinner, goldsmith, and hardware/spice seller.

[b] Sefrou-born descendants of the Prophet (sherifs of the Alawi line). These are strongly represented in three trades, grocer, vegetable seller, and silk merchant/spinner (about 20% of their total in each); moderately represented in the butcher trade (12%); with the rest thinly scattered in tailor, cloth seller, weaver, and other "light" trades.

[c] Berbers from the Sus, the southwestern part of Morocco. They are famed all over the country as especially aggressive traders, particularly in the grocery trade. About 70% in Sefrou are grocers. The only other trade of significance among the Sefrou Sussis is ready-made clothes seller (10%).

[d] A lumped category of three immediately adjacent mountain Berber nisbas. They are strong in vegetable selfing (30%); moderate in tailor and grocer (20% each) and in farm produce selling (10%).

[e] From a developed village (or a near-town) a few miles north of Sefrou; Arab speaking. They are strong in grocer (30%) and tailor (20%); moderate in barber (10%); the

rest scattered, mostly in marginal trades like odds-and-ends seller, ready-to-eat-food seller.

[f] A lumped category of two immediately adjacent plains Berber nisbas. About 43% are grocers, 23% vegetable and fruit sellers, 13% cafe keepers, and of the small-scale variety in each case. The remainder are scattered.

[g] All Sefrou-born. A third are cloth sellers. The only other significant category is produce seller (17%). Jewish occupations are "abnormally" scattered by the need to have one each of some major occupations as parallel, within-the-community trades owing to dietary and other religious considerations: butcher, grocer, baker, bathhouse keeper, tailor, shoemaker. Owing to the now-small total number, these "enclave" occupations lead the index to be misleadingly low, and a group that is actually very highly concentrated so far as bazaar occupations generally are concerned (besides cloth and produce, the only other occupation in the general sphere, is represented by the two Jewish goldsmiths) looks much more diffuse than it is.

[h] Rural Arabs immigrant to Sefrou from the region (Jebel) north and east of Fez. Various nisbas (Branti, Ghewani, Tuli, etc.) are involved, but they are known generally in Sefrou as Jebli. They are strong in the grocer (26%) and tailor (18%) trades; moderate in cloth selling (13%) and vegetable and fruit selling (11%). The rest are scattered, mostly in marginal trades: prepared food, tobacconists, barbers, shoemakers.

[i] Sefrou-born Arab speakers, but residing in a separate walled quarter (*l-Qlaʿa*), originally a rather separate community. They are very heavily concentrated as (mostly quite small) grocers (47%). The rest are scattered widely over a large number of occupations, at one or two apiece. Thus, rather like the Jews, the group is in fact more concentrated than our measure suggests.

[j] Members of the largest Arab tribe in the immediate Sefrou hinterland. Their main trades are grocer (26%) and tailor (22%), the smaller ones in both cases. They are moderately represented in vegetable and fruit selling (12%) and in ready-made clothes selling (7%). The rest are more or less randomly scattered.

The bazaar, which, as we shall see later in more detail, lacks much collective organization of any sort, has essentially only two axes along which to organize itself: (1) the division of labor, which gives rise to occupational types; and (2) the a-man-is-his-provenance discrimination of persons, which gives rise to nisba types. The development of these two classifications to extraordinary levels of differentiation, together with their partial but quite real interfusion, provides the bazaar with both map and mold, an image of its form that is also a matrix for its formation.

The Sefrou bazaar (and beyond it the Moroccan and, I suspect, the Middle Eastern) is a great heterogeneous collection of individuals sorted out partly by trade and partly by what one can only call, invoking again a grammatical term, attributive identity. As noted, the attribute involved can be quite various: Fassis are people from a particular town. Jeblis or Sussis are people from a particular region (and speaking a particular language: a Berber speaker from the Jebel is called a Riffi; an Arab speaker from the same region is called a Jebli; an Arab speaker from the Sus is called a Seharawi; a Berber speaker, a Sussi). Alawis are people descended from the Prophet; Adlunis are members of a particular patrilineage; Yahudis are adherents of a religious faith; Bhalulis are people from a large village a few kilometers from Sefrou; Qlawis are inhabitants of a quarter of Sefrou; Yazghis are members of a particular tribe. And so on. As has been noted, occupations themselves can form the basis of a nisba, as can allegiance to a religious brotherhood, a political commitment, or even individual circumstances. What is regular here is the attributive principle, the adjectival ascription to individuals of some dimension of their social setting and the use of such ascriptions as a framework, at once conceptual and institutional, of bazaar activity. Like all social systems, the Sefrou bazaar is but partly ordered; but the degree to which it is derives in no mean part from the habit of seeing men as named by their backgrounds.

Islam and the bazaar

Beyond the nisba and nisbalike categorization of individuals, the other cultural force with a shaping effect on the Sefrou bazaar is, as would be expected in a country notorious for a clamorous sort of piety, Islam. A good deal of this effect is diffuse, a general coloring of style and attitude in commercial relationships that only extended ethnographic description could capture, and then but obliquely. Some of it, also, is only skin deep – Quranic prohibitions against interest taking, gambling, or trafficking in gold that seem to exist mainly to be circumvented. But some of it is both precise and powerful, built into specific institutional forms whose impact on commercial life is as readily visible as that of transport, taxation, or the rhythm of the seasons. Among the world religions, Islam has always been notable for its ability to sort its utopian and its pragmatic aspects into distinct and only partially communicating spheres – the former left as ideals to be affirmed, explicated, codified, and taught; the latter cast into ingenious pieces of social machinery regulating the detailed processes of community life.

In Sefrou, the two most important such pieces of machinery have been the *ḥabus* and the *zāwia*. Habus, material property dedicated to the spiritual welfare of the Islamic community (mortmain, Muslim style) has already been mentioned in connection with the classical funduq, but it survived the caravan economy period to be an even more critical institution in the bazaar economy. Zawia, in Moroccan usage, refers to a Sufi brotherhood, and though the heyday of such brotherhoods has apparently passed, they played a central role in the formation of the bazaar economy in the first half of the century. Between them, the habus and the zawia provided the kind of organizational framework for locally centered, marketplace trade that the funduq, the qirad, and the zettata had played for long-distance, passage trade.

The habus

The economic importance of the habus institution in Sefrou can be gauged from a few preliminary statistics. A total of 183 shops and ateliers in the town is under one form or another of habus ownership. So are four ovens, four funduqs, three public baths, four grain warehouses, and a slaughterhouse. In addition to such commercial properties in the narrow sense, the habus owns forty houses, twenty-eight rooms within houses, and forty water-supply systems for houses. Beyond that, there are, in the countryside immediately around the town, 103 gardens (mostly irrigated), 305 fields (mainly in rainfall wheat), literally thousands of olive trees, and because, like rooms in houses, they can be separately dedicated, even branches of olive trees. The total income for 1965 from all these properties was about $20,000 and the expenditures about $17,000, the surplus being deposited in a bank for eventual use in acquiring new properties. Of the income, about three-quarters came from the urban properties (most of it from the commercial ones, because the houses, rooms, and water systems are rented for wholly nominal prices) and a quarter from agriculture.[42] Along with the government, which manages several former French farms now nationalized, and perhaps a half dozen private individuals, the habus is clearly one of the major landholders in the region. In the town – public facilities such as roads, parks, bureaus, and so on aside – it is *the* largest property owner by far. In the bazaar, it is the only one of any scale at all.[43]

Aside from lending a religious justification to commerce as a useful and praiseworthy activity – something not all the world religions have been able to do with such equanimity – the heavy involvement of the Islamic establishment in the bazaar in the form of the habus has exercised an effect on the economic life of the town in three quite specific ways: through monetary expenditure, through usufruct auctioning, and through fixing rents. In Sefrou, the religious institution (to use Gibb and Bowen's useful substitute for church in clergyless Islam) does not merely sanction trade: It engages in it.[44]

On the expenditure side, habus funds mainly go for the upkeep of religious properties (mosques, Quranic schools, shrines, etc.) and to support various sorts of religious functionaries. The former provides employment for a certain number of people in the construction trades, such as painters, carpenters, masons, and tile layers; but the latter is the more important. The nadir's payroll runs to about 250 persons, including, besides the small staff of his own office, the prayer leaders (*imām*), prayer callers (*muaḏḏin*), and sermon givers (*ḵaṭīb*) of all the major mosques, as well as their janitors, timekeepers, plumbers, and so on. (In the main mosque, there is even a man hired to warm the lustral water on cold mornings.) Further, there is a large number of, as it were, piecework celebrants: men who hand out the Qurans on Friday; men who chant for a quarter hour on Monday and Friday afternoons before evening prayers; men (thirty altogether) who read a section of the Quran (*ḥizb*) in the morning and in the afternoon, getting through the sixty into which it is evenly divided in a month. And finally, many Quranic schoolteachers, religious students, and so on receive small subsidies. As virtually all these people – known collectively, the janitors and such aside, as *ṭulba* (sq. *ṭāleb*), "religious scholars" (literally, "devoted, eternal students") – are also market traders, often prominent and influential ones, habus money not only mostly gets back into the bazaar economy from which, mostly, it originally comes, but acts to fuse the religious and economic elites of the town.[45]

The habus's activities in usufruct auctioning merely reinforce the connection. The main products involved are cereals (wheat, barley, occasionally maize) and olives. In the case of cereals, access to plots of land is auctioned; in the case of olives, rights to harvest particular trees. The land auctions take place in the late summer just before fall plowing, and the leases run for a growing season with right of renewal for a second season at the same price. In the case of olives, the auction takes place in midwinter, just before the harvest, the legal opening date for which is set by the government. The trees, in lots containing from two or three up to 200 or 300, are bid upon, and the purchaser obtains the harvest from them for that year.

The auctions, in both cases completed in a single morning, are conducted by the nadir in a small square in the center of the old city; the bidders are mainly bazaar traders in cereals and olive oil. The traders then either hire sharecroppers for the land or pieceworkers for the olive drive and sell the product on site to millers' agents, who deliver it to the mills by hired truck, or, as is perfectly permissible, resell the leases to yet other traders. Details aside, the placing of a significant proportion of the area's cereal and olive production on the market in the form of short-term usufruct leases brings the bazaar trader far deeper into the rural economy than as a mere purchaser of agricultural products carried to market. Under the agency of the habus the bazaar not only capitalizes a significant part of that economy, but, in effect, manages it.

The most important contribution of the habus institution to the functioning of the bazaar economy comes through neither its expenditures nor its agricultural operations, but through its role in setting rents on urban commercial properties. The shops, ateliers, funduqs, and so on that the habus owns are also distributed to lessees through an auction system. But here the leases are not short term but long – in fact, lifelong. Once a trader has bid and won the right to use a vacant habus property, it is his for as long as he wishes to keep it, assuming he neither defaults on the rent, commits a crime, or moves away. If he retires or, as is very common, becomes engaged in other activities, he may sublet it freely. Indeed, it is for all intents and purposes heritable because, though his death necessitates a new auction, other traders do not normally bid against his heir. Finally, and most importantly, rents of commercial properties are almost never renegotiated, with the result that, given the general expansion of the Sefrou economy over the last fifty or sixty years, they are, in market terms, extremely low. Of all the subsidies the habus institution provides to the bazaar economy this letting of sites, buildings, and even in some cases certain sorts of equipment (e.g., forges, looms, mills) at extremely low and almost perfectly stable rents is surely the greatest.[46] Rent as a factor in bazaar calculations is reduced to virtual unimportance. Land is not precisely a free factor of production in the bazaar economy (though low, rents are, as the fact that they bring in about $15,000 a year demonstrates, not trivial), but it is a very cheap one.[47]

This stabilization of rents at abnormally low levels is not a result of any provision of Maliki law or of any general policy on the part of the Ministry of Habus. The law permits adjustments in response to market forces and the ministry, which is only just now beginning to organize itself into an effective force, still has little practical control over matters so traditionally regarded as local concerns. What holds habus rents down is simply the unified desire of the Sefrou trading community that they be held down. Here, as in so much else, the operation of the habus reflects the fact that the leaders of the religious institution and (if we may call it that) the commercial institution are the same people; that the main locus of the orthodox, sunni community in Sefrou, the *umma* in the strict sense of the term, is the bazaar. Normative Islam – as contrasted, on the one side, to the so-called saint worship or maraboutism characteristic of the countryside and the urban poor and, on the other, to the indifferentism of the Western-educated national elite – has emerged in direct association with the emergence of a recognizable commercial class that has both advanced the cause of scripturalist orthodoxy and benefited from its provisions.[48]

The habus's importance in the development of the bazaar was even greater in the early days of its formation, the first three or four decades of the century, than it is now. In the first place, an even greater proportion of commercial property was then in habus – indeed, virtually all of it – because the building of shops, ateliers, and the like outside the medina by the government and by various private parties has mostly taken place since the end of World War II. In the second place, the French encroachment upon habus properties, particularly agricultural ones, grew during the Protectorate period to fairly serious proportions, reducing the resources, and thus the power, of the institution quite significantly. And third, recent reforms, still minor but increasing in scope, on the part of the newly independent state have begun to limit the habus's role still further. But whatever the future of the habus as a factor in the bazaar economy, its role in that economy's development was of central importance, and the deep bond between commerce and orthodoxy it helped to forge will not soon be broken.

The zawia

In its dictionary definition, *zāwia* means "cubicle" or "corner of a room, especially in a mosque" (i.e., a prayer nook), but in Morocco it means about what *iḵwān* ("brethren") or *ṭarīqa* ("path," "way") mean elsewhere: a sufi sect. Properly, the zawia is the building, a kind of small mosque or prayer house; the ikhwan is the social body, the sect as such; and the tariqa is the observance, what the members of the sect do in the building. But colloquially zawia is used for all three of these, whether taken separately or as a single whole.

The religious and organizational dimensions of the Sefrou zawias, which are essentially identical to those of Morocco and North Africa generally, need not be described here in any detail.[49] Massignon's (surely incomplete) list of brotherhoods in Islam mentions thirty-four, past and present, as existing in Morocco, though much depends in these matters on how you count.[50] The major zawias during the period with which we are concerned – that is, since 1910 – were (in order of estimated memberships), the *Tijānīya*, the *Darqāwa*, the *Naṣirīya*, the *Qādarīya*, the *Wazzānīya*, the *ʿIsāwa*, and the *Kittānīya*, all of which, save the Wazzaniya, which had only a few isolated followers, were present in strength in Sefrou, as were several less prominent ones locally popular.[51]

Part of the importance of the zawia in the development of the bazaar economy lies in the simple fact that its members were, at least until the 1950s, almost all merchants and artisans, and almost all merchants and artisans were members.[52] Like the habus, the zawia drew piety and trade together into a single world. The darkened prayer house lined with men telling beads, and the cobbled alleyway thronged with men striking bargains, were separated only by a doorsill: Outside, one could hear the chants as one passed; inside, the clatter as one knelt. But a larger part was that, also like the habus, the zawia played an organizing role in that economy, lent it structure, gave it form. What the habus did for the property system, the zawia did for the occupational: outlined it, stabilized it, and, so doing, reinforced it.

To understand how this was so, and to avoid the misinterpretations that have arisen from a too-ready use of the word *guild* in the Moroccan context, we must become involved in yet a few more intra-Arabic ordinary language distinctions, that tiresome sorting of semisynonyms and partial contrasts necessary to make exotic social arrangements understandable. In Sefrou, at least, *zāwia* must be set beside two other terms, *ḥerfa* ("profession," "vocation") and *ḥenṭa* ("pious society," "mutual aid group"), in order to delineate a very complex interaction of conceptions underlying an equally complex set of social forms. Some of these conceptions were religious, some economic, and some moral; together they defined an unusual institutional pattern whose exact nature the application of standard terms from Western economic history has done more to obscure than to clarify.[53]

In themselves, the three terms are easily enough understood; it is their conjunction that raises the problems. Zawia, as indicated, refers to a religious group of, in Protectorate Sefrou, twenty or thirty to seventy or eighty men, following one or another style of Sufistic practice under the leadership of a religious adept, known as a *muqaddem* (a general word, meaning "leader," "overseer," "headman"), himself usually a disciple of a regional or all-Morocco tariqa leader called a *šai̱k* ("chief," "patriarch," "master"). The group, as a body, possessed a prayer building, as well as some habus property deeded to it by deceased members to support it.[54]

The actual practices, all directed toward the attainment of some level of mystical experience, varied from sedate chanting of classical religious phrases over and over again to exalted dancing and drumming, playing with fire, handling of snakes, swallowing glass, self-mutilation with knives or hatchets. In more general terms, this variation in "way" from the ecstatics of order to those of frenzy, was expressed as a gradation between "clean" (*nqi*) sects and "dirty" (*mūssek̲*). Even small differences in practice, such as whether one stood or sat to chant (it was cleaner to sit, cleaner yet not to chant aloud but under one's breath) played a role in the classification that ran from the Malin Dalil, Mulay Ali Sherif, and Tijani at the clean pole, through the various Darqawa sects (b-l-Larbi, Kittani, b-l-Khadira, and l-Ghazi), to the Nasiriyins, Sadqiyins, and Q̱adariyins in the dirtier direction; the dionysian Aissawa and Hamadsha (the first eating fire and leaping about, the latter opening their heads with hatchets) held down the farther end.

The importance for the bazaar economy of this classification of zawias into clean and dirty was that the various trades and professions, the herfas, were similarly classified, and the classifications in the one domain were, in a broad but yet clearly outlined way, parallel to those in the other. That is, individuals pursuing cleaner occupations (e.g., cloth selling, wool trading, silk handling, tailoring, grocering) tended to belong to cleaner zawias, and those pursuing dirtier occupations (e.g., butchers, vegetable and fruit sellers, blacksmiths, odds-and-ends peddlers) tended to belong to dirtier zawias.

As with the nisba, it is important to understand the highly relative, even probabilistic, nature of this pattern and not to oversubstantivize it into a precise and stable structure. First, the classification, on both the sect side and the trade side, was only partly consensual. Whether Zawia b-l-Khadira was cleaner than Zawia b-l-Larbi, or whether tile making was a dirtier way to earn a living than wheat selling, was to some degree an arguable matter and often enough argued. Second, though in some vague moral and even metaphysical sense "clean" was a more estimable thing for either a profession or a sect to be than "dirty," the system was not in fact hierarchical. Clean trades and brotherhoods did not dominate dirtier ones, and whatever dispraise was involved (which, this being Morocco, was a great deal) flowed freely in all directions. *Caste* is no more appropriate a characterization of occupational organization in the bazaar than *guild*. Third, though the membership correlation was real, recognized, approved, and encouraged, it was nowhere near perfect; nor was it expected to be. Most cloth traders belonged to Malin Dalil (and no butchers did); but some cloth traders belonged to Mohammed b-l-Larbi or Mulay Ali Sherif. Though grocers clearly dominated b-l-Khadira, there were a fair number of ready-made clothes sellers and hardware and spice merchants in that zawia also, as well as an odd barber or café keeper. And so on, down the line. Finally, some traders – especially footloose ones like musicians and auctioneers – were not specifically associated with any zawia, but were either scattered about fairly randomly or did not belong at all.

Yet, for all this, the match between the classification of sects according to their liturgical style and the trades according to their sort of work was reasonably systematic. And, being so, it was as critical in the evolution of the social form of the central place network of the bazaar economy from the point-to-point network of the caravan economy as were the nisba system, the habus, or, as we shall see, the florescence of Jewish paternalism.[55]

A partial list (partial because not all the correlations are recoverable from after-the-fact interviews, and so far as I have been able to discover, there are no written sources on the subject) of trade-sect connections in Sefrou around 1920 is given in Table 6.[56]

Given this clean–dirty interplay between bazaar vocations (herfas) and religious tendencies (zawias), the nature of the third, and most problematical, element in the complex, the henta, can be grasped without invoking external parallels. From one point of view, the henta was the herfa in its religious dimension; from another, it was the zawia in its secular dimension. In the henta the impulse of the trader to relate his career to the deeper reality Islam defined and the desire of the adept (in any case, the same man) to realize his piety in the practical world met and confirmed one another.

The hybrid nature of the henta as a social group was reflected in its membership, which consisted of those practitioners of a particular herfa who were also members of a particular zawia. As indicated, this was rarely, if ever, either all the practitioners of the vocation or all the adherents of the sect.[57] Rather the henta was but a part element in both the zawia and the herfa: a socially focused subgroup within the sect and a religiously focused subgroup within the trade. The clothseller henta, which was located in Malin Dalil, contained neither all the cloth sellers nor all the members of Malin Dalil. Similarly for the grocers in b-l-Khadira or the blacksmiths in Aissawa. The henta formed where the occupational structure and the devotional intersected, but it was an independent entity, with its own activities, purposes, and rationale.[58]

Table 6. *Trades and sects in Sefrou, ca. 1920*

Trade (ḤERFA)[a,b]	Sect (ZĀWIA)[c]
Cloth seller	Malin Dalil, Abdelhayy l-Kittani, Sidi Ahmad l-Tijani, Mulay Ali Sherif
Silk merchant	Mulay Ali Sherif, Tijani,
Kittani, Malin Dalil	
Tailor	Mohammed b-l-Larbi, Mulay Ali Sherif, Kittani, Malin Dalil
Wool trader	b-l-Larbi, Kittani, Mulay Abdelqader l-Jillali
Ready-made clothes seller	b-l-Larbi, b-l-Khadira, Abdelqader l-Jillali
Grocer	b-l-Khadira, Abdelqader l-Jillali, Mohammed ben Nasser, Sidi Hamid b-l-Abdelsadeq
Wheat trader	b-l-Khadira, ben Nasser
Tobacconist	b-l-Khadira, b-l-Larbi
Hardware/spice seller	b-l-Khadira, Abdelqader l-Jillali, ben Nasser
Café keeper	b-l-Larbi, b-l-Khadira
Miller	Abdelqader l-Jillali
Funduq keeper	Abdelqader l-Jillali
Bathhouse keeper	Abdelqader l-Jillali
Weaver	ben Nasser, Abdelqader l-Jillali, Sidi l-Ghazi
Saddlepack maker	l-Ghazi
Cord maker	l-Ghazi
Carpenter	Abdelqader l-Jillali, b-l-Abdelsadeq, ben Nasser
Mason	b-l-Abdelsadeq, Abdelqader
	l-Jillali
Baker	ben Nasser, Abdelqader l-Jillali, b-l-Abdelsadeq
Shoemaker	ben Nasser, Abdelqader l-Jillali

Barber	Abdelqader l-Jillali, ben Nasser, Sidi Lahcen Yusi
Vegetable and fruit seller	Aissawa, Sidi Lahcen Yusi, ben Nasser
Butcher	Aissawa, Abdelqader l-Jillali
Blacksmith	Aissawa
Cooked-food seller	Sidi Ali Hamdush, Aissawa
Odds-and-ends peddler	Aissawa, Sidi Ali Hamdush
Porter	Aissawa, Sidi Ali Hamdush

[a] Trades are listed in sequence from clean to dirty.

[b] Trades that had no, unknown, or scattered affiliations with zawias were musicians, auctioneers, charcoal sellers. Goldsmithing and tinsmithing were largely Jewish trades (as were significant parts of the shoemaker and butcher trades). Those government officials, teachers, etc., who belonged to local zawias (a number belonged to Fez ones) were mostly affiliated with the Tijaniya. Those farmers (i.e., a few, large, urban-dwelling ones) who were members, belonged to the Kittaniya, which, in Sefrou, was dominated by a single, powerful, landed family, the Adluns. For the Arabic names for these trades, see Annex A.

[c] Sects are listed, for each trade, in approximate order of popularity.

Source: Interviews with older informants who had been both traders and zawia members in the 1920s and earlier, some even before the Protectorate.

The particular activities involved were multiple and not identical from one instance to the next, but the majority fell into one or another of three broad categories: (1) general sociability, (2) mutual assistance, (3) collective participation in ritualized civic events. It is difficult to argue that any one of these was fundamental to the others, for they flowed into one another to give the henta the part private club, part protective society, part social faction quality that has made it so difficult for outsiders to comprehend.

The informal socializing aspect ought not, in any case, to be underestimated simply because of the natural difficulties of obtaining circumstantial reports about it decades after the fact. The common interest of the members, deriving from a single profession, promoted socializing, of course; like any business club, the henta was an excellent place to strike deals over drinks, even if the drinks were nonalcoholic. But the mere day-to-day routine of zawia life also promoted socializing: the five daily prayers, usually followed by tea and cakes for those who had time to tarry; a meal after the noon prayer on Friday (itself usually performed in one of the major mosques); major feasts on the religious holidays; and the special "nights" (*lilāt*; sg. *līla*) of mystical practice, also usually connected with conviviality. For those who belonged to one, the henta was their main home away from home. For their wives, meeting on Fridays in the house of one or another members, the henta provided, along with the bath, almost the only legitimate extrafamilial social life. "The henta," the saying said, "is better than the family."

It was better, too, because of its mutual assistance functions, a much more formalized matter.[59] Such assistance consisted of collective rallying around bereaved and mourning members; attendance with appropriate gifts and appropriate prayers at birth, marriage, and circumcision ceremonies; visiting the sick; as well as material help, whether in the form of individual donations, "contribution club" type insurance schemes, or whatever.

The funeral aspect was clearly the most important and the one most often pointed to in reminiscence. The henta usually undertook the whole of the burial expenses, dug the grave (which, for a particularly prominent figure, might be in the zawia floor rather than the public graveyard), provided monetary and moral support to the immediate survivors, and offered up a stream of prayers, sometimes continuing periodically for years, for the deceased's soul. But the obligation to present gifts, cook food, and the like at the happier rites of passage; to aid and comfort the ill (often with curative talismans from the zawia sheikh); and even at particular crises, including business crises, to lend money was also quite strong. The large and wealthy hentas were not only powerful solidary groups in Protectorate and immediate pre-Protectorate Sefrou (i.e., in roughly the first half of the twentieth century), they were virtually the only such groups in the entire bazaar context (to some degree in the entire society), otherwise a radically one-on-one, man-to-man affair.[60]

The third type of activity, group representation in the annual saint festivals, projected the henta, as socializing and mutual aid did not, out of the world of personal interrelations into the public arena; and it thus has been the activity most often noticed.[61] So far as the henta was concerned, there were two main sorts of such festivals (*mwāsīm*, sg. *musim* – literally, "time of the year," "season," "harvest"): those honoring the saint associated with the henta particularly, and those honoring the saint associated with the town as a whole. The former connection was based on the zawia affiliation of the henta: The blacksmiths, being in Aissawa, participated in the musim for Sidi ben Aissa; the tailors in that for Sidi b-l-Larbi; the carpenters in that for Sidi Abdelqader; the weavers in that for Sidi Ali Hamdush. The latter connection, that for the town saint, Sidi Ali Buseghine, a legendary miracle worker migrant to Sefrou from some distant place at some distant time, was based on the mere fact of residence, and all the hentas participated, though they did so severally, not cooperatively, as distinct and independent units.

The zawia musims were each on different, traditionally fixed days of the year. As the shrine (*qubba*) *of* the brotherhood saint was, for Sefrouis, always elsewhere – ben Aissa's in Meknes, b-l-Larbi's in the Rharb, Hamdush's in Zerhun, ben Nasser's in the pre-Sahara – the henta usually held a celebration in Sefrou just prior to the musim proper, parading around town with the henta banners and music to signal the event, and then either went off in a body or sent a delegation to the festival itself. The musim for the local saint (his shrine, a small white cupola structure, sits atop a high hill rising directly behind the town) was held for two days in early October and, until the French suppressed it in the 1930s, was, along with the usual *ᶜid* celebrations, the main communal ritual of the city as a whole.[62]

The members of each henta, carrying banners and various sorts of insignia, marched in a body around the town and then up to the shrine, where they camped in a particular place on the knoll behind the structure. Most hentas endeavored to sacrifice a bull, or even two, or failing that at least several sheep. Some, for example, silk merchants and weavers, brought samples of their craftwork to adorn the shrine. Some chanted, sang, or danced, often to the point of trance. Some provided meat, couscous, soup, tea, cigarettes, and so on for invited guests from comparable hentas in other towns, for the "children of the siyyid" (i.e., the guardians of the shrine, considered to be the saint's descendants), or for the tribal peoples from the surrounding countryside who engaged in the riding and shooting displays that were the high point, in secular terms, of the festival. And they all prayed in turn, though, so far as one can now discover, in no fixed order, before the tomb of the saint. At no other point in the normal course of town life did the henta emerge so emphatically into public view, and in no other context were the foundations of that life in the workings of the bazaar asserted in so explicit a symbolism.

As has been suggested, if obliquely, the hentas are no more. The herfas, the occupational groupings, remain, more or less as they were and structured as they were, except that a few new ones – truck and bus drivers and garage mechanics, most notably – have been added.[63] Most of the zawias also remain, but as shadows of their former selves: mere prayer houses, to which a dwindling band of aging members, survivors from the institution's heyday, repair for chanting and conversation. Indeed, as the florescence of the zawia in effect created the henta, its retrogression has destroyed it – a retrogression caused less by economic or religious factors (though these played a role as well) than by political ones.[64] Nationalism destroyed the zawias and with them the interaction between the work-type classification of the trades and the liturgy-type classification of the sects, the clean–dirty correspondence, that made the henta possible.

The first indication that the zawias were beginning to be projected, or to project themselves, into the political arena came with the French prohibition of the town musim in 1931.[65] This prohibition was part of the general reaction of the Protectorate government to the upsurge of mass religiopolitical protests by the Moroccan urban population following the proclamation of the so-called Berber Decree in 1930, a policy that seemed designed to separate the Berber-speaking population from the Arab, and even from Islam. All over Morocco, mass prayers of supplication, called *laṭīf* (from *ya laṭīf,* "O, Kind One!," the shout that goes up at them), were held in protest, the first truly popular nationalist outcries.[66] The Sefrou saint musim was banned on the basis of the (correct) suspicion that the nationalist, anti-Berber Decree stalwarts were seeking to turn it into such a political latif and had indeed partly done so the year before.

The irony of the situation as it developed for the established zawias was that, initially suspected by the French (to some degree accurately) as seed grounds for rebellion, they became increasingly identified, and in part identified themselves, with the established order, sharing finally in the radical discrediting of that order when at length it fell. The reasons for this are complex, and not all of them are relevant to an understanding of the bazaar economy. But surely the most important reason was the rise, under the combined stimulus of religious reformism and radical nationalism, of a new sort of zawia: the Istiqlal (*istiqlāl,* "independence"), Morocco's first mass political party.[67]

The casting of the Istiqlal (formally founded in 1943 but preceded by a number of clandestine cadre organizations from 1930) into the zawia form has often been noted. Stimulated originally by the Islamic reform movement, *s-salafīya,* the Istiqlal was opposed to the existing zawias, as indeed they tended to be to one another, and put itself forward, as they had before it, as an improved, more authentic version of the brotherhood tradition. The proto-Istiqlal group, the organization that grew out of the latif agitation, actually called itself the Zawia, and its head, later the leader of Istiqlal proper and Morocco's most prominent nationalist, Allal Al-Fassi, was considered its sheikh; the group was referred to, on the usual model, as the Allaliya, its adherents as Allaliyins. The chapters were called *ṭā'ifa* ("part," "portion"), in Morocco a synonym for zawia; the dues were called *ziāra,* on the pattern of contributions by the members to the sheikhs and muqqadems in the older zawias; the nationalist slogans were recited in the style of the traditional prayer chants; the members referred to one another as *ik̲wan* ("brethren"). And so on. As the movement developed, the zawia idiom weakened somewhat at the leadership levels in favor of the political party idiom. But in the countryside and in small towns like Sefrou – and, for that matter, among the urban masses – the zawia form remained strong. And in the revolution it, and the organizational pattern it reflected, served the movement and its cause well.

The earliest phases of the Istiqlal (i.e., those prior to its official foundation) seem to have had no formal representation in Sefrou, though from the latif agitation forward there were a number of sympathizers and even a dedicated adherent or two. The party itself was established in Sefrou in 1943, coincident with its national appearance, and of the original twenty-one members, all but three were bazaar traders or artisans.[68]

This bazaar economy aspect of the movement became crucial in the revolution. In 1946, a number of the leaders of the Istiqlal in Fez, including Allal Al-Fassi's brother, called the inner core of the Sefrou Istiqlal, together with a few militants from various smaller settlements in the area, to a midnight meeting at the house of a prominent Fez merchant living in Sefrou. At the meeting, the central leadership of the party offered to put up 100,000 rials (about $5,000) to each of eight men to set up grocery stores in various places in the Sefrou region to serve as centers for Istiqlal organization. The money, donated to the party by rich Fez merchants, was not turned over to the shopkeepers directly, but given as a credit to the most prominent of the Sefrou grocers, an immigrant from the Sus in south Morocco, who then provided goods to the storekeepers, most of whom were themselves Sefrou townsmen. The storekeepers, who also traveled to rural markets, set up secondary satellite stores of their own, traded as usual, and prospered. But the main purpose was not commerce; it was the setting up of a nationalist network in the Sefrou area, a network that turned out to be extraordinarily effective. The French never uncovered it, and Sefrou became one of the strongholds of the Istiqlal party.[69]

As the Istiqlal rose as the nationalist zawia as well as the bearer of Islamic reform, the older established zawias, led by the Kettaniyin, which was headed on the national level by a long-time Fez rival of Al-Fassi, Abdel Hayy Al-Kettani, became increasingly identified with the Protectorate. Except for the Kettaniyin, which grew more and more powerful in the countryside during this period, the older zawias do not seem to have actively cooperated with the French, but indeed to have been hostile to them, as to Christian domination of the Muslim world generally. But on the principle of "the enemy of my enemy is my friend," they generally supported, in a passive and even somewhat reluctant way (they would have really liked to find a way to be apolitical), Abdel Hayy's anti-Istiqlal, and eventually anti-king, activities. When Istiqlal, and even more clearly, the king, triumphed, they participated in Abdel Hayy's disgrace and have never fully recovered.[70] But though, at least for the moment, the zawia is no longer a central institution in Sefrou, it was critical in the formation of the bazaar economy and has left its stamp permanently on that economy. Indeed, as its spiritual style – a passionate devotionalism trained on charismatic figures – remains intense, the brotherhood pattern may again revive to give shape to the evolution not only of religious but of commercial and political life.

The Jewish community

The Jewish trading community provides, when set beside the Muslim, a model case in the delicacies of sociological comparison: From many points of view it looks exactly like the Muslim community; from as many others, totally different. The Jews were at once Sefrouis like any others and resoundingly themselves. Many of their institutions – in the bazaar setting, most of them – were direct counterparts to Muslim ones; often even the terminology was not changed. But the way those institutions were put together to form a pattern, the organizational whole they add to, was in such sharp contrast to the Muslim way as to be almost an answer to it. It is not possible to treat the Jews as just one moré "tribe" in the Moroccan conglomerate, another nisba, though they were certainly that. Nor is it possible to treat them as a set-apart pariah community, deviant and self-contained, though they were as certainly that too. Moroccan to the core and Jewish to the same core, they were heritors of a tradition double and indivisible and in no way marginal.[71]

This curious just-the-same, utterly different image the Jews presented was made possible by the street cosmopolitanism, domestic communalism pattern of social integration mentioned earlier in connection with nisba classification. In public contexts, and most especially the bazaar (where, it will be recalled from Tables 1 and 2, nearly 90 percent of adult male Jews were in one way or another employed), Jews mixed with Muslims under uniform ground rules, which, to an extent difficult to credit for those whose ideas about Jews in traditional trade are based on the role they played in premodern Europe, were indifferent to religious status. There was, of course, some penetration of communal concerns into the bazaar setting (exclusively Jewish trades, like goldworking and tinsmithing, and such special phenomena as kosher butchers), but what is remarkable is not how much there was but how little. The cash nexus was here quite real; the Jew was cloth seller, peddler, shopkeeper, shoemaker, or porter before he was Jew, and dealt and was dealt with as such.[72] Contrariwise, there was some penetration of general Moroccan patterns of life into the communal area: Jewish kinship patterns were not all that unlike Muslim; Jews not only had saints of their own but often honored Muslim ones as well; and Arabic, not Hebrew, was the language of the home. But this penetration too was minor: As a community (Heb. *qahal*), the Jewish population formed a world very much its own.

The Jews in the mellah

That world was marked by three main characteristics: hyperorganization, thoroughgoing plutocracy, and intense piety. Pressed in behind the walls of their own quarter, the *mellāh*, where, until the Protectorate they were obliged to live, the Jews seem to have concentrated their social personality as the Muslims diffused theirs. Locked each night in their quarter (no non-Jew could enter after dark), an increasingly crowded and unexpandable ghetto, whose buildings raised up like miniskyscrapers to accommodate the pressure, the Jews developed a society whose closest counterpart, the religiosity perhaps somewhat aside, seems to be the merchant oligarchies of Renaissance Italy.[73]

Hyperorganization was the aspect in which the Jewish community was most strikingly different from the Muslim. The dominating institution was a small band of magnates called "the committee" (Heb. *hama'amad*)[74] In Sefrou, the committee had four members up until the 1940s, when a minirevolt by younger, "evolved" Jews forced it to expand to six. Nominally elected, the members were in fact inevitably the richest mercantile figures in the community, and once in place they stayed there until it was time, through aging or death, to coopt their replacements. The plutocracy thus created was further extended by a formal division of the community into five classes of steeply increasing numbers and even more steeply declining wealth: (1) those who had to pay 1,000 rials (in the 1930s, about $50) every six months at the two holiday seasons, Passover and the High Holy Days; (2) those who had to pay 500 rials; (3) those who had to pay 250 rials; (4) those who had to pay 125 rials; and (5) those, the poor, who had to pay nothing and to whom the committee, whose job it was to organize the holidays, distributed this money on behalf of the community. The committee's monopolization of charity, at least of this sort, was official: It was explicitly forbidden for individuals to give private alms (or to beg), and few seem to have done so. This hierarchy of welfare obligations, which was at the same time an economic, a social, and a political hierarchy, was the general backbone of the social pattern I referred to earlier as plutocratic paternalism. "On peut," as Le Tourneau said with respect to the slightly larger Fez committee (it had ten members), "le considérer comme un conseil de gestion de la 'firme Mellah.'"[75]

As such a "conseil de gestion" of such a "firme," the committee faced in several directions: outward, toward the Muslim government, and later the French; downward, toward an enormously complex set of public sodalities controlled and regulated by it; and sideways, so to speak, toward a culturally powerful rabbinate standing moral guard over its, and everyone else's, behavior.

Of these, the connection with the state was perhaps the least important, because in the wider world of Moroccan society individual Jews defended their own interests on the same terms, and through the same maneuvers and institutions, as did the Muslims. A few formal matters aside, the general society and its rulers did not deal with the Jews as an undivided collectivity, but as just so many separate Jews scattered in among so many separate Muslims.[76] What was needed in the role of official representative to the state – the *šaīḵ l-Yahūd* (Heb. *nagīd*) – was someone nerveless enough to haggle with the established powers, Muslim or French, concerning Jewish rights, constraints, grievances, hopes, and obligations. In Sefrou, a single wealthy family, popularly regarded as "stubborn but not intelligent" provided the sheikh al-Yahud for several generations in the nineteenth and early twentieth centuries until an excess of stubbornness at the expense of intelligence led the sultan to inform Sefrou's Jews that he did not much care whom they had for their sheikh so long as he did not come from that family, a suggestion – it came in the form of a decree – to which the community instantly, and apparently with some enthusiasm, acceded. The sheikh, who was simultaneously chairman of the committee, was mainly concerned with relations to the authorities; the internal functions often ascribed, usually rather vaguely, to him in the literature (enforcement of committee decisions, collection of contributions, maintenance of peace) seem to have been reflexes of his formal leadership of the committee and not independent, personal powers. Externally of some consequence because of his contacts with the local qaids and pashas, and occasionally with the royal court itself, his role inside the community was about the same as that of his peers: one of the ruling clique of affluent merchants. As he was not even necessarily the most substantial of them, they could be counted on to contain any "king of the Jews" ambitions he might harbor.[77]

Of the public sodalities (Ar. *ribāᶜ*, sg. *rabᶜ*-, Heb. *ḥebrah*) that were regulated by the committee and formed the internal structure of the community, the most important was one that embraced the entire population and was named after one of the saints venerated in a nearby cave, the Jewish equivalent of Sidi Ali Buseghine, Rabbi Simaun. The Simaun rebaa had three sections (also referred to as rebaa), each with its own chairman, vice chairman, and "messenger." Section membership for both men and women was by patrifiliation: One belonged to the section to which one's father belonged. The functions of the organization were broadly social. At burial, the relevant section prepared the corpse, conducted the funeral, and comforted the survivors. When Jews quarreled among themselves, the section officers sought to settle the matter before it exploded into a public dispute, in which case the committee settled it, usually with advice from the rabbinate. Indeed, all intra-Jewish issues, conflictual or not, were handled within the Simaun rebaa whenever possible.[78] But besides the Simaun rebaa there was a large number – informants speak, vaguely, of *bezzef* ("lots"), and I managed to elicit about a dozen – of less formal, voluntary sodalities, engaged in various social, religious, and philanthropic activities: making clothes for the poor, helping them get married, finding housing for them, supporting orphanages, financing synagogues, reading the Torah, founding schools.[79] In comparison with the Muslim community, where about the only corporate groups worthy of the name, and those but barely, were the zawias and hentas, the Jewish community was a maze of intensely solidary associations dominated in every case by members of the same small band – fifteen, twenty, or twenty-five at the most – of very rich merchants, a thoroughly interlocked directorate of which the committee was but the visible arm.[80]

Yet, for all the committee's power, there was another institution that constrained the oligarchy's behavior from within the community as the

Muslim or French state constrained it from without: the rabbinical court (Heb. *bēth dīn*). The religious life of the community need not be described in any detail here. In its formal outlines it was not different from that of other maghrebi communities, and its tone, rigorous to the point of zealotry, would take a monograph to convey. The point is that, like the institutions of Islam in the wider society, Jewish institutions had more than spiritual consequences. As the Muslim community had its tolba (individuals claiming some degree of religious learning, skill, or piety beyond the normal run of men and regarding themselves as the spiritual conscience of the population), the Jewish had its *ḥazzānīn* (a Hebrew term strictly meaning "cantor[s]," but popularly extended by the general Muslim population, and in colloquial contexts by the Jews themselves, to apply to the religious class generally: scholars, ritual slaughterers, teachers in Talmudic schools, rabbis, judges, even just especially pious men). Of these, three, headed by the chief rabbi of the community, called *rāv* ("master") or *ḥaḵām* ("sage"), sat on the religious court and were known as *dayyānīn* ("judges"). The jurisdiction of the court extended, as did the differently organized qadi court among the Muslims, only to those aspects of social life explicitly covered by religious law: most especially marriage, divorce, and inheritance.[81] The main impact of the religious tribunal on the economic and political life of the community stemmed from its ability to criticize dominant figures from a spiritually secured moral base. The effectiveness with which the tribunal accomplished this and thus formed, with the hazzan class generally, a genuine counterweight to the merchant oligarchy, varied with individuals and circumstances. Depending upon the character of the judges, especially the rav, one could get a narrowly legalistic conception of the judge's office, the hazzan role, and indeed of religious life generally that left the plutocrats a largely free hand, or one could get a broadly moral conception that subjected the plutocrats to a drumfire of prophetlike criticism from the local agents of God's justice. But whatever the momentary situation, the rabbinical court was, aside from its particular judicial functions, a potential counterbalance to the power of the committee and its clientele.

The Jews in the bazaar

When one turns from this brief description of the internal structure of the Jewish community to the integration of its labor force into the bazaar, it is first necessary to forestall a common misconception, one even many Moroccans (though none who have themselves spent any

Table 7. *Comparative percent of Muslim and Jewish bazaar workers in large-, medium-, and small-scale activities, 1960*[a]

	Large scale	Medium scale	Small scale
Muslims			
(N = 1,966)	3	38	59
Jews			
(N = 526)	3	44	53

[a] The large-, medium-, and small-scale classifications are by occupational category and were made totally independently of ethnic considerations. Employment of alternative culting points does not alter the picture appreciably.

Source: Data from official 1960 Census of Sefrou.

Table 8. *Comparative percent of Muslim and Jewish bazaar workers in commerce and artisanry, 1960*

	Commerce	Artisanry
Muslims	28	72
Jews	46	54

Source: Data from official 1960 Census of Sefrou.

significant amount of time in bazaar occupations) hold: namely, that the Jews as a group had a specially privileged role within the bazaar. In Sefrou, at least, this was not the case. As Table 7 shows, the distribution of Jewish merchants and artisans across the economic class structure was, to the degree one can measure it, very similar to that of the Muslim.[82]

If, however, one looks at the situation in terms not of scale of operation but of types (Table 8), a striking difference between the two groups appears: Whereas the Jews are rather equally divided between commercial and artisanal occupations, the Muslims are heavily weighted toward the artisan side.[83] In part, this merely reflects certain value differences between the two groups, the Muslims regarding craft labor more highly than the Jews. In part, it reflects history, the Jews having been relatively more prominent in the largely nonartisanal caravan trade in nineteenth-century Sefrou. But in the main it reflects the nature of the Jewish role as it developed, given those values and that history, in the evolving opportunity structure of the bazaar economy: The Jews became the intermediaries between the (largely) Arab-speaking population of the town and the (largely) Berber-speaking population of the countryside.[84]

As remarked above, the role of the Jews in connecting Sefrou's region-focusing bazaar to the cloud of locality-focusing bazaars growing up around it was crucial from the earliest stages of the transition from passage to central place trade and to some extent even preceded them. Just why this should have been so, why the Arabic speakers of: Sais Plain Morocco and the Berber speakers of Middle Atlas should have needed a third element distinct from them both to relate them commercially, can only be a matter for speculation. The desire of intensely competitive groups – suspicious of each other's actions, jealous of each other's power, and frightened of each other's ambitions – to conduct their trade through politically impotent agents, individuals who could bring neither force nor authority to bear in the exchange process and could achieve nothing more than wealth by means of it, is perhaps part of the answer. A related desire to divest trading activities of any meaning beyond the cash and carry and so blunt their acculturative force may be another. But whatever the reason, the fact had a profound impact, virtually a determining one, on the shaping of Jewish activities in the bazaar economy.

In the first place, it meant that Jewish trade was heavily rural-oriented. Not only were many Jews engaged in itinerant petty commerce, but as artisans they were heavily concentrated in a very few light crafts, particularly shoemaking and tailoring, specifically oriented to a rural clientele.[85] In the second place, it meant that, within the town, the various strands of trade were drawn up into a very few hands, those again of the dominant figures of the community. In contrast to the Muslim pattern of long sequences of ad hoc two-person connections between traders of every size and description, running in diverse directions and crossing and recrossing one another in hopeless complexity, now and then converging momentarily on some more formidable figure emerging from the crowd and then immediately scattering again, the Jewish pattern consisted of a large mass of marginal and semimarginal operators directly and almost totally dependent on one or another of a dozen or two established financiers. The similar distribution of Muslim and Jewish traders across the very gross categories of large, small, and medium scale shown in Table 7 thus masks a sharp difference in the nature of the relations among individuals in those categories in the two groups. Among the Muslims, the leading traders stood out from the rest; among the Jews, they stood over the rest.

Each of the major figures – the "sitting" (*gles*) Jews referred to earlier – had attached exclusively and more or less permanently to him a number of itinerant merchants – "riding" (*rkeb*) Jews.[86] The riding Jews traveled about the countryside, often in twos and threes, their goods loaded onto donkeys. They camped in areas where their backers had established updated versions of the old mezrag tradeplace arrangement with a local power (the major sitting Jews seem to have parceled out spheres of influence in the countryside in a conscious, precise, and systematic manner, to the point where exactly whose writ ran exactly where is still recallable today) at the edge of one or another Berber settlement. There they set up a makeshift shop out of which, as well as in the local periodic bazaar and even – only a Jew could approach a Berber woman in her home – door to door, they peddled cloth, ready-made clothes, shoes, domestic implements, soap, sugar, salt, tea, matches, perfumes, medicines, oil, spices, jewelry, talismans, and, increasingly, cheap imported manufactures such as combs, clocks, and mirrors. On the buying side they purchased, again both directly and more and more in the expanding local suqs, hides, wool, animals, olives, and grain, which the Berbers themselves then carried to the sitting Jews in town. They lent money, either outright or through taking pawns, and they arranged share contracts (oral, as all these arrangements) concerning animals or olives in which the Jews purchased beasts or trees, the Berbers raised and cared for them, and the returns were, by one or another elaborate formula, divided. After a month or six weeks of this the Jews moved on to another location of the same sort, repeated the process, and then moved on again.

The riding Jews were, in fact, riding, camp to camp, suq to suq, virtually the whole of the year, returning to Sefrou for any length of time only during the two main holiday seasons.[87] In town, the sitting Jews sat, sources not only of capital for the riding Jews, but of food and housing, and indeed of a whole range of welfare services, for the latter's families, including governance of their moral and religious life. Though not explicitly conceived as such, the riding Jews were almost as much the sitting Jews' servants as their agents. Toward the artisans, most of whom, especially in shoemaking and tailoring, were also dirt poor, the financiers had a similar relation, capitalizing them, engrossing their output, and providing for their subsistence almost as an extension of an expanded family economy. The welfare hierarchy that governed community life generally provided the framework for commercial relations within the community as well. Outside the community, whether dealing with a

Berber pastoralist, a town weaver, or a Fez importer, the Jews fitted, as mentioned, into the more general structure of the bazaar as a whole. Indeed, in Sefrou at least, tying town and country together, permanent suq and periodic, they helped create the bazaar.[88]

This done, they then turned, as the Protectorate period advanced, toward yet another form of commercial pioneering, the development of the modern business district, the show-window bazaar connecting the European community – by the 1930s some 700 or 800 people – commercially to the local economy. The first modern-type grocery stores, called épiceries rather than hanuts, along the highroad were opened by Jews, soon followed by other European-oriented businesses: bars, furniture stores, gas stations, garages, pharmacies, bicycle shops, (Western) tailors, and eventually a motion picture house. In time, some Muslims became involved in this expansion, but the formative phase (which ended, as did so much else, in 1940) seems to have been largely Jewish.[89] By 1969, when the European population had fallen to less than 100, and the Jewish to less than 400, about ten out of the thirty-five or forty business-district-type enterprises were still Jewish-owned. But the end of that development, like the end of the community generally, was drawing near. Having helped in turn to project Sefrou into the caravan trade, link it to the rural bazaar, and adjust it to enclave capitalism, the Jews disappeared from the scene to apply their practiced ability to change with change in another history.

The bazaar as an economic institution

Product of a transformation of long-distance caravan trade into short-distance central place trade, set in the context of Moroccan ideas of piety, community, and personal identity, and animated by a jumble of received practices, borrowed tastes, and changing possibilities, the bazaar is also, of course, a social mechanism for the production and exchange of goods and services: an economic system. It is not there, in the first instance, to express Moroccan religious conceptions or to exemplify Moroccan social arrangements, but to bring supply crowds and demand crowds usefully together. The institutional structures and practical procedures through which it does this (and changes them thus from mere crowds to formed webs of personal connection) are as distinctive a characteristic as nisba categorization, habus property law, or the moral impact of zawia mysticism.

Looked at in this light – as a ramifying pattern of material transactions, most of them face to face – the bazaar consists in the integration of physically separated marketplaces into a continuous system. In part, this integration is accomplished spatiotemporally, as one market-day area overlaps with the next, chain-mail fashion, across virtually the whole of Morocco. In part, it is accomplished hierarchically, as national emporiums, region-focusing markets, and locality-focusing markets reach out toward one another in a center and subcenter, headquarters and outpost fashion. And in part it is accomplished functionally, as the wheat-dominated markets of the plain, the wool-dominated ones of the steppe, the olive markets of the piedmont, and the manufactures ones of the coast balance off their specialties.

But it is not the marketplaces that do all this. It is those who frequent them: the *sūwwāqa*.

Sūwwāq (sg.) is a term for which no precise equivalent exists in English. It covers anyone who attends markets, of whatever size and for whatever purpose, with some regularity; an habitue of suqs. It includes the countryman bringing his two or three sheep or his basket of barley into a mountain bazaar in search of a little cash, together with the great Fez or Marrakech engrosser pyramiding deals in his urban warehouse. It includes buyer and seller, producer and consumer, master and apprentice, transporter, auctioneer, moneylender, and market official. It includes the man who squats on a carpet and tells sad stories of the death of kings, the man who wanders through the crowd with a zawia pennant collecting pious contributions, the man who sits behind a small table and writes whorled, grandiloquent letters to order; and it includes the gambler, the pickpocket, the snake charmer, the prostitute, even the idler just hanging around as part of the life (a secondary meaning of *sūwwāqa* is "rabble," "mob"), so long as they pursue their occupations in a place called a suq. What sets any one Moroccan marketplace off from any other one, and one section of such a marketplace from another section, is less where it is located, how it is housed, or even its size, than the types of suwwaqs characteristically found there.

This point is of some importance because of a tendency in what literature there is on Moroccan suqs to draw sharp contrasts between them along rural-urban lines, and in particular to characterize so-called tribal markets as a distinct economic type.[90] The fact is that, at least so far as Morocco is concerned, the rural or "tribal" market and the urban or "bourgeois" market are, in analytical terms, the same institution. Suqs may be developed or undeveloped, permanent or periodic, crowded alleyway quarters in built-up towns or sprawling tent camps set up for the day in an open field, and they may serve whole sections of the country or a handful or nearby villages. But their basic organization and mode of functioning vary very little. A suq is a suq, in Fez or in the Atlas, in cloth or in camels. The players differ (and the stakes), but not the shape of the game.[91]

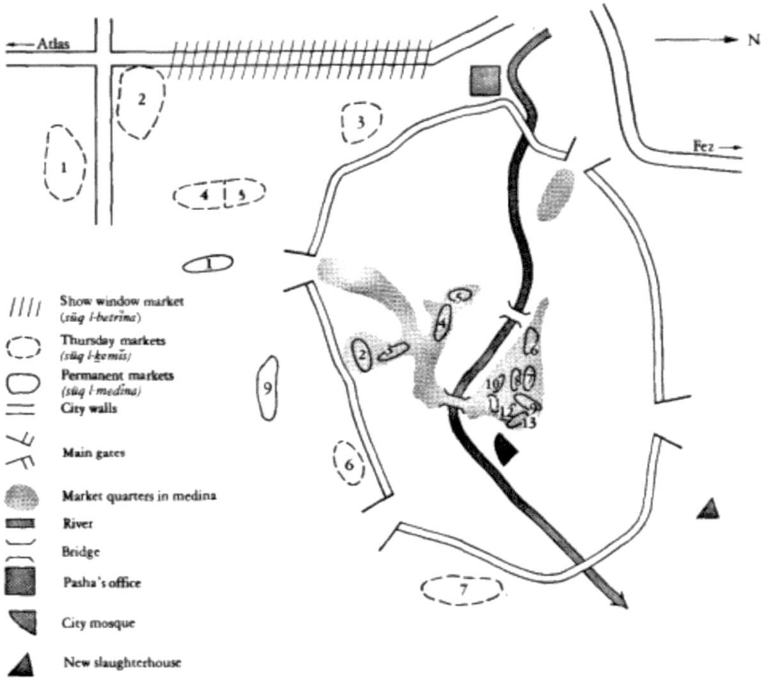

Figure 4. The markets of Sefrou, 1968–9.
Thursday markets
1 *Sūq l-ḵodra*: vegetables, fruits, spices
2 *Sūq l-ksiba*: (*l-behayim, l-begra*): sheep, goats, cattle, donkeys
3 *Sūq s-sella*: baskets, woven mats, chickens, eggs, salt
4 *Sūq z-zraᶜ*: (*l-gemeh*): grain, beans
5 *Sūq s-suf-*: wool
6 *Jutiya* (*kerīa*)*:* secondhand goods, flea market
7 *Sūq z-zrābi*: rugs, textiles, clothes, medicines, storytellers, odds and ends
Permanent markets
1 *Terrāfīn*: shoemakers, shoe repairers
2 *Swiqa* (*ḵeddāra*): vegetables, fruits
3 *Blasa* (*gezzāra*): butchers

4 *Ḵiyyāta*: tailors
5 *Harrāra*: silk
6 *Qīsarīya* (*bezzāziyin*): cloth, jewelry
7 *Bradʿiya* (*semmārin*): saddlemakers, horseshoers
8 *Haddādin*: blacksmiths
9 *Najjārin*: carpenters (two locations)
10 *Qsadriya*: tinsmiths
11 *Tiyyabin* (*kiffitiyin*): cooked food
12 *Thiniya* (*kebbazin*): flour, baked bread, sweet rolls
13 *Hajjamin*: barbers, cuppers

Note to Figure 4: Suqs are referred to in various ways, and I have given in each case what seems to me the most popular (and where two seem about equally current, an alternative in parenthesis) in Sefrou ca. 1968–9. Suqs named after occupations may be designated by either the masculine (*terrāfin, nejjārīn, haddādīn*) or the feminine (*terrāfa, nejjāra, ḥaddāda*) sound plural. I have again given what seems to me the more common usage in each case, but the alternative (*kvyyātin, hajjāma*) is almost always also current. It is usually possible, particularly when a sort of good (e.g., flour, silk) rather than a type of skill (e.g., tailoring, carpentry) is involved, to use the combining form, as with the Thursday markets-*sūq l-thīn* ("flour market"), *sūq l-hrīr* ("silk market") – or the "owners of" (*mwālin*, sg. *mūl*) form – *mwālin l-thin* ("flour owners"), *mwālīn l-hrīr* ("silk owners"). Finally, for almost all trades, not just the *thīnīya, bradʿīya*, etc. of the list, where it is preferred, the plural of the occupational nisba – *hrārīya* ("silk-merchantish" or "silks area", a barbarous translation, but the closest I can get); *nejjārīya* ("carpenterish area") – is usually acceptable. It is possible that actual choices in these matters reflect subtle conceptual, and thus sociological, differences, rather than being mere free variants. If so, I cannot yet sort them out.

Ecology: the suq on the ground

Three aspects of a suq, as suq, need to be addressed in describing it: (1) its physical form – how it is laid out, populated, sectioned into parts; (2) its social form – how practical relationships (seller and buyer, lender and borrower, master and apprentice, professional and layman) are ordered and regulated with it; and (3) its dynamics, the characteristic patterns of activity it sustains – how bazaar actors behave and why. For convention's sake, we begin with the first; hard data give a place to stand, or seem to. But we might as well have started with either of the other two, for they are all, in actuality, interfused – part of a single reality suwwaqs inhabit.

To reprise an earlier discussion, the main sub-elements of the Sefrou bazaar are (1) "the old city bazaar" (*sūq l-medīna*), which during the past thirty years or so has spilled over into the newer quarters immediately outside the walls; (2) "the Thursday bazaar" (*sūq l-ḵemīs*), which connects Sefrou with the periodic market system of the region generally and thus integrates it into the wheat-sheep-and-olive economy of the countryside; and (3) "the show-window bazaar" (*sūq l-betrīna*) of the French-built new town, which integrates Sefrou into the cosmopolitan economy of developed Morocco – Fez, Rabat, Casablanca, and beyond. The layout of these various bazaars can be seen in detail in Annex A, where each established enterprise is mapped and classified. A general picture can be obtained from Figure 4, which summarizes in schematic form what is recounted in Annex A.[92] The figure shows the Sefrou market at its fullest extent, on market day, when the population of the town probably doubles or more as, by foot, donkey, mule, bus, and truck, the countrymen (and suwwaqs from other towns) stream in to trade.

The first thing that leaps to notice from Figure 4 is that all the Thursday markets, each quite definitely specialized, are located outside the walls in the new quarters to the south. As reference to Annex B ("The Markets of Sefrou around 1910") will make apparent, this has not always been the case. Each of these markets was originally inside the medina amid the permanent ones, which latter were themselves then rather more periodic affairs, functioning with much force only on Thursdays, than they have since become. By 1936, when Le Tourneau made a brief survey of the periodic markets in Sefrou town (he paid only glancing attention to the permanent ones, which were just then beginning to become truly such), all save the flea market had moved out to a single location – the place where the wool and grain markets are today. At that time, the animal market immediately adjoined this "vaste enclos bordé de boutiques et de magasins," to which it was physically connected by an arcade. In addition to wool, wheat, barley, maize, and beans, such items as salt, rugs, charcoal, pots, baskets, mats, fruit, vegetables, chickens, and eggs were sold in this French-built (1931) *marsi* (i.e., Fr. *marché*).[93] By 1951, when Si Bekkai, then pasha of Sefrou, made an even more cursory survey (though one that did distinguish the periodic and permanent aspects of the bazaar, a contrast it was no longer possible to miss), the animal market had been moved, "pour des raisons faciles a concevoir," to its present location. At the same time, the rug and basket traders had drifted, or been pushed, to their separate places, leaving the "vaste enclos" (it is only about 1,000 square meters) exclusively to wool at one end and cereals, legumes, fruits, and vegetables at the other.[94] The establishment of an external Thursday market in vegetables and fruits, separate both from a refurbished permanent vegetable market within the medina and from the wool-wheat extramural one, in the late 1960s completed the process; no periodic market remained within the old city.[95]

The reasons for this evolution, if that is what it should be called, are the obvious ones: expansion and solidification of commerce (including a sharpening differentiation of permanent bazaar trade from periodic); overcrowding of the medina, mainly as a result of rural in-migration; and French (and now Moroccan) attempts at more systematic, "functional" zoning.[96] There are government plans to rationalize further the Sefrou market layout to the point where all commercial and industrial activity will be located outside the medina, leaving the latter wholly residential – an archaic slum awaiting only the next lurch toward "modernity" to be razed altogether.

As for the permanent markets (of which only those more commonly referred to are indicated in Figure 4), perhaps the most striking thing about them is that they exist. Despite the enormous expansion in numbers of traders (since 1900, over 300 percent, as indicated in Table 1), trades (about a third of the trades of Sefrou postdate the establishment of the Protectorate), and volume of trade (difficult to estimate numerically, but universally attested to by knowledgeable informants), activity remains strongly localized in occupational terms, as demonstrated in Tables 9 through 11. It is still the case, as it was in 1910, 1935, and 1950, that most forms of commercial and artisanal activity cluster together in definite – usually quite small – sections of the town.[97]

The permanent, periodic, and show-window bazaars differ in physical appearance as well.

The last, with its glass-fronted stores, sidewalk cafés, and motion picture houses strung out along the main street (Boulevard Mohammed V), with signs proclaiming what they are and often the owner's name and telephone number, looks about like any small-town business district – complete with sidewalks, parking zones, a stoplight, and the inevitable *ronde pointe* – in provincial France.

The periodic marketplaces consist of large cleared areas, on a lively day packed beyond imagination with would-be buyers and sellers: a collection of small-scale medieval fairs. The animal marketplace is enclosed by walls, the sellers of goats, sheep, cattle, donkeys, and mules, occupying distinct regions within it. They stay put with their animal(s) while the buyers wander among them, inspecting, bargaining, choosing. The wool, grain, and bean marketplace is bordered, as Le Tourneau noted, with shoplike buildings, except that all of them now are used either to house motor-driven mills (sg. *ṭāḥūna*) or as storage houses (sg. *ḵzīn*). The grain, beans, and wool are piled by their vendors in large heaps around the open plaza, also according to established place, and a group of scale owners (sg. *mūl l-mīzān*) occupies a weighing shed at one end. The other periodic marketplaces show a similar pattern: The offerer of rugs or baskets or clothes or vegetables sits at his place, his *mūḍaᶜ*, as possible buyers wander by to look, haggle, and decide. Sellers (auctioneers, of whom more later, aside) virtually never wander about hawking their wares.

Table 9. *Distribution of strongly localized trades in Sefrou, 1968–9*

Trade	Number in suq area[a]	Total number	Percent in suq area
Blacksmith (*ḥaddād*)	15	15	100
Saddlemaker/horseshoer (*bradᶜī/semmār*)	7	7	100
Vegetable and fruit seller (*k̲eḍḍar*)	82	90	91
Butcher (*gczzār*)	20	22	91
Prepared-food seller (*tiyyāb*)	12	15	80
Cloth merchant (*mūl l-kettān, mūl t-tūb*)	25	35	71
Tinsmith (*qṣādrī*)	7	10	70
Tailor (*k̲iyyāt*)[b]	52	73	70
Weaver (*derrāz*)	15	22	68
Hardware/spice seller (*mūl l-ḥadīd*)[c]	6	10	60
Silk merchant (*barrār, brārī*)	13	33	59
Carpenter (*nejjār*)[d]	10	18	56
Odds-and-ends seller (*k̲ordāwī*)	9	17	53
Shoemaker (*ṭerrāf*)	16	31	52
Barber/cupper (*ḥajjām*)[e]	20	42	48
Miller (*ṭeḥḥān*)[f]	5	12	42
Ready-made clothes seller	16	36	41
Overall	330	488	68

[a] By suq area is meant the part of the town informants regard as the place where members of the trade are normally to be found, their *mūḍaᶜ* or *reḥba* ("place," "space").

Such areas, which are named, in various ways, after the trade concerned (see Figure 4), are admittedly fuzzy at the edges, necessitating some practical judgments on the part of the ethnographer about where to draw the line. But their overall location is perfectly consensual for all informants. All are quite small, never more than a few hundred square meters, most a good deal less.

[b] The tailors are in two locations, rather than one. Thirty-four (47%) are in the old khiyyata of Figure 4; eighteen more have clustered near the cloth market, the Qisariya, giving the composite 70% figure.

[c] All (six) of the traditional-type hardware/spice traders are in one region (*Reḥbt l-ᶜaued*: see Figure A.13, Annex A). The other four, somewhat more "modern" in form, are in the new quarter, Derb l-Miter (Sections A.5 and A.6 on Figure A.1 of Annex A).

[d] Only two carpenters remain in the old area of Annex B; the new carpenters' suq is outside the medina in Derb l-Miter.

[e] All old-fashioned barbers (those who also serve as cuppers) are in the old hajjama suq; the appearance of new-style barbers in the new quarters is quite recent.

[f] Four of the five millers run modern machine-driven grain mills located around the Thursday grain market. The scattered millers are the remnants, all outside the medina, of the water-driven-mill (*rḥa b-l-mā*) industry, once quite large, which the 1950 flood more or less wiped out.

Source: Based on data presented in Annex A plus informants' judgments about the location of the various suqs.

Various marginal trades such as (traditional) plumber (*qwādsī*), musician (*šaiḵ*), tile maker (*zellaižī*), cord maker (*šerrāt*) are not considered. What representatives of them still exist are scattered randomly about.

Source: Based on data presented in Annex A plus informants' judgments about the location of the various suqs.

In the permanent marketplaces, the "sitting pattern," which is what selling there is commonly called (*gles f-l-ḥanūt*, "sitting in a shop") is even more pronounced. Each trader has a small, usually wooden cubicle (a hanut) a couple of meters wide, deep, and high in most cases, rarely more than 3 or 4 meters, where he squats with his goods about him as market goers stream by in front of him (see Figure 5). Craft ateliers, also called hanuts, are about the same, except that they are oriented toward the workplace inside the cubicle rather than toward the street, and, of course, the interior layout is adjusted to the particular demands of the craft.

The various bazaars of Sefrou thus are distinctive in layout, architecture, and the flow of traffic. Yet, because they all at base *are* bazaars of one sort or another, highly specialized areas set apart exclusively for craft and trade, the distinctions, though real, have not hardened into divisions.[98]

Table 10. *Distribution of moderately and weakly localized trades in Sefrou, 1968–9*

Trade	Location
Moderately localized trades	
Wheat and bean trader (*mūl z-zraʿ; mūl l-fūl*)	Operate mainly in Thursday market where many have storage houses and some own or share in mills. Also travel to rural markets.
Wool trader (*mūl ṣ-ṣuf*)	Operate in Thursday market and travel to rural ones.
Café keeper (*qehwāji*)	Mainly clustered along Fez road and near gates to medina.
Baker (*mūl l-ferrān; ḵebbāz*)	Distributed by quarter, theoretically (and for most part actually) one to each quarter.
Bathhouse keeper (*mūl l-ḥammām*) Lime kiln (*kūša*)	As bakers. Bakers and bathhouse keepers are only trades not confined to properly suq areas of town, but commonly found in midst of residential areas. See separate listing in Annex B. There are ten or so lime kilns for making whitewash located in the rocky hillsides just south of town in a definite cluster (not mapped in Annex A). Most are owned by old Sefroui townsmen and worked by rural in-migrants. Product is sold mainly by hardware/spice merchants.
Prostitute (*qaḥba*)	Prostitutes are difficult to census for obvious reasons, but most live in and around mellah, which has turned into a slum-cum-red-light district since departure of Jews to the new quarters. Ready-made clothes dealers, café keepers, etc., act as pimps.
Flour and bread seller (*mūl l-ṭḥīn wa l-ḵubz*)	The four or five who are left still in tihiniya. Flour is now mostly sold in grocery stores.
Porter (*ḥernmāl; zerzaī*)	Hang out, waiting for jobs, just outside the major gates of town. Some have crude handcarts; some merely bear things on their backs.

Trade	Location
Casual laborer (*ḵeddām*)	Casual laborers, whose numbers fluctuate with season and circumstance between about ten and about a hundred, hang out, waiting for pickup work, around plaza in front of Mkam gates, along edge of park in front of pasha's office, and near public works and public welfare offices in Derb l-Miter (see Figures A.5 and A.11, Annex A).
Scribe (*kātib*) *Weakly or nonlocalized trades*	Sit at small tables in arcade in front of Merbaᶜ gate and in various Thursday markets.
Grocer (*beqqāl*)	Small grocers are found almost everywhere in suq areas outside medina. However, the very largest ones (their stores are called *herī,* roughly "depot," "emporium"), who serve as suppliers to many of the others and to small shops in villages, are concentrated just outside Merbaᶜ gate (see Figure A.5, Annex A).
Mason (*bennaāī*)	Masons have no business abode in most cases, though a few large ones have storage yards in the new quarters.
Tobacconist (*saka*)	Tobacconists are randomly scattered.
Auctioneer (*dellāl*), broker	These are unlocalized by profession.
(*semsār*), arbitrager (*sebaībī*)	They are discussed further in text.
Home spinner (*ḡezzāla*)	Home spinning is connected to the wool trade and carried out by women in their homes under a putting-out system, mediated by women engrossers, who then sell the produce in a special women's market. This is discussed in text.
Hashish seller (*mūl l-kīf*)	Hashish selling is at least formally illegal and is conducted semi-clandestinely at various well-known points scattered around town. Most hashish comes into Sefrou area from Rif area of northeast Morocco.

Table 11. *Distribution of modern trades in Sefrou, 1968–9*[a]

Wholly new trades
Bicycle seller and repairman (*sīklist*)[b]
Radio repairman (*kehrabī*)[c]
Electrical supplies seller (radios, refrigerators, fans, lighting fixtures, etc.) (*mūl l-'ālāt*
l-kehrahā)[c]
Watchmaker (*mūl l-mwāgen*)[b]
Gasoline station keeper (*pumpī*st)[c]
Garage mechanic, auto parts seller (*garājīst*)[d]
Transport worker: trucker (*mūl l-kamiūn*), bus owner or driver (*mūl l-kār*), taxi owner
or driver (*mūl ṭ-ṭaksi*)[e]
Electrician (*mūl ḍ-ḍū*)[c]
Movie house owner (*mūl s-itnima*)[c]
Pharmacist (*mūl d-dwā*)[c]
Photographer (*ṣuwwūr*)[c]
Physician (*ṭabīb*)
Modem versions of older trades
Grocer (*pīserī*)[c]
Tailor (*ṭaīyūr*)[c]
Barber (*kuāfūr*)[c]
Plumber (*plumbī*)[b]
Carpenter, sawmill owner (*menīsiwī*)
Innkeeper (*mūl l-uṭīl*)[c]

[a] Modern trades may be loosely divided (though Sefrouis do not) into those that are wholly new, imported from the West, and those that are modernized versions of older trades. Some modern trades have Arabic names (*suwwū*, photographer), some have Arabized French names (*menīsiwī*, carpenter, sawmill owner, from *menuisier*), and some have a mixture of both (*mūl l-utīl*, innkeeper).

[b] Trades located in Derb l-Miter (see Figures A.5–A.7, Annex A).

[c] Trades located in show-window bazaar (see Figures A.2–A.4, Annex A).

[d] Clustered at upper end of Derb l-Miter (see Figures A.3 and A.5, Annex A).

e Vehicles garaged at, and buses and taxis operate out of, station in front of Mkam Gate (see Figure A.11, Annex A).

Source: Based on data presented in Annex A plus informants' judgments about the location of the various suqs.

There is the boutiquier propriety of the business district; there is the Carnivalesque, country-fair hubbub of the animal, grain, or rug markets; there is the casbah mysteriousness of the winding, cobblestone thoroughfares of the medina, some covered with lattices and none wide or level enough to accommodate wheeled vehicles; and there is the neither-this-nor-that, square-buildings, gridstreet attempt at urban regularity of the new quarters (Derb l-Miter, "Metric Street[s]") that the persistence of older styles of doing things has turned into a medina housed in a bourgade. These are all discernible enough to the eye of the suwwaq, as are the subareas and the sub-subareas within them. But they are, to that same eye, also mere locales, various arenas in a single, continuous, entangled whole: *Sūq Ṣ-Ṣefru.*

Organization: the structures of order

If, in describing the ecology of the suq, one begins, naturally, with the physical layout, one begins, equally naturally, with the division of labor in describing its social form. But, as with physical layout, such a description must be cast in terms of the perceptions of those caught up in bazaar life, not in terms of some conventional grid of occupational differentiation impressed upon that life from outside. The network of conceptual distinctions suwwaqs use to divide themselves into general categories, those general categories into more focused component categories, and those more focused component categories into particular roles or role types needs to be uncovered. An attempt to do this, in a form still far too gross to be adequate to the enormous delicacy of discrimination that is actually there, is shown in Figure 6, a tree-diagram of suwwaq classification, the indigenous typology of work, as it exists in Sefrou.

The division of labor

Figure 6 presents the main types of bazaar roles (e.g., shopkeeper, arbitrager, craftmaster, target seller) as the Sefrouis see them, and indicates how the Sefrouis conceive of the relations among these roles.[99] Below, indicated by the dotted lines, the tree branches into the separate trades and crafts: cloth sellers, carpenters, wool traders, bathhouse keepers, sheep vendors, rug auctioneers, cattle brokers, and so on. Above, similarly indicated, the suwwaq "market participant" category is in contrast with the other overall occupational domains in Sefrou, of which the main ones

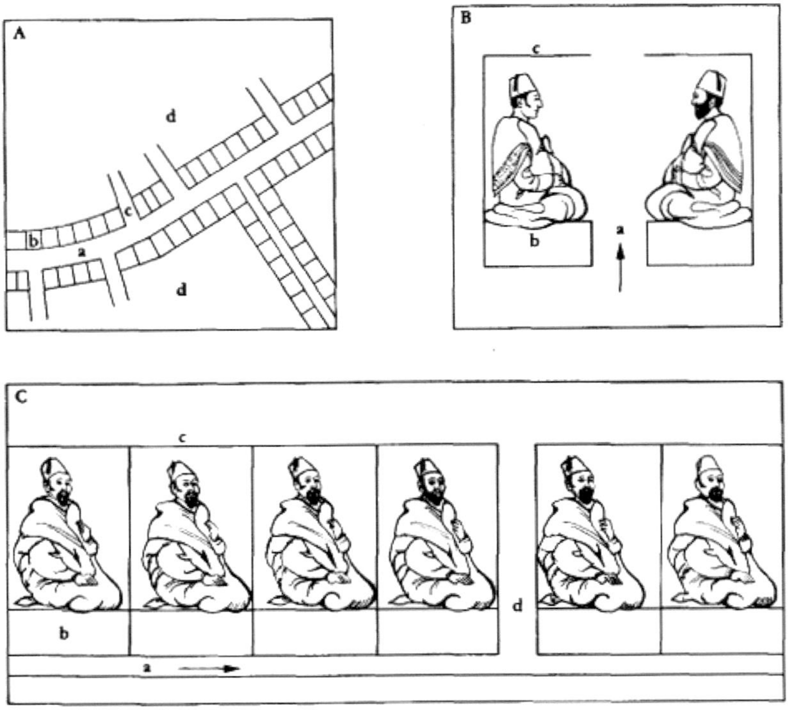

Figure 5. Permanent shops. *A. Air* view of shop layout in part of permanent market: *a*, street (*zenqa*); *b*, shop (*ḥānūt*); *c*, alley (*derb*); *d*, residential quarter (*ḥūma*). *B*. Cross section of shops: *a*, street; *b*, sitting platform; *c*, roof. *C*. Front view of shops: *a*, street; *b*, sitting platform; *c*, roof; *d*, alley. (Constructed after the mode of presentation used by Le Tourneau [*Fès avant le Protectorat*, Casablanca, 1949, p. 316] for Fez, which in this regard hardly differs from Sefrou.)

are *fellāh* ("farmer") and *mūḍḍaf* (strictly, "government clerical worker," but now applied to office workers generally), each of which has its own internal pattern of division. The middle-range categorizations shown in the figure, the ones we are concerned with here, bring the spectacular complexity of the division of labor at the level of particular activities – of which even the 110 trade abbreviations listed in Annex A represent a simplified picture – into a comprehensible order. They outline the overall structure of the bazaar economy as an occupational world for those who have, each day, to operate within it.[100]

The major contrast within the bazaar domain between "buyer-seller" and "artisan" is extremely sharp and completely consensual. Special cases aside, there are virtually no examples of artisans who themselves hawk their manufactures directly in the marketplace. Either they contract jobs with particular clients who seek them out, by far the more common pattern, or they sell their product to buyer-sellers who then sell them in turn to consumers (or, as commonly, to other buyer-sellers). Inversely, though buyer-sellers will put out special contract jobs, usually rather small-scale ones, to particular artisans, thus engrossing their output for a few weeks, I was unable to find a single case where an artisan was an employee of a buyer-seller (i.e., where a buyer-seller owned an atelier run for him by a craftmaster subordinate to him) or even a case where a master was so deeply in debt to a buyer-seller that it amounted to the same thing. (The explicit fear of precisely this on the part of many artisans, and their conscious effort to avoid contracting the bulk of their output to any one buyer-seller, suggests, however, that it does on occasion occur.) Except for one or two modern furniture enterprises, there are no integrated craft-commercial enterprises of significance in Sefrou, and there seem never to have been any.[101] One either makes (or repairs) things, or one vends them; almost never both.

On the buying and selling side, the absence of a single term (or at least one in common use) for *merchant* is itself indicative. Buying and selling are regarded as a unitary activity to be looked at simultaneously from the wholly interchangeable perspectives of the man who is passing goods to a trading partner and the man who is passing money, a difference in itself of no essential import. Both *biᶜ* ("to sell") and *šri* ("to buy") have one another's primary meaning as their own secondary one, so that each really signifies something like "to make, or conclude, a deal, a bargain, a contract, an exchange." This implies, in turn, that even an ordinary customer – what is here glossed as a "target buyer" (and of whom more in a moment) – is viewed as himself a kind of trader, and there is no clear contrast between wholesale, in the sense of trader-to-trader, and retail, in the sense of trader-to-consumer, commerce.[102] In the universe of the suq, which *is* a universe, and, conceptually at least, a closed one, all are suwwaqs of one sort or another. There is no general public.

The next two levels of discrimination on the buyer-seller side (they have no application on the artisan side) are adjectival, not nominative; they are not themselves roles, but rather groupings of roles, genres of occupation. The "fixed"/"ambulant" distinction has already been mentioned several times, and is in any case fairly transparent in its meaning. The only remark still left to be made is that the distinction does not rest on whether the role occupant ever moves from his accustomed place.

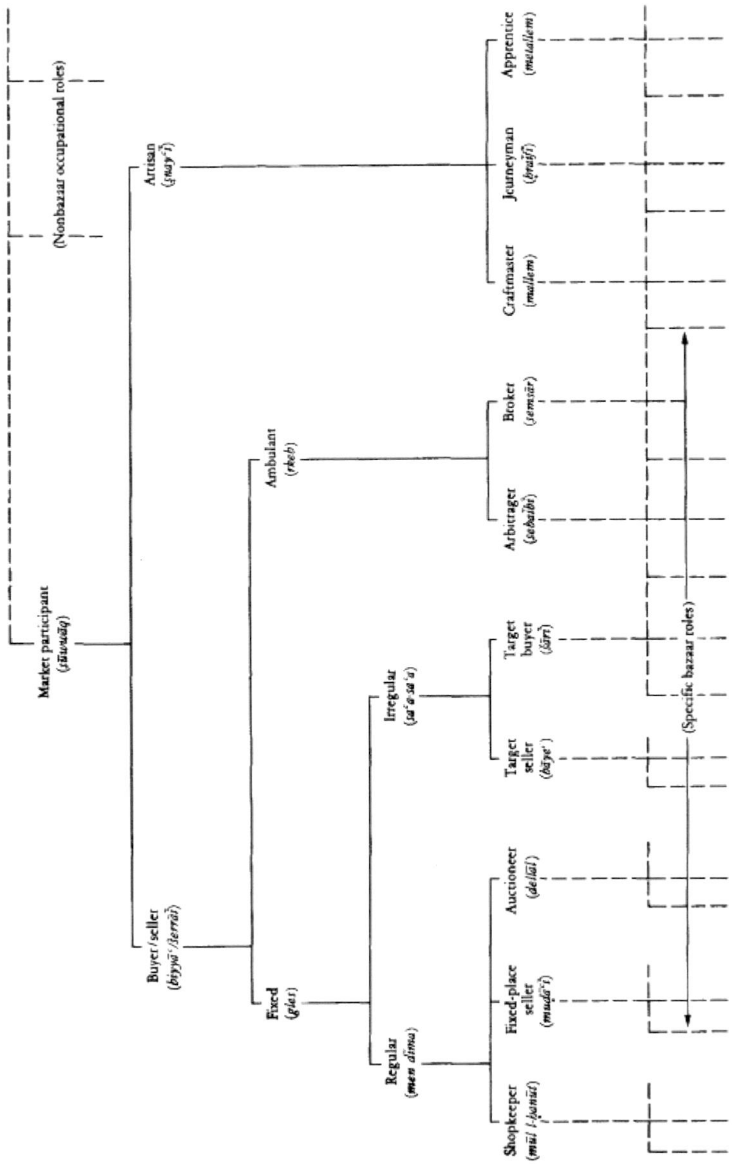
Market participant
(Nonbazaar occupational roles)
Artisan
Buyer/seller
Ambulant
Fixed
Irregular
Regular
Apprentice
Journeyman
Craftmaster
Broker
Arbitrager
Target buyer
Target seller
Auctioneer
Fixed-place seller
Shopkeeper
(Specific bazaar roles)

Figure 6

Almost no suwwaqs, a restless lot in a restless society, stay put all, or even most, of the time. On the contrary, they wander about constantly. Even shopkeepers, the most settled group, are half the time off somewhere up to something possibly profitable, their young sons or nephews left in place to inform inquirers innocent enough to believe them that father or uncle will "soon" be back. The distinction projected here is between those conceived, and who conceive themselves, to have a defined place – a shop, a customary selling spot, a particular market – where they, so to speak, belong and can at least normally be found, and those who, in the nature of the case, by virtue of their function, move among several such places. No one in the bazaar can afford to remain immobile; it's a scrambler's life. ("Move and you will confound your enemies," a Moroccan proverb runs, "sit and they will confound you; *fī l-ḥaraka, baraka*," "there is blessing in movement," runs an even more famous one.) But some suwwaqs are footloose by profession, and some, by profession, are anchored.

The "regular"/"irregular" contrast within the fixed category (all "ambulant" roles are "regular") discriminates those suwwaqs who engage in trade day in and day out or, in periodic markets, week in and week out, from those who engage in it only when the impulse, need, or occasion takes them. On the regular side, shopkeepers and fixed-place sellers have already been discussed, and more detail about them can be found in Annexes A and C. It remains only to say something about auctioneers, a disappearing phenomenon in the bazaar economy, before turning to the irregular target seller and target buyer categories, whose crystallization is responsible for the disappearance.

Auctioneers (*dellāla*; sg. *dellāl*, from a root meaning "to show," "demonstrate," "display") were once a major element in the Sefrou suq. In the years before World War II, there were forty or fifty of them engaged in various sorts of trade; today (1968–9), there are but nine or ten marginal figures, dealing mainly in cheap cloth, yarn, and second-hand goods, the tattered remnants of a once flourishing and colorful profession.[103]

The main function of the auctioneers was to bridge the gap between buyer-sellers knowledgeable in commerce and those who, though wishing to trade in the suq, were not so knowledgeable. By shifting price making into the hands of buyers forced to compete among themselves for the right to purchase – which is what any form of auctioning does – both the farmer and the craftsman could avoid the direct bargaining pattern most of them felt gave all the advantage to the professional merchants and leave the latter to joust with one another. The dellal took an item of trade, most commonly but not exclusively, a craft item, on which its owner set a floor price, and walked about among the crowds of the suq carrying it, or a sample of it, with him, crying out for all to hear first the floor price and then, as individuals bid upward (usually in terms of customarily fixed intervals), the most recent offer until, bids ceasing to come, the last bidder was sought out and the item sold to him.[104] Clearly there was great room for chicanery in all this – misrepresentation, kickbacks, sheer embezzlement – and the dellal (who received a commission, usually two percent, on the sale) had to have an unmarked reputation for honesty, in the eyes both of his clients and of his potential bidders, something not that easy to come by in the suq and even harder to maintain. Of all the trades in Sefrou, that of the auctioneer, inevitably a Muslim, was, through mechanisms we will come to presently, among the most regulated, both internally and from the side of the government. (Only the moneylender, inevitably a Jew, was more ambiguous and more watched.) The uncertainty of the system and the aura of shadyness surrounding it finally weakened it as, the bazaar economy firmly in place, artisans and primary producers grew knowledgeable and confident enough to participate in the bazaar directly. The competence gap between regular buyer-sellers and irregular ones narrowed, the irregular ones developed roles of their own, and the auctioneer, who had been, so to speak, their commercial stand-in, was rendered less and less necessary.

When they come to stand in for themselves, such irregular market goers are no longer external to the suwwaq domain, but, in the form of the target trader roles, an integral part of it. The term target seller – someone who, in need of a certain amount of cash for some purpose or other, brings something of his (a quantity of wheat or some animals) to market to sell – has come to have a certain currency in recent anthropological work on "traditional markets."[105] The majority of grain and animal sellers in Sefrou periodic markets, even those of the town, are target sellers in this sense and are recognized to be such. They sell sporadically in response to their need for cash (which is not to say they are insensitive to price conjunctures, unaware of inventory issues, or uninterested in accumulating balances) and, essentially farmers, do not deal in commodities as such. Though there are, of course, also fully commercial figures, the people with the money, in the throngs crowded into a periodic grain or animal market (we shall come to them in a moment), the *bāyeʿ* is by far the most common type: a man who has come to a particular, for him familiar, "known," suq to convert something he has himself produced into cash.[106]

The transfer of the "target" idea from sellers (or laborers) to buyers is, so far as market studies go, an innovation, but one the suwwaq buying-is-selling and selling-is-buying view of things demands. Individuals (still, as noted earlier, predominantly men, and twenty or thirty years ago almost entirely so) concerned to purchase some item or another, whether it be a basket or a cow, are not regarded as members of some general external, residual class called "customers" or "consumers," but of an internal class on a par with other sorts of suwwaqs and distinguished only by the fact of a particular focus on a particular end. Whether the purchased item is consumed or itself target-sold in turn is a matter of no consequence (and quite often indeterminable, so far as the seller is concerned); the *šārī* role is regarded as fully a professional one as any other, and the occupant of it is treated as such. Not only is competence in "shopping" (a word, with its connotation of idle search, save for tourists a rare phenomenon in Morocco, that is precisely the wrong one here) something a target buyer is expected to have – and if he does not, so much the worse for him – but the instiutions of the market, from price bargaining and the intricate division of labor to the purposeful destandardization of quality and long-term clientelization, all ensure that the amateur will be at as great a disadvantage in the target buyer role as in any other. Some of the implications of this fact – perhaps the most important are that, a "fixed" activity, one "shops," as one "vends," only in specific, well-known environments and that target buyers and target sellers almost never confront one another directly – will be touched op later. The general point is that the noisy communication-network nature of the suq makes of even the consumer role, in advanced economies but an aspect of family roles and in "primitive" ones but a reflex of structural position, a commercial occupation.[107]

As a fixed or sitting buyer-seller, whether quotidian or occasional, is one associated, both in his own mind and those of others, with a particular suq or section of one, an ambulant or riding buyer-seller is one associated with at least two and most commonly several.[108] Of these, there are two main classes: arbitragers and brokers. Arbitragers are traders who gain their living out of the differential between what something sells for in one marketplace and what it sells for in another to which they can readily transport it. Brokers are those who act as the agents in one market of a trader (or traders) sitting in another. There are some other types of ambulant merchants – peddlers who travel around door to door in the countryside, for example – but these two are by far the most important.[109]

Most arbitragers (*sebaībīya*) have a more or less fixed itinerary, though what that itinerary is varies widely from individual to individual, to the point where one hardly encounters two that are precisely identical. As itineraries involving more than nine markets and less than four are relatively rare, and as almost all Sefrou arbitragers contrive to be there on Thursdays, the typical sebaibi trades in the Sefrou suq and anywhere from three or four to seven or eight others. The others may be nearby locality-focusing markets, relatively distant region-focusing ones, or even locality-focusing ones in other regions than Sefrou. Just which markets a given sebaibi operates in, as well as what he buys and sells in them, depend on his personal contacts and his familiarity with local situations, products, in turn, of his particular background and experience. His direct and detailed knowledge of diverse bazaar environments, or rather of a definite, limited set of them, and his ability to move effectively among them capturing the profit of price discrepancies are the basis of his living – a living that can range from the extremely marginal to the quite considerable.[110]

Unlike other sorts of buyer-sellers, sebaibis deal in a variety of goods rather than focusing on one or two. The specializations of the markets they frequent shape their activities somewhat. Those who go to Guigou are likely to be looking for hides or cattle, to Marmoucha for rugs or wool, to El Menzel for wickerwork, to Immouzer for fruits, to Kucheta for wheat. But in general they trade in whatever seems profitable at the moment. One Sefrou sebaibi I traveled with to Marmoucha for the Tuesday market (he also works, in an intricate schedule, Missour, El Menzel, Guigou, and, of course, Sefrou) first bought two head of cattle. One he immediately resold locally to a sebaibi from Guigou; the other he contracted with another Sefrou sebaibi on a share arrangement to carry back in the latter's truck to Sefrou for sale there the following Thursday. Then he bought some chickens and a half a sack of wheat, which we carried back with us. And finally he bought some textiles, which he consigned, qirad fashion, to another Sefrou sebaibi, who took them off to Enjil by bus for the following day's market there. A series of such cases could be recounted, many of them far more complex than this. But the main point would emerge in them all – that sebaibis (who almost never hold goods for more than a few days) live by suq-to-suq trading, jobbing an income out of a sort of commercial cosmopolitanism.[111]

Semsār, which translates quite unproblematically as "broker," is a rather more familiar role in Western eyes, and less needs to be said therefore to describe it. Strictly, the term is used for real estate brokers, a function of minor importance in Sefrou, but generally it is extended to anyone who acts as a commission-paid agent for someone else in a commercial transaction. (Indeed, in any transaction: The feminine form, *semsira*, means "matchmaker.")

In Sefrou, semsars are most prominent in the commodity trades, especially animals, wool, and wheat, where they are major actors, though they can appear in virtually any commercial context. In the commodity trades most of them are agents of large Fez merchants buying up local goods on behalf of their patron. Most animal sales, especially of cattle and sheep, are to semsars, rather than to butchers, arbitragers, or target buyers. Many of the largest transactions in wool and grain and virtually all in olives involve them as well.[112] Le Tourneau estimates for the 1933–6 period that about three-fifths of the cattle and about half the cereal sales in the Thursday market went, via semsars, most of whom were local, to Fez. Having tried, over a much longer research period, to devise a way to estimate such matters with any precision and failed, I am unable to take Le Tourneau's figures as more than offhand guesses disguised as calculations. But the picture of the critical role of the semsar in connecting Sefrou to higher nodes (and not just Fez) in the bazaar hierarchy is clearly accurate.[113] As but an undocumented assertion, I would hazard that at least three- quarters, and quite possibly more, of the primary product flow from the Sefrou region toward the more developed regions of central Morocco, the Atlantic coast, and beyond, takes place through the agency of local semsars working on commission for engrossers in the superordinate bazaars of those regions. If the sebaibi connects suqs laterally, the semsar connects them hierarchically.

On the artisan side of the tree, the role pattern is either extremely simple or forbiddingly complex: simple, if one has the courage to leave details to themselves; complex, if one has not. The general discrimination of statuses into those who are acquiring a skill, those who have acquired it, and those who have conquered it applies more or less across the board; it is found in similar form in virtually every craft, save odd cases like watchman or curer.[114] But exactly how these statuses are defined and how the relations among them are organized vary markedly from one craft to the next depending on technical requirements and the work traditions that have grown up around the crafts. The integration of masters, journeymen, and apprentices into the productive process is clearly going to be rather different among tailors than among blacksmiths, weavers, butchers, or masons, because the process is different. Yet for all that, the critical feature of artisan roles from the point of view of bazaar economics is one that marks them all: their complete independence from any sort of corporate organization. Mallems, hraifis, and metallems alike are not employers or employees, bosses or workers, but rather so many tinsmiths or shoemakers more or less expert. However good they are or are not at what they do, and however dependent they may be in fact, they are free professionals, and their relations with one another are as contractual as with those who buy their products or hire their skills, and very nearly as fragile.

Which of the three statuses any particular artisan occupies is clear enough in the vast majority of cases. (A master craftsman is commonly referred to and addressed as such, "Mallem Mohammed"; and an established journeyman is frequently called by the nisba of his profession, "Khiyyati Mohammed.") But there is no formal process of movement, ritual or legal, from one such status to the next in any trade; there is no public marking, save for the terms themselves, of the occupants; and there are no collectively defined rules allotting duties, rights, or powers to them. Any one who owns an atelier is in the nature of the case a master and takes on whom he will as journeyman or apprentice (which is not to say he does so randomly, as earlier discussion should have made clear), and organizes his enterprise as seems to him, and whomever he takes on, appropriate. There are, of course, customs and precedents in these matters, a certain amount of civil law, and even some guidance (not much) from the Sharia, which provide Durkheim's "noncontractual bases of contract" and thus constrain the shapes such arrangements take. But – another nail in the coffin of the guild stereotype – there are no tradewide regulations or, for that matter, any body that could enforce them if there were.

An atelier, in whatever craft, is essentially a partnership (*šerka*) between artisans of varying skill, and whether one is master, journeyman, or apprentice depends upon what sort of partnership one has contrived to make. At base, all partnerships in the bazaar, commercial as well as industrial, are conceived of as between two persons, more complex arrangements being regarded as compounds of these. One variety of partnership is distinguished from another by the sort (and size) of the contribution each participant makes to it and the reward each in consequence draws from it. A craft atelier is a web of diverse partnerships in this sense converging on the master (or masters, for there may be more than one). And indeed, the diversity is greater than the general threefold distinction is capable of expressing. Specific outcomes of specific negotiations, hardly any two arrangements are exactly the same. Though reflective of age, experience, and expertise, and connected organizationally to technical function, at base the craft role categories indicate types of dyadic contract prevalent between artisans-forms of reltionships, not bundles of skills.[115]

The complexity of such contractual ties varies enormously, both from craft to craft and from atelier to atelier within a given craft. A fair number of smaller artisans, especially in the barbering, butchering, and shoemaking trades, is not involved in them at all, but works alone. At the other extreme there are ateliers with two or three masters locked in an intricacy of arrangements probably no single participant completely understands. There are master weavers with twenty looms, not all of them in the same place, in contract with various sorts of masters, journeymen, and apprentices up to nearly a hundred, and there are master weavers with one loom and a boy to keep the yarn straight. Blacksmithing demands a group of at least three for effective operation, but it cannot really utilize more than five or six. Large-scale tailoring establishments are uncommon, but most tailors have at least an apprentice or two to assist the master, and some have eight or nine, ranked with three or four levels and including children as young as six. Journeyman/apprentice contrasts are sharp in carpentry, blurred in baking; master/journeyman contrasts are sharp in milling, blurred in café keeping. Family connections underpin contractual relations importantly in tailoring and blacksmithing, weakly in café keeping and silk spinning. And so on. Only an extended, and rather wearisome, recounting of concrete descriptions of work organization could capture the variety. And even then not much more could be said as summary than "other cases, other arrangements."[116]

The amin system

A universe of roles sorted into types and gathered into classes, the suq is thus a structured domain of human activity, a bounded field of meaningful goings-on. But like all such universes, domains, and fields, it does not maintain itself; it takes more than a map of distinctions to keep a world in order. The map must have a force neither its formal beauties nor its functional convenience can themselves assure. Custom, the sheer weight of social habit, provides much of this force in any society, and ritual, law, and government contribute most of the rest. But in the suq world, an unusual institution, drawing somewhat on the authority of each of these and yet not readily identifiable with any of them, supplies most of the force: the amin system.

Amin (pl. *umanā*, occasionally *amīnāt*), from the root for "faithful," "reliable," "trustworthy," "safe," means a "trustee," "guarantor," "custodian," "superintendent," "guardian" – more or less. In Morocco, it is applied to a selected member of an occupation, eminent, trusted, and usually pious and elderly, as well as comfortably situated, whose function it is to mediate disputes both between practitioners of that occupation and between them and dissatisfied clients. There are (ca. 1965) forty-eight amins in Sefrou, some of them of great weight in the life of the market, others of essentially none, covering everything from doughnut sellers to goldsmiths, quranic scholars to garage mechanics. A list of them (or rather, as their personal names are of no significance here, the occupations they serve) is given in Table 12.[117]

One thing is apparent from this list, merely from inspection: Whatever amins are, their distribution is no mere reflex of occupational structure. Jewish cloth sellers and shoe repairmen are distinguished from Muslim cloth sellers and shoe repairmen. Truck, taxi, and bus operators are lumped together. Shoe repairmen and shoemakers are separated (even though the majority of the one are also the other), as are cloak tailors and ready-made clothes tailors (though few of the one are also the other). There are no amins for such major trades as silk merchant or hardware seller, 'whereas distinctly marginal trades such as scribe, musician, and quarry worker boast them. Farmer is not a bazaar occupation, and religious scholar not really an occupation at all, as its members, a few Quran teachers aside, actually earn their living at something else.

Nor do any of the by now familiar suq distinctions seem to apply with genuine strictness: modern/traditional: garage mechanics and horseshoers have amins, bicycle repairmen and rug merchants do not; permanent market/periodic market: carpenters and charcoal sellers do, silk merchants and herbalists do not; large/small occupations: grocers and plowmakers versus ready-made clothes sellers and potters; skilled/unskilled: goldsmiths and porters, tile makers and lime kiln workers. And, of course, the great merchant/artisan divide does not sort either: grocers, auctioneers, cord makers, and masons have amins; tobacconists, odds-and-ends sellers, glaziers, and buttonmakers do not.

The amin functions in the suq setting, and only there, but his sociological foundations are elsewhere: in the culturewide Moroccan (and to some extent generally Mid-Eastern) idea that the possibility of effective

Table 12. *Occupations possessing amins in Sefrou, ca. 1965*

Auctioneer	Jewish shoe repairman
Baker	Jewish slipper maker
Barber	Mason
Bathhouse keeper	Miller
Blacksmith	Musician/singer
Bread seller	Porter
Butcher	Plowmaker
Carpenter	Plumber
Charcoal seller	Religious scholar
Cloth seller	Saddlemaker
Coffeeshop keeper	Scribe
Cooked-food seller	Shoemaker
Cord maker	Shoe repairman
Farmer	Slipper maker
Floor layer/excavator	Stone cutter/quarry worker
Flour seller	Tailor of cloaks
Fried doughnut seller	Tailor of ready-made clothes
Funduq keeper	Tinsmith
Garage mechanic	Truck, taxi, bus operator
Goldsmith/jeweler	Vegetable and fruit seller
Grocer	Weaver
Horseshoer	Weigher/measurer
Jewish cloth seller	Wheat/bean trader
Jewish grocer	Wool/hide trader

Source: Sefrou municipality office (the Baladiya).

settlement of public disputes between diversely interested individuals depends, at base, upon the existence of a single, splendid, and very hard to find figure – the reliable witness.

To trace out the reasons why the reliable witness is such a critical figure in Moroccan life would take us far afield into the intricacies of authority, morality, and public discourse in that life, as well as into peculiar corners of Islamic doctrine and North African history. But the uncertainty of information quality already attributed to the suq, and inferentially to the society as a whole, clearly has something to do with it: Where fact is elusive, the man who can fix it is a prize resource. And that, not an imperious *Zunftmeister*, is what the amin is and, in Sefrou anyway, always has been.

"Amin" is actually one of a set of such reliable witness roles found throughout the society. In irrigation, there is the *jāri* (from the root for "to run," "flow," "stream"), who is not an oriental water bureaucrat managing matters, but a countryside water expert monitoring them. For descendants of the Prophet (Alawis, Idrissis, and so on, the so-called *šurfa*) and certain other special groups there is the *mezwār* (from the Berber *amzuaru,* "first"), who, whatever his personal influence, does not govern them but attests to the fact that they are what they say they are and serves as a kind of notary public for them. In the religious (qadi) court, the *ᶜadel* (from "to act justly," "equitably") fulfills a similar professional attestor function, and in the secular court (the *maḥkama*) an official called an *ᶜarīf* (from "to know," "be aware of," "recognize," "discover") or a *k̲ebīr* (from "to know by experience," "be acquainted with") is sent out by the judge to visit the scene of the dispute and report back what the facts of the case "really" are.[118] At marriage, a woman must have a (male) *wali* to attest before the qadi to her status, her propriety, and her very desires. The justness of market scales are guaranteed by the sworn declaration of four religious scholars (*ṭolba*). Even lower-level, local administrative officials – the village or quarter muqqadems – serve more this reliable witness function than a decision-making and enforcing one.

From this point of view, the amin is merely the suq variant in a bracketed series of official, quasi-official, or as in the old tribal oathswearing patterns, extraofficial reliable witnesses, specialized as to domain, upon which another, similar series of law- (or custom-) applying officials – the pasha, the qaid, the qadi, the hakim, and, in the suq, the *muḥtaseb* ("the market inspector," of whom more in a moment) – rely for the empirical foundations of their judgment. The amin system is an expression of a distinctive style of social control, a dialectic of "fact legitimators" and "norm appliers," which, rooted in some of the most general concepts of Maghrebi culture, extends far beyond itself. No more than the zawia, the habus, or the nisba is it a simple product of the suq; no less than they is it a force there.

Amins are chosen (usually for indefinite terms, occasionally for set ones) by a process of negotiation between the members of the trade and the government – the royal bureaucracy in the pre- and post-Protectorate periods, the colonial bureaucracy during the Protectorate. As in all negotiational processes in Moroccan society, the weight of the two parties, and thus the balance of the outcome, varies with places, times, personalities, and situations. Sometimes amins are essentially elected functionaries of the traders they serve upon whom the government has passively placed its official imprimature. Sometimes they are essentially government appointees the traders have had necessarily to accept. Most often they are the result of a compromise between the sort of man the traders would prefer (one capable of spitting in a pasha's eye) and the sort the government feels it must have (one who does what he is damn well told).

As one would imagine, the general trend over the half century we are concerned with here has been toward the cat's-paw side of things as central rule has grown, consolidated, and come to think of itself in modern terms. But there is still much variation, not only from suq to suq – smaller or more far-flung ones having more autonomy – but even within a single suq, such as Sefrou, where some trades (cloth seller, blacksmith, porter, funduq keeper) maintain a fair degree of independence and others (tailor, grocer, mason, auctioneer) rather less. By now, however, all important Sefrou amins are at least as much arms of the government as they are agents of their colleagues.[119]

In any case, when a trader has a dispute with respect to workmanship, prices, debts, quality of material, contract provisions, and so forth, either with another trader or with a customer, which cannot be directly resolved through the usual exchange of insults, excuses, concessions, and promises, the dispute is taken to the amin (or if representatives of different trades are involved, amins) for determination. The amin, who has no formal judicial powers, simply endeavors to discover what the facts of the matter are, a task in which he seems inevitably to consider himself successful. Normally this ends the matter, because if the disgruntled disputant carries things to the muhtaseb, who does have formal judicial powers (and a court in which to exercise them), the amin will be called upon as the reliable witness and but repeat his conclusions. Moroccans being an argumentative and headstrong lot, not much given to letting well enough alone, this does nonetheless happen with some frequency, the usual outcome being that the intransigent protester ends up with an even less favorable resolution than he had to begin with.

Whether the muhtaseb has formally to decide the case or it resolves itself at the amin level, the settlement is effected in terms of a combination of customary, religious, and civil commercial law, a kind of half-codified morality of the market, called the *hisba*. Strictly, the hisba (which is mentioned in connection with North Africa at least as early as Ibn Khaldun) is the authority to supervise markets, an authority vested ultimately in the caliph, and there is a fairly sizable classical literature, within Morocco and without, concerning it. Concretely, the hisba consists of the principles, some of them stemming from government edict (*ḍahīr*), some from Islamic law (*šraᶜ*), and some – in a place like Sefrou, a great many – from local practice (*ᶜurf*), that the amin, and if need be, the muhtaseb use in regulating suq activities.[120] The balance of importance among these three main sources of the hisba has also shifted toward the governmental pole in the past half century or so, and the muhtaseb, once, with the pasha (or qaid) and the qadi, "le seconde personnage de la trinite" of local government, the amin of amins, presiding over a separate realm of law, has been reduced to but another government functionary.[121]

In any case, whatever the recent, and far from definitive, weakening in favor of state power, the amins as "reliable commercial witnesses" and the muhtaseb as "commercial norm applier" were the main agents of social control in the bazaar, containing disruption in a society where enmities tend rather easily to become both intense and long lasting and to spread rapidly from their source to involve more and more people. In the marketplace, where individuals from all sorts of background, with all sorts of loyalties, and possessed of all sorts of intentions meet in an atmosphere of hectic interaction, the possibility of discord mounting to "explosion," to use Francisco Benet's only somewhat dramatized image, is clearly much enhanced.[122]

The fear of *nefra* (the "sudden, panicky 'snapping' which breaks the peace of the *sūq*," scattering its occupants in all directions and leaving it a pole of avoidance rather than a pole of attraction) is alive in even the best regulated of markets; and in the not-so-well-regulated ones it hangs in the air like a premonition.[123] Where the occupational structure is not developed enough or the population of the market not stable enough – in small markets, in remote ones, in new ones – to support an effective amin system, other reliable witnesses and norm appliers are brought into play: religious scholars (*ṭulba*); descendants of the Prophet (*šurfa*); members of saintly lineages (*murābtīn*; Br. *igurramen*); generally recognized "market masters" (*mwālīn s-sūq*, unofficial muhtasebs); brotherhood muqaddems; local political leaders of one sort or another; and, of course, nowadays, uniformed representatives of state standing about with repeating rifles. Saint shrines cast a general beneficence over the marketplace and provide sacred ground (where violence or lying under oath bring supernatural disaster) for peaceful resolution of conflict. Customary law forbids the carrying of firearms, the unsheathing of knives, and so on, and is popularly enforced to the point of lapidation or the gouging out of eyes. Adjacent tribes guarantee each other's safety under zettata-like protection pacts. The marketplace is physically and institutionally insulated from virtually all the other contexts of social life (normally one should not even discuss extra-commercial disputes there). All these ingenious cultural devices, and others, work to protect the precious and delicate peace of the marketplace.

Behind the amin system and behind the hisba, what Benet well calls "the covenant of the market," lies more than an abstract thirst for justice. Behind them lies a quite unabstract fear of anarchy – *nefra*, *sība*, *fitna*, *hāraž*; the Moroccan vocabulary of disorder is rich and nuanced – rising in the bazaar, "*the* danger spot in the social structure," and raging out from there across the whole landscape of collective life.[124]

Exchange: toward a communication model of the bazaar economy

To the foreign eye, a mid-Eastern bazaar, Sefrou's like any other, is a tumbling chaos: hundreds of men, this one in rags, that one in silken robe, the next in some outlandish mountain costume, jammed into alleyways, squatting in cubicles, milling in plazas, shouting in each others' faces, whispering in each others' ears, smothering each other in cascades of gestures, grimaces, glares – the whole enveloped in a smell of donkeys, a clatter of carts, and an accumulation of material objects God himself could not inventory, and some of which He could probably not even identify . . . sensory confusion brought to a majestic pitch. To an indigenous eye, it looks much the same; but with one essential difference. Embodied in all this high commotion, and in fact actualized by it, is, Revelation (maybe) aside, the most powerful organizing force in social life: *mbādla* ("exchange"). What holds everything more or less together in this knockabout world is that men want what others have and find it, normally, easier to chaffer it out of them than force it.

In attempting to reduce the surface tumult of bazaar economies to the deep calm of social theory, anthropologists who have turned their attention to such economies have found themselves entangled in a received idea they could neither escape nor make much of: Now that so much of the world is filled with corporation directors and advertising men, the bazaar is the nearest thing to be found in reality to the purely competitive market of neoclassical economics, the one place in the world where isolated, interest-rivalrous, profit-maximizing sellers still actually confront isolated, nonpropagandized, utility-maximizing consumers on equal ground, deterministic actors in the cosmic drama of supply and demand. Some have embraced the idea in the hope that, applied to exotics, it would somehow get them somewhere economists had not already been; some have angrily rejected it as just so much more Western ethnocentrism, an attempt to make all the world look like natural capitalists; more have striven to construct some "yes, but" middle way – "my people are rational, but in their own peculiar fashion."[125] But few have been able to turn entirely away from the idea with the unconcern it seems most to deserve. As a speculative instrument, the concept of "the perfect market" yields, when applied to a system like the Sefrou suq, mere banalities (surely we need no more demonstrations that, left to themselves, prices equilibrate wants to resources) or wanderings off in unhelpful directions (that trade localization functions to minimize travel costs is not so much false as obscurant of more interesting truths; e.g., that it focuses search). The tumult of the suq, all that goods crying and arm waving, must be approached directly. And the first step in approaching is to understand that, whatever the state of competition may be (and it is not, in fact, all that Marshallian), that of communication is a good deal less than pure, perfect, and undistorted.[126]

To say that is not to say, however, that one ought to turn from the distracting formalisms of market theory to the even more misleading ones of information theory, which accentuate the measurabilities of communication while washing out its import.[127] The need is for (1) a qualitative formulation of the information situation in the suq as the Moroccans themselves conceive it, followed by (2) an analysis of the relation of that situation thus conceived to the process of exchange as it actually takes place (or fails to take place) in the ordered muddle of bazaar encounter.

The information situation

A description of what the suq looks like in information and communication terms from within, from the point of view of those who have or are looking for the information and doing or not doing the communicating, takes us first into the realm of ideas, and that in turn entangles us once more in the arabesques of Arabic. Not only is what goes on in the suq mainly talk (*klām*, literally "words"; figuratively, as we shall see, very much more), but the meta-talk in which that talk is talked about defines the conceptual space in which the exchange process moves. "The linguistic turn" that has transformed so great a part of modern social thought has, as yet, barely touched economics; but here it must, briefly, hesitantly, and more than a little elliptically, be made. In the suq, the flow of words and the flow of values are not two things; they are two aspects of the same thing.

There is no simple way (and possibly no complicated one either) to convey the exact shape of the conceptual world of the suq or to outline with any firmness or exhaustiveness the language games that sustain it. All that can be done is to work through a small catalogue of words relevant to that world in such a way that its general character will be at least broadly invoked. But though this is a limited aim, it is not a misdirected one. For it is just such a general sense of a diffuse situation, not a precise theory of a definite state of affairs, that the Moroccans, struggling like the rest of us to order indistinct experiences with inadequate ideas, themselves have. Wittgenstein's remark to the effect that an accurate picture of a vague object does not consist in a clear picture but a vague one applies here with a special force.

But prior even to discussing particular words, something must be said about Arabic in general, for even the word *word* does not translate easily between Arabic and English. The heart of the matter is, of course, the famous Semitic root system in which a (usually) triconsonantal cluster is worked out through a series of (mostly) vocalic modulations to yield a set of lexemes with (generally) related meanings. We have already seen something of this in connection with the discussions of *sūq* (*s-w-q*) and *nisba* (*n-s-b*), but it is a matter hard to formulate and impossible to ignore in any attempt beyond the most mechanical to gloss Arabic words in English. The Arabic root and modulation system connects – morphologically connects – a set of words in such a way as to set up an overall semantic field within which the particular meaning of a particular word has its being. Each word, to change the metaphor, is but a more or less defined semantic cloud in a diffuse and general, yet readily enough sensed, atmosphere of meaning projected by the root.[128]

As an orienting example, let us look at a word we shall find playing a role of some importance in the suq "information situation": *ṣdiq*. In itself, *ṣdiq* means "truth," "trueness," "sincerity," "candor," "honesty." One says of a man, *fi-h ṣdiq* ("he is honest," "there is, *ṣdiq* in him"); or of an assertion, *kantkellem-mᶜa-k b-ṣ-ṣdiq* ("I tell you sincerely," "I speak with you with *ṣdiq*"), or even *ma-kayn ma-ḥsen men ṣ-ṣdiq* ("honesty is the best policy," "there is nothing that is better than *ṣdiq*").

Here, in no particular order, are some other derivations of the same root (*ṣ-d-q*):

Ṣadīq	Friend, friendly, connected by bonds of friendship (pl. *aṣdiqā*)
Ṣdeq	To be right, to guess right, to succeed, to turn out well (a venture, a meal, etc.)
Ṣdāq	A dowry, a marriage contract
Ṣādiq	True, reliable, accurate, authentic
Ṣeddeq	To believe, to accept as truthful, to verify, to give alms, to donate to charity
Ṣedeq	To tell the truth, be candid with
Ṣiddīq	Strictly veracious, righteous, upright, loyal, saintly
Ṣadāqa	Alms, charitable gift, religious tax, offerings
Ṣedāqa	Friendship, loyalty, clientship
Taṣdīq	Belief, faith, consent, agreement, covenant
Meṣaddeq	Credible, believable, reliable, trustworthy[129]

One gets the picture, even if the picture is difficult to focus. The point is that there is nothing special about *ṣdiq* as an example: All the words we will consider are set in a similar field of root-conditioned meanings. In the discussion this field will be assumed rather than as here systematically displayed, and, largely ignoring the niceties of morphological class and grammatical function, absorbed into their definitions. Thus, in our example, the "friendship," "marriage contract," "alms," and "loyalty" intimations of *ṣdiq* – its "human relationship" penumbra – will be invoked in explicating what "truth" here means, without actually parading related forms and meanings justifying the interpretation or going, save glancingly, into the hardly unimportant matter of its place in the structure of Arabic *langue*.

The words to be thus treated – those that can lead us into some sense of how Moroccan suwwaqs conceive the bazaar in information terms – are: *zḥām* ("crowd"), *klām* ("words"), and *ḵbar* ("news"); *ṣdiq* ("honest"), *maʿrūf* ("known"), and *ṣḥiḥ* ("unblemished"); and *maʿqūl* ("reasonable"), *ḥaqq* ("right"), *kdūb* ("lying"), and *bāṭel* ("worthless"). These ten (the rationale for the subgrouping will be presented in a moment) are hardly the only such words that might have been chosen, and certainly they are not all that could be. But because they recur in both the rhetoric of bazaar exchange as such and in participants' attempts to represent to themselves (and to inquiring ethnographers) what goes on in such exchange, to unpack their meaning is to unpack as well a good deal of what the suq comes to as a cultural system.[130]

The first three words – zḥām, klām, and ḵbar – are mostly employed in characterizing the "phenomenal" aspects of the bazaar information situation: how it appears, if not quite unreflectively, at least more or less immediately, to someone caught up directly in it. They are describing terms. The second three – *ṣdiq, maʿrūf*, and *ṣḥīḥ* – on the contrary, define considerations brought to bear on phenomenal information in estimating its worth. They are appraisive terms. And the last four – *maʿqūl, ḥaqq, bāṭel*, and *kdūb* – are judgment terms: conclusions the appraisal of things seen and heard jostling about in the suq lead finally on to. This categorization, modeled, of course, on Austinian procedures, is admittedly not without a certain arbitrariness and makes the process of finding out what the devil is going on in the bazaar look far more mechanical and clear-cut than it in any way is. Nevertheless, the classification does outline reasonably well the logical (or, perhaps more exactly, the semiological) structure within which that process unfolds and can serve, therefore, as a useful frame for a general account of it.

Description: crowds, words, news. Zḥām, which means "crowd," "mob," "throng," "swarm," "crush," but connects to forms meaning to "push," "shove," "jostle," "elbow," "harass," or "beset" someone; to forms meaning "jammed," "packed in," "(over)stuffed," "teeming," or "crammed (with)"; to forms meaning "competition" and "rivalry," and "competitor" and "rival"; and, along more imaginative lines, to a form meaning "a convulsive fit" or "an acute attack of dysentery" is simply the word most commonly used to characterize the suq as a social setting: *Hiya zḥām* ("it's a shoving, pushing, elbowing crowd"). The competitiveness of the bazaar is imaged not as a set of isolated confrontations, hand-to-hand tests of strength, but as a mass of people jammed into a space too narrow to accommodate half of them, harassed individuals struggling to maintain their footing in a crush. For the suwwaq, the first thing about the bazaar is that it's a mob.[131]

The second thing is that it's a talkative mob. As noted, *klām* (like *zḥām* a collective noun – the singular is *kelma*), which means "words" and beyond that "language," "speech," "speaking," "utterance," "phrase," "statement," "trope," "proverb," "dialect," "discussion," "argument," "debate," and – the informing twist – "power" or "influence," is a word to conjure with in Arabic. The central conceptual node of the semantic field in which it is enclosed is quite clearly "talk." The verbal forms mean to "speak," "say," "utter," "express," "address (someone)," "converse with (someone)"; the nounal forms refer to a "speaker," "spokesman," "orator," "(good) conversationalist"; and the adjectival forms invoke such qualities as "talkative," "fluent," "loquacious," "eloquent." But the peculiar status of "talk" in the Arab world, and especially the Muslim part of it, with its concept of the Quran as the direct speech of God (*klām allāh*), give to that core meaning an almost energic dimension. *Klām* is not just an attribute people have; it is a force they wield.[132]

For all the actual jostling that goes on in a bazaar mob, something most people take more or less in stride, the real pushing and shoving is done with talk. The varieties of *klām* Moroccans perceive and index with fixed idioms are virtually endless: *klām ḡādi u māji* ("words coming and going," "rumor"); *klām ḵāwi* ("empty words," "insipid, vapid speech"); *klām meblūz* ("words of a blunderer," "inappropriate, awkward, speech"); *klām merr* ("bitter talk"); *klām qāseḥ* ("hard, wounding talk"); *klām b-l-maʿna* ("significant, serious words," "polite, polished, formal speech"); *klām fertek* ("words ripped apart at the seams," "disjointed, incoherent talk"); *klām qbīh* ("rotten, spoiled words," "distasteful, unpleasant talk"); *klām l-mḵasma* ("quarrel words," "invective"); *klām ṭiyyeb* ("pleasant, delicious words," a "compliment"); *klām siyāsa* ("political, diplomatic words," an "insinuation"). And there are more complex locutions constructed around *klām* to mean: "to speak in a boring manner" ("boring talk," "a bore"), "to digress," "to interrupt," "to contradict," "to deny," "to be speechless with rage," "to perseverate," "to turn a phrase," "to attack someone's reputation," "to compromise one's own reputation," and so on through a jungle of expressions constantly heard to the one most often heard – *ʿand-u klām* (or *kelma*) ("he has words [word]," "he has [the] power, the 'say'"). To "have words," to speak with carrying force in a given situation, is to be the one whose wishes count. And the hubbub in the market is in great part a scramble to gain just that: to have, as we would put it, the last word.

So the tumult of the marketplace is largely a tumult of words (and various paralinguistic signs, *išārāt*, a subject in itself), or anyway is seen as such. But for all the richness of classification of types of "words," "talk," "statements," and so on, and for all the judgmental quality of many of the characterizations involved in that classification, the attitude toward the particular things actually said in the marketplace, the *klām* in fact emitted there, is, in epistemological terms, radically agnostic. "Bitter," "wounding," "distasteful," even "insipid" or "disjointed" talk may be, for all that, well worth believing and acting on – truly informative; "polite," "pleasant," or "fluent" talk may equally well not be – stylishly deceptive. "Invective," "compliment," "rumor," and "insinuation" may be either clarifying or misleading with respect to the exchange process. The talk of the market is, like the crowd that populates it, merely prodigiously there. How reasonable, creditable, veracious, or useful it is is altogether another question, separately asked, separately answered. "A tale," the proverb goes, "is a tale; talk is talk."

It is this sheer appearance view of what is heard (and seen) in the market that the word *k̲bar*, the term most commonly used to sum it up, projects. *K̲bar* means "news," "report," "tidings," "message," "communication," "story," "indication," "notification," but it means these things in a manner that bleaches them of any implication beyond their simple phenomenal existence – pure, brute, received intelligence. Connected to forms for "direct experience of," "immediate awareness of," "knowledge-by-acquaintance of" on the one hand, and to forms for "empirical inquiry," "to seek information about" on the other (the man sent out by the judge to explore the facts in a dispute [see above] is called a *k̲ebir*, a *muk̲bīr* is a newspaper reporter or a detective, a *k̲ebbār* is a police spy, a *muk̲ebāra* is an interview or an investigation, a *bīt ik̲tiber dwa* ["room for inspecting 'medicine'"] is a laboratory), *k̲bar* sums up the information situation the suwwaq confronts in the bazaar in resolutely noncommittal terms. There is no lack of messages; but one is as actual as the next.

Descriptively, then, the suwwaq's suq is a crowd of rivals, a clatter of words, and a vast collection of ponderable news. Pondering it (although the English word is much too contemplative, equable, and altogether passive in tone to characterize accurately what in fact goes on) and coming to decisions about what to make of it is the critical matter for the suwwaq and what distinguishes, in his eyes at least, the numberless failures of this world from the handful of successes. Keeping your feet in the bazaar mob is mainly a matter of deciding whom, what, and how much to believe and, believing (or half-believing), what and how much – and in whom – to confide.

Appraisal: candor, consensus, wholeness. A suwwaq faced with a particular piece of marketplace news – a price quotation, a wage offer, a representation concerning quality, a promise to do something or other – and obliged to decide what to make of it normally proceeds by placing the news simultaneously in three different contextual frames: the identity of its purveyor, the current state of bazaar opinion, and the accepted norms of credibility. *Ṣdiq*, *maʿrūf*, and *ṣḥīḥ*, each of which should properly be written with a question mark following it ("is he being honest with me?" "does it square with the consensus?" "is it sound?"), set these frames. They point appraisal toward its appropriate concerns: personal relationships, community attitudes, and the defining feature of sane belief.

Ṣdiq has already been partly explicated. It has to do, as Smith has suggested, with "the truth of persons."[133] What holds together the "sincerity," "friendship," "alms," "marriage contract," "loyalty," and "faith" dimensions of *ṣ-d-q* is that they all have to do with assertions, celebrations, demonstrations, promises, tokens of individual reliability, of being someone whose integrity empowers his words. Smith's summary of the meaning of *taṣdiq*, the "faith" derivative, though cast in the accents of the mosque rather than those of the bazaar, puts the matter exactly:

> [*Taṣdīq*] can mean, to regard as true, and this is indeed its most general connotation; but we must remember that "true" here is in the personalist sense. Its primary object is a person . . . so that *ṣaddaqahu* [the second, "causative" form of the verb plus a *hu* "him" object suffix], or "he gave him *taṣdīq*" may mean "he held him to be a speaker of the truth" – he believed him . . . because he trusted him . . . he held him to be *ṣādiq*, a speaker of truth on a particular occasion, "or held him to be *ṣiddīq*, an habitual teller of the truth by moral character . . ."
>
> Another standard usage, moreover, is that it mean, not "He found him to be a speaker of the truth," but rather, "He found him to be so." One may hear a man's statement, and only subsequently find reason or to know that the man was no liar.
>
> Thirdly, it may indicate this sort of notion but with a more active, resolute type of finding: that is, "he proved him to be a speaker of the truth," or confirmed or verified it. Thus the common phrase *ṣaddaqa al-khabara al-khabru*: "the experience verified the report" . . . [or better, given the personalist meaning *of ṣ-d-q*] "the [experience] verified the report and the reporter."
>
> Fourthly . . . *taṣdīq* may mean "to render true," "to take steps to make come true" – for instance, one's own promise (a radically important matter), or another's promise, or another's remark . . .
>
> Throughout this *taṣdīq* form, the sincerity involved may be on the part of the subject of the secondary form, as well as or perhaps even rather than of the primary subject; so that if I *taṣdīq* some statement, I not merely establish its truth in the world outside me, but incorporate it into my own moral integrity as a person . . .
>
> *Taṣdīq* is to recognize a truth, to appropriate it, to affirm it, to actualize it. And the truth, in each case is personalist.[134]

There are many implications of this "personalist" view of truth so far as bazaar exchange is concerned, among them that candor is about as rare as saintliness. But by far the most important are that a reputation for speaking (relatively) honestly is a valuable resource for a suwwaq to have and that such a reputation (or lack thereof) is not a general, context-free, "characterological" quality of an individual, like his temperament, taste, or political orientation, but, is embedded in particular, concrete, person-to-person relationships from which it cannot be even conceptually disentangled. One is honest (or not honest or not quite honest) *with* someone, *about* something, in a given instance, not as such. The "friendship," "marriage contract," "covenant," "alms giving" aspects of honesty are not mere secondary connotations, metaphorical extensions, of the notion of "being (or, what is the same thing, 'speaking') true"; they are part of its defining essence. Strictly, a bazaar trader or artisan does not have a reputation, good or bad. He has reputations, dozens of them.[135]

The very nature of the bazaar – the enormous multiplicity of participants, combined with the absence of advertising, brands, or even store names – makes this inevitably the case, renders the establishment of a general reputation next to impossible. The most the average suwwaq can hope for is that those in his corner of the suq or (which, given localization, may be the same thing) in his trade, may have some overall opinion, preferably not too bad, of him. And even that opinion, so far as it exists, will be highly diffuse and not very important to his actual day-to-day functioning. The people in whose eyes he really has a reputation – "reputations" – in the proper sense of the term are those with whom he actually conducts exchanges repeatedly. The clientelization of trade (which is marked, and of which more later) means that a given suwwaq does not relate to the bazaar mob as an undifferentiated whole. He relates to a more or less defined (though, as relationships ripen and sour, changing) set of individuals within it. And the issues raised by the question, *Waš kayṣedeq mᶜa-ya?* ("Is he being honest with me?"), always, of course, a reciprocal one, crystallize and are at least tentatively resolved with respect to each particular case. Except for the most minor or passing transaction, or in cases where advantage is so obvious as to override caution, people deal largely with people they know; and the evolution of those dealings, the concrete exchange experience of particular pairs of individuals, forms the foundation for *ṣdiq* "truth-of-persons" type appraisals of bazaar news. It is the state of the relationship between the two parties that matters – men are true or false (or, most commonly, something uncertainly in between) to each other, not in themselves.[136]

The relationship of oneself and the person whose news one is considering – are you or aren't you *aṣdiqā* (truth-telling "friends") – is not, however, the only criterion one can employ in appraising it. The degree to which the news conforms to the prevailing consensus about what is "normal," "customary," "usual," "conventional," or "standard" is another, no less important, criterion.

The word for this is *maʿrūf*, which means (something) "known," "well known," "familiar," "widely recognized," "generally acknowledged," "universally accepted"; as well as (something) "fitting," "proper," "fair," or "equitable"; and, by extension from that, "a favor," "a courtesy," "a kindness," or a "good deed." In Quranic usage (where it is always *al-maʿrūf*), and in the moral system that spreads out from it, *maʿrūf* means "good," in the sense of acts in consonance with God's commands, and therefore "recommended." Thus, behind the notion lies the conviction that public consensus is a trustworthy guide for behavior because God commands only that which all unimpaired men (an unimpaired woman is a contradiction in terms) are capable of knowing and following and unless, as is, alas, too often the case, blinded by divisive lies and illusions, will in fact know and follow. "God's community," as the maxim has it, "cannot unite in error."

So far as the bazaar is concerned, this means that one way to decide the worth of what a particular suwwaq says or does is to measure it against settled social opinion: *ʿurf* ("practice," "custom," "tradition," "mores," "customary law," or, considering the root, "the known," "the accepted," "the recognized," "the acknowledged"). There, too, cognition, consensus, and virtue are internally connected in such a way that though the community may divide in error, and chronically does, it can agree only in truth.[137]

The range of the *maʿrūf – the* generally acknowledged, the equitable, and the recommended – is as wide as the bazaar and as differentiated as its parts. There are established practices for virtually every trade, every marketplace, and every situation. The *ʿurf* of the suq – its commonplace ethic – is a palpable presence at every point in it. Part of getting into a trade is learning the relevant details of it (and part of keeping people out is preventing them from doing so). It is what the amin and muhtaseb rely on, or should, in clarifying and settling disputes and the ultimate foundation of their authority. Everything from the day, hours, and place of a suq, through who has a right to be in which part of it doing what, to the rules governing bargaining, partnership, working conditions, clientship obligations, habus rights, craft standards, credit relations, and general public comportment – indeed, just about anything that goes on in the suq that has anything remotely to do with exchange – is governed by *ᶜurf*.[138] Appealing to what is "known" is central both to the rhetoric of the bazaar and to the process of determining what in that rhetoric should be credited and what not.

Yet despite its more public, collective status, the consensus of the suq concerning any particular matter, what really is considered fair and proper dealing, is not that much more easily determined than is the honesty of personal intention. Such consensus varies from place to place, trade to trade, time to time, and issue to issue. And when you get down to it, individuals, more divided in error and interest than they are united in truth and obedience, in fact differ, even for one place, trade, time, and issue in their expressed views about what the concensus is. Finding out what the ground rules are with respect to having a cloak made, or buying raw wool, or patronizing a client butcher, or advancing a grocer credit, or selling mules in the Thursday market does not in general work out to be a set and straightforward task, but a vexed and problematic one. Like *ṣdiq*, *maᶜrūf* poses an appraisive question: *Waš hād šī maᶜruf?* ("Does this thing [proposed, argued, reported, claimed, asserted, promised, insinuated, demanded] square with recognized practice?"). Answering – actually making the appraisal – is a more difficult matter.

In any case, besides personal relations and community perceptions, the worth of bazaar news can also be appraised in terms of what we would call more "objective" considerations: its inherent plausibility, its credibility as such. Plausibility and credibility are, however, not quite the right glosses. For the Arabic word that invokes this range of considerations, *ṣḥīḥ*, trails a stream of associations that connect it not with likelihood, probability, chance, logic, demonstration, argument, but with health, strength, vigor, wholesomeness, salubriousness, lack of impairment, absence of blemish, recuperation, healing, cure. The entire concept pivots around the notion either of being whole or of restoring wholeness – an almost medical view of truth as a state of disease-free well-being: scatheless, blotchless completeness.

The Arab, and especially the Muslim Arab, concern with bodily integrity, the tendency to identify physical imperfection with moral, has often been noted. (There is even a special morphological class for adjectives denoting defects – "mute," "blind," "deaf," "lame," "scabrous," "demented," "moronic," "pregnant.") So has the connection between that idea and the evaluation of statements, documents, traditions, reports, and the like. A chain of "healthy," "unblemished" witnesses to a purported fact, whole and intact in both the material and spiritual senses, is a guarantee of the fact's validity; the discovery of one "weak" or "damaged" link in such a chain undermines it. That which is worthy of belief is that which is sound in the most literal sense of the term, in which no hidden infirmity of the slightest sort can be uncovered. So far as matters seen or heard in the bazaar are concerned, none of which reach such immaculate levels, what one looks for (and looks for, and looks for) are defects, especially unobvious ones. Like most conceptions of health, *ṣḥīḥ* turns the attention toward a concern with signs of its absence – the symptoms of falsehood, not the evidences of truth.

Around the idea of *ṣḥīḥ* ("well," "strong," "whole," "valid," "credible," "sound") is formed a whole doctrine of suspicion, a catalogue, though hardly a systematic one, of the pathologies of communication and their outward expressions. Like *ṣdiq* and *maʿruf*, *ṣḥīḥ* is more a sceptical question expecting a negative answer than an expression of confidence or an affirmation of belief. One searches for what may be wrong – a juggled measure, a product switch, a disguised cost – and for the false signals – an evasive response, an overready agreement, an excessive promise – that reveal its presence. In the message-saturated world of the bazaar, where everyone is trying to lead everyone else down the garden path, mistrust is an adaptive attitude and ethically a quite proper one. The credulous do not thrive. "The power of the people of the Sous is lying," the song of Al Hiba says of that quintessential suwwaq group. "All that comes from the Sous is [vegetable] oil, locusts, and a great deal of misinformation."[139] The development of a fine sense for the deceptive and devious hidden within the apparently *ṣḥīḥ* (the "not healthy" disguised as the "healthy") and the skill to correct for it, *ṣeḥḥeḥ* ("restore to health," "heal," "emend," "rectify," "repair"), is prerequisite to any sort of success in the market. Or in life generally: A person who hears some news he does not believe, Westermarck remarks in *Wit and Wisdom*, asks ironically: *Kull mā smaʿt f-s-sūq ṣḥīḥ?* ("Everything heard in the market, is it true?").[140]

No. Nor are all the men one meets trustworthy or all the propositions one is tendered proper. The information situation in the market is itself seriously defective – a hum of locusts. Coping with that fact, trying to filter out of all that outpouring of earnest declaration just what, whom, and how much even to begin to believe, is what *ṣdiq*, *maʿrūf*, and *ṣḥīḥ* (trueness as friendship, trueness as consensus, and trueness as health) are all about. They are names for ways of weighing talk.

Judgment: *reason*, *reality*, *deception*, *vanity*. The judgments – verdicts, if you will – to which the appraisals of bazaar news, the weighings of talk, lead are extremely various and hardly to be captured in four isolated terms. Yet as a general classification of those judgments, or verdicts, an overall typology of them, the oft-heard and intricately deployed words, *maᶜqūl*, *ḥaqq*, *kdūb*, *bāṭel*, do well enough. The categories they evoke are ultimately metaphysical ones: The first two bespeak a movement toward God, the second two a movement away from Him; but brought down into the marketplace as concrete conclusions about mundane matters, they sort what happens there into what seem to Moroccans natural varieties. In a sense, everything one confronts in the bazaar – persons, talk, and actions alike – is rational, authentic, fraudulent, or vacuous; and conclusions about which is which are as impossible to avoid as they are difficult to arrive at.

Maᶜqūl simply means "reasonable," "sensible," "understandable," in the sense of "restrained," "controlled," "unexcessive," "not carried away by passion," "prudent." Historically, the root seems to have referred (the joke is not wholly a joke) to the hobbling of a camel, and it still secondarily means to "confine," "control," "tie up," "fetter," "curb," "bind," even to "impound," "detain," or "arrest." How far this set of "constraint" meanings interworks with the "reason" set in the minds of contemporary speakers is not altogether clear. But that "the understanding" (*ᶜaql*) is conceived in terms of a bridle for "the appetites" (*nafs*) is beyond much question. Reason, here, is neither a mirror nor a lamp, but a tether, a holding in, a curbing, a hobbling – of desire, passion, vitality – in the interest of a moral, ordered life.[141] In the market, *maᶜqūl* is mainly heard in approval or, negated, in disapproval of a price, a contract, a proposal, as, in this sense, "within (or not within) bounds." Though the theological penumbra surrounding it is somewhat different, referring less to notions of natural law than to the necessary containment of the appetitive faculties by the intellectual in any redeemable world, a *taman maᶜqūl* is about what was known in the premodern West as a "just price," and is – as is a "just wage," "just rent," or "just partnership" – a powerful moral idea in bazaar exchange. And if, as in the Western case, no one can define very exactly what a "just price" is and precisely why it is just when a price half or twice its size is not, the sense for the contrary is, nevertheless, quite keen. *Mā šī maᶜqūl; wāk̲k̲a maᶜqūl* ("It isn't just"; "yes, it is so just") is probably the exchange of protestations most often heard in the higgling apologetics of the bazaar.

But where *maᶜqūl* is a fairly easy notion for English speakers to grasp, at least so long as subtleties are bypassed, *ḥaqq*, one of the Quran's most resonant words and one of colloquial speech's most idiomatic, is almost impossible to explain to someone who has never been faced with the problem of having actually to use it. The standard translation is "real," or in the nounal form (*ḥaqīqa*), "reality"; this is not incorrect, just rather unhelpful if one has no idea of what the concept of reality involved might be. "In Arabic, *ḥaqq*," Smith remarks, struggling heroically to summarize the matter in a paragraph,

> refers to what is real, genuine, true in and of itself by dint of metaphysical or cosmic status. It is a term par excellence of God. In fact, it refers absolutely to Him, and indeed *al-Ḥaqq* is a name of God not merely in the sense of an attribute but of a denotation. *Huwa al-Ḥaqq*: He is reality ["The Real"] as such. Yet every other thing that is genuine is also *ḥaqq* – and some of the mystics went on to say, is therefore divine. Yet it means reality first, and God only second, for those [i.e., Muslims] who equate Him with reality. It is somewhat interesting . . . that this in a sense makes it more realistic to talk about atheism in Arabic than in English, since in Arabic the question can become whether one believes in Reality, whether one trusts Reality, whether one commits oneself to Reality, and the like. But I let that pass. We simply note that *Ḥaqq* is truth in the sense of the real, with or without the capital R.[142]

The critical point, however, is that, like God, *ḥaqq* is a deeply moralized, active, demanding real, not a neutral, ontological "being" merely sitting there awaiting observation and reflection; a real of prophets not of philosophers. Thus besides "real," and more profoundly, *ḥaqq* means "right." "correct," "obligatory," "necessary," "just," "lawful," "legitimate," "merited," "authentic," and therefore "a right, title, or claim to something," "rightful possession," "property," "one's due," "one's duty, responsibility," "accountability," and a number of other things our notion of the "real," an affair of objects not imperatives, does not encompass. The play of prepositions around the term generates a whole series of judgmental categories constantly applied in the suq and out: *ʿand-ik l-ḥaqq* ("you are right," "right is on your side"); *fī-k l-ḥaqq* ("you are in the wrong"); *min ḥaqq-ek* ("you're entitled to it," "it's your due"); *ḥaqq ʿalī-k* ("it is your duty, responsibility," "you must," "you are obligated to").[143] And as with *klām*, the phrases run on *ḥaqq* seem endless: a beneficiary, a participant in a business deal, a legitimate share in something (a profit, a bundle of goods), a contracted duty, a general responsibility in some matter, a due bill, a fine or indemnity – all are indicated by idioms constructed around *ḥaqq*. And in its plural, the word means "jurisprudence."

Clearly, *ḥaqq* is a rather extreme example of the tendency we have been tracing of Arabic to link a set of disparate ideas into a single morphologically marked off conceptual field no one lexeme can even begin to sum up. (The listing in Wehr here runs to four full columns and dozens of entries and subentries.)[144] But concerning the information situation in the suq, what is important is that the term characterizes the distribution of rights and duties in the frame of conclusions about where (or with whom) reality lies. The rightful and the genuine are fused, and to determine the one is to determine the other. The metaphysical optimism and practical skepticism we have found already in *maʿruf* and *ṣḥīḥ* is here finally reinforced. The facts, in the bazaar or anywhere else, are normative; it is no more possible for them to diverge from the good than for God to lie. What is possible is for men, who can lie and inveterately do, to lose sight of what the facts really are.

That lying (*kdūb*) is not just one sin among many in Islam, but in many ways the premier sin, is apparent from the intense Quranic imprecations against it: "Who does more wrong, or who is more unjust than he who forges against God a lie?" "Forge not a lie against God, lest He destroy you with punishment."[145] But the condemnation of lying is not less intense in everyday life, where, as prevalent as it is decried, it is seen as the main source of just about every sort of evil. "The Moors," Westermarck remarks with what sounds like prejudice but would not be thought so by Sefroui suwwaqs, "have a large number of proverbs condemning lying, although they cannot be called a truthful race."[146] Whether they are more given to falsehood than anybody else is, of course, both doubtful and beside the point. But that they are obsessed with its malignity, the way Greeks were with that of hubris or Calvinists with that of indolence, is very much to it.

It should be clear from what has already been said why this is so, for the deliberate purveying of falsehoods contravenes almost every norm we have reviewed. The liar is personally not reliable; lies divide opinion, dissolve consensus, and destroy community; lying blemishes, sickens, enfeebles communication. False words or other representations do not just conceal reality, they disown it – resist it, reject it, refuse to accept its demands. On the religious plane, contradictory of "the words of God," lying is quite simply unbelief:

> [A] particular sacrosanctity is attributed in the Quran to the word "Truth," *ḥaqq*. and consequently, all use of language which contradicts it in any way is considered to be glaring blasphemy against God

> and His religion. It is not at all surprising, then, that we find *kadhib*, "falsehood," or "lying," talked of in the *Qur'ān* as a heinous sin. It constitutes one of the most salient features of a *Kāfir*.[147]

On the secular plane lying, a willful undermining of trust in the words of men, is but marginally less serious. So far as the bazaar is concerned, lying – active, deliberate, systematic lying – is the main disruptive force, leading, if it is uncontained, to the feared "snapping of the market," the transformation of relations of exchange into ones of violence. "Greet a liar," says yet another proverb, grimly, "in arms."

Yet lying, though perhaps the most worrisome, is not the only sort of falsity that exists in the world: Ignorance, cant, prattle, slander, cajolery, boasting, inanity, imprudence, deviousness, venality, and that hard to define but easy to detect form of smoke blowing, moral cowardice, are others. The most general term for such things and for the ostensible "information" produced by them is *bāṭel* ("worthless," "vain," "futile," "vacuous," "baseless") or, as Moroccans say in one of their most settled idioms, *kif wālu* ("like nothing," "zeroesville"). Often directly contrasted with *ḥaqq* in the Quran ("The *ḥaqq* has come and the *bāṭil* has vanished," XVII 83/31), *bāṭel* is sometimes glossed as "unreality"; but its connections are not so much with "illusion," "fantasy," or "hallucination" as with "pointlessness," "uselessness," "inactiveness." *Bṭala* is "unemployment," "absence from school," "a vacation," "an interruption (of an action)"; *bṭel* is "to be canceled, called off," "to be omitted, left out," "to expire, become invalid," "to be dismissed" (a suit, claim, etc.); a *beṭṭāl* is a person out of work or simply "lazy"; *beṭṭel* is "to be absent," "to abolish," "to abrogate," and, with the word for "work" as object, "to go on strike"; *mebṭūl* is "amputated" (a hand, arm, etc.). In the suq context, *bāṭel* essentially means something not worth paying attention to – the vain and vacuous noise emitted more by the weak and foolish of the bazaar (the favorite image is the sound of an empty water jar when struck with the knuckles) than by its accomplished knaves.

Sorting lies and nonsense from the reasonable and the real is the information problem as it finally appears to the suwwaq. Beginning with the hodgepodge of people, words, and news he encounters in the suq (as well as, of course, adding his small bit of confusion to it), he tries to contextualize what he hears, sees, and thinks he understands in terms of his exchange experience with particular individuals, what he knows of general suq practice, and some sort of symptomatology of market deceit to divide it into that which perhaps can be somewhat relied upon (exceedingly the smaller part) and that which very likely cannot (enormously the greater). Three things are true about market information: It is luxuriant, it is unreliable, and there are more ways of getting lost in it than there are of finding paths through it. Virtually the whole institutional structure of the market is, in one way or another, a response to the problem of organizing exchange in such an unpromising situation. Even more remarkably, it is an effective response: Trade goes on, at great pace and some efficiency, in a moral climate that seems almost designed to prevent it.

The shape of trade

The cast of thought – *mentalité*, *Geisteshaltung*, *ēthos*, *ʿaqalīya* – which the rhetoric of exchange projects is not, therefore, a bodiless subjectivity lodged somewhere in the darker reaches of "the Moroccan mind"; it is an overt, observable feature of a well-lit public arena in Moroccan society.[148] The intricate system of customs, rules, and practical arrangements that marks the suq is at once an adaptation to this cast of thought and the best example of it. More than mere instruments of commerce, the institutions of the bazaar give to trade a distinctive form.

To identify that form, to show that there is such a system and not mere conglomerate of usages and devices inherited from a checkered past, it is necessary to establish that its elements, the parts of the system, in fact constrain one another; that taken together they constitute a whole within which their presence is logical, their interrelationships motivated, and their workings comprehensible. The terminology here ("constrain," "logical," "motivated," "comprehensible") derives less from a causal idiom, the worn formulas of social mechanics, than from a hermeneutical one, and the choice is deliberate. Extremely complex webs of causal connection cross and recross the whole field of bazaar life, but not only are they extremely difficult, if not impossible, to isolate, they are not germane (or, anyway, not immediately so) to what we here want to display, how the institutions of the suq combine to provide a coherent framework for the processes of exchange and how those processes, in turn, fit intelligibly within that framework. The constraints are partial, the logic approximate, the motivations incomplete, the comprehensibility limited – and the system, thus, as all social systems, far from fully coherent. But, however imperfect, the organization of bazaar institutions into an ordered whole with properties of its own is real. It can be described. And described, it can extend our understanding of how the suq operates and why; can clarify just what sort of animal the bazaar economy is. The deeper physiology of the beast, assuming it has one, will have to wait.

With this proposition as premise, Table 13 has been constructed. It attempts to list, in more or less systematic form, the leading characteristics of the institutional pattern of the bazaar as it has here been described in terms of the information perspective as it has here been defined.[149]

Most of these characteristics, as well as the subpoints extending them, modifying them, or spelling them out, have already been explicitly discussed; others have at least been alluded to, and others will be touched on shortly. It is clear that small enterprises, a finely drawn division of labor, person-to-person transactions, inhomogeneous goods, equivocal signaling systems, the predominance of trading skills, unitary exchange roles, a reliance on personal contract, and a broad dispersion of coordinating mechanisms are prominent features of the bazaar and that, from a communication systems point of view, they somehow go together. What is not so clear – hence the "somehow" – is just what "going together" means in this context.

Table 13. *The bazaar as a communication system: general characteristics*

A. There is a great multiplicity of *small-sized enterprises.* 1. The commercial class is large in relation to the population as a whole. 2. There are almost no multifunctional or multitrade enterprises. 3. Most enterprises have very low fixed costs in terms of rents, machinery, housing, inventory, etc. 4. There is a continuous gradation from very small, man-on-a-mat enterprises to quite moderately sized (two or three major partners) ones, with the overwhelming majority lying toward the smaller end.
B. There is a very *finely drawn division of labor* in technical, social, and spatial terms. 1. Occupational specialization is extremely intensive. 2. Trades are fairly clearly differentiated in ethnic-like (nisba) terms. 3. There is a significant degree of trade-type localization, especially within bazaars, but also, to an extent, among them. 4. Temporal coordination of trading sites by means of a periodic marketplace system is highly developed.
C. *Transactions are mostly interpersonal.* They take place between individuals as individuals, not as representatives of collective economic entities (e.g., firms, companies, cooperatives).

1. There is an enormous plurality of small transactions, each more or less independent of the next.
2. The overwhelming proportion of those transactions involves two persons, and hardly ever more than three or four persons.
3. The overwhelming proportion of transactions is face-to-face.
4. Initial-seller to final-buyer chains are often long and circuitous, involving a arge number of intermediary transactions.

D. *Goods and services are inhomogeneous.* Those that flow through the bazaar are, for the most part, highly divisible, extremely various consumption items that are unstandardized, of mixed provenance, and very hard to evaluate.

1. Trademarks and brand names are absent, and the qualitative classification of goods is markedly subjective and ad hoc.
2. There is essentially no advertising, even in the form of artful display, and reputation is personal and changing, not corporate and stable. Differential educational attainment (which is not great) plays essentially no role in labor market signaling.
3. There are no institutions specifically devoted to assembling and distributing market information (e.g., price quotations, production reports, employment agencies, consumer guides).

E. *Formal signaling systems are undeveloped*, both irregular and unreliable, and their outputs are consequently ambiguous and difficult to interpret.

1. There are virtually no aggregate statistics generally available to market participants concerning any economic variable.
2. Price dispersion is high, and price movements erratic.
3. Accounting techniques are unsystematic, clumsy, and unanalytical.
4. Weight and measure systems are intricate and incompletely standardized. The same is true of grading systems.
5. Price feedback to production and inventory decisions is poor.

F. *Exchange skills predominate* over either managerial or technical ones.

1. Both technical and managerial skills are but modestly developed, and within any one trade they are too evenly diffused to yield much in the way of competitive advantage.
2. Exchange skills are very elaborately developed. Differential possession of them is marked and is the primary determinant of who prospers in the bazaar and who does not, as much among craftsmen and laborers as among storekeepers and commodity traders.
3. Haggling, in the strict sense of arguing, wrangling, caviling over terms with respect to any aspect or condition of exchange (i.e., not just price bargaining), is pervasive, strenuous, and unremitting.

G. As general processes, *buying and selling are virtually undifferentiated.* Essentially a single activity, the assumptions and procedures governing the one are the same as for the other. 1. Tastes are autonomous: They are still mainly traditionally set and the operation of the market has at best a marginal and/or very long-term impact upon them. 2. Trading involves a serial search for specific partners, not the mere offering of goods to the general public. 3. Intensive search (i.e., pursuing matters with a given partner) is primary; extensive search (surveying competing offers) is but ancillary to it. 4. Clientship to and between specific merchants and craftsmen is very common. Free shopping in an anonymous market is avoided.
H. The (normally oral, sometimes written) *personal contract is the main legal form of relationship.* 1. Partnerships are preferred to employer-employee organization. 2. Socialization into trades and crafts is by an apprenticeship system considered as a special form of (unequal) partnership. 3. The regulation of disputes involves the testimony by reliable witnesses to factual matters, not the weighing of competing juridical principles.
I. *Overall integrative institutions are diffuse,* informal, and generally weak. 1. Governmental controls over marketplace activity are marginal, decentralized, and mostly rhetorical. 2. There is virtually no hierarchical coordination of enterprises in wholesale/retail, headquarters/branch, supplier/distributor organization. Firm bureaucracy is extremely rare. 3. There are no true guilds consolidating trades into corporate units, but rather an interaction of various crosscutting forms of trade classification. Functioning trade unions, business associations, consumer organizations are also absent.

Primarily it means that, taken together, these features create an exchange situation in which the first problems, and often the last, facing would-be participants are to obtain reasonably reliable information of even the most elementary sort about the relevant economic variables (not all of which – e.g., whether the participants are *aṣdiqā* ["friends"] – are economic in the stricter sense) and having obtained such information, to use the knowledge differential it creates to advantage. The very difficulty of doing this in a diffuse, highly personal, highly fractionated setting without the aid of settled standards, unambiguous signals, or believable statistics raises the natural enough desire not to operate in the dark to the level of a ruling passion and heightens enormously the utility of even partially succeeding. When information is both widely scattered and poorly encoded, as well as transmitted along channels it would be flattery to call noisy, it takes on a special prominence. The usual vicissitudes of life and trade aside (and most suwwaqs regard them as wholly beyond the reach of man), the only thing that can really hurt you in the bazaar is what you don't know . . . and someone else does.

There are at least two consequences of this state of affairs: (1) any notion of attacking, altering, or systematically manipulating the general framework of economic life is absent; and (2) search is the paramount economic activity, the one upon which virtually everything else turns, and much of the apparatus of the marketplace is concerned with rendering it practicable.

Aside from sporadic protests concerning government regulations – usually those having to do with taxation or the attempt to fix prices - collective action in favor of one or another sort of economic policy simply does not appear.[150] Indeed, the very idea of policy (to say nothing of planning, a notion that has not managed to diffuse the few hundred meters from the city hall where, in the form of *planification,* it is, in a theoretical way, quite popular) is foreign in a context where what matters is capitalizing on dysfunctions, not correcting them. The nationalist activity of the Independence period already described, which comes as close to concerted effort by suwwaqs as suwwaqs as has ever occurred in Sefrou, was dedicated to a rather simple political aim, not an economic or even politico-economic one. And that half-exception half aside, what has been, and remains, remarkable about the bazaar class (and not merely in Sefrou) is that, given its large size, its great vigor, its enormous strategic importance, and its reputation for explosiveness, it has neither exercised nor made any effort to exercise any conscious, organized influence on the conditions of its existence. In commerce, as in the cosmos, parameters are parameters.[151]

The given being so flatly given, the energies of the suwwaq that are not absorbed in the more routine demands of his occupation are freed for what is, when all is said and done, the critical task: combing the suq for usable signs, clues to how particular matters at the immediate moment specifically stand. The matters investigated may include everything from the industriousness of a prospective co-worker or the reliability of a certain craftsman to regional variations in taste or the supply situation in agricultural products. But the two most persistent concerns, which more or less sum and enfold all the others, are with price and the quality of goods. The overwhelming centrality of exchange skills – as against those involved in production or coordination – puts tremendous emphasis on knowing what particular things are actually selling for and what sort of thing they precisely are. And it is toward gaining such knowledge, or at least reducing one's ignorance somewhat, that search, the really advanced art in the suq, is directed.[162]

From such a perspective, the various elements of the institutional structure of the bazaar can be seen in terms of the degree to which they, on the one hand, render search a high and difficult, thus costly, enterprise or, on the other, serve to facilitate it and so bring its costs (the main one of which is time) within practical limits. Not that all those elements line up neatly on one side of the ledger or the other. Most have effects in both directions, for suwwaqs are about as interested in making search bootless for others as they are in making it effectual for themselves. The desire to know what is really going on is matched by the desire to deal with people who do not but imagine they do (in that direction profit lies), and so the structures enabling search and those casting obstructions in its path are thoroughly intertwined. Indeed, they are often the same structures.

Some of the features of bazaar trade evoked in Table 13 seem, on balance, to be fairly clearly search impeding: the multiplicity of units, the inhomogeneity of goods, price dispersion (a measure, in part of inhomogeneity and, beyond it, of the general difficulty "participants in the market have [in] collecting information about their environments"), the amorphousness of business reputation.[153] Others, on the same balance, seem to be as clearly search facilitating: the localization (and "nisbazation") of markets, the elaboration of exchange skills, the pervasiveness of clientship. Yet others – discriminatory (sliding) prices, the interpersonal quality of exchange, the intensive division of labor – are more ambiguous in their effects. But it is the overall pattern – the interaction of such institutions as they set the conditions for search – that needs to be understood if we are to see how would-be exchangers find their way through the jungle of prices and cacophony of goods the suq represents to some commercial consummation. And for this, a brief consideration of the two most important search procedures – clientelization and bargaining – can be of use. The one concerned with finding an exchange partner, the other with what to do with him once you have found him, the two procedures bring almost all aspects of the bazaar system in some way within their ken.

Search: clientelization. Strictly, clientelization applies to the tendency, very marked in the suq, for repetitive purchasers of certain goods and services – whether consumption ones like vegetables or barbering, or intracommercial ones like bulk weaving or porterage – to establish continuing relationships with certain purveyors, occasionally one, much more often a half dozen or so, instead of searching widely through the market at each occasion of need. More broadly it applies to the establishment of relatively enduring exchange relations of any sort, for in essence the phenomenon is the same, whether the client is a household head buying his morning piece of lamb, a cloth seller laying in his weekly stock of jellaba materials, an adolescent apprenticing himself to a carpenter, or an arbitrager consigning his gathered-up goods to a carter or truck driver to be taken off to another market. Within what looks like brownian movement of randomly colliding suwwaqs is concealed (concealed, at least, to casual observation) a definite and surprisingly resilient pattern of specific, if informal, personal connections. Whether or not "buyers and sellers, blindfolded by a lack of knowledge simply grop[ing] about until they bump into one another" is, as has been proposed, a reasonable description of modern labor markets (and anybody who has been in one would hardly think so), it certainly is not of the suq, whose buyers and sellers, moving along the grooved channels clientelization lays down, find their way again and again to the same adversaries.[154]

"Adversaries" is the correct word, for, some apprenticeship and some credit arrangements partially aside (and the vanished sitting Jew/riding Jew systems wholly so), clientship relations are not, either in fact or in conception, dependency relations: They are competitive ones. Given the unitary view of buying and selling, the avoidance of explicitly hierarchical organizational forms, and the preference for face-to-face dealings, clientship is perceived as at once symmetrical, egalitarian, and oppositional. There are, a few half-exceptions again apart, no real patrons, in the master and man sense, here. Whatever the relative power (wealth, knowledge, skill, status) of the participants – and it can be spectacularly uneven – clientship is a reciprocal matter, and the butcher, wool seller, tailor, or coffeeshop keeper is tied to his regular customers in precisely the same terms as they are to him. By partitioning the bazaar crowd into those who, from the point of view of a man in the middle of it, are genuine candidates for his attention and those, infinitely the larger group, who are merely theoretically such, clientelization reduces search to manageable proportions, transforms a diffuse, anonymous mob into a reasonably stable collection of familiar antagonists.[155]

This use of repetitive exchange between acquainted partners as the main behavioral strategy for limiting the time costs of search (others, such as the employment of agents, bulk purchasing and selling, formal subcontracting, collective pooling of information, do exist, but they are much less important) is both a practical consequence of the overall institutional structure of the suq and an element within that structure itself – a reflex of the rules by which the game of trade is defined and a procedural device that makes the game playable.

In the first place, the high degree of submarket specialization in technical, spatial, and quasi-ethnic terms simplifies the process of finding plausible clients and stabilizes its achievements. If one wants a kaftan or a mule pack made, one knows where, how, and for what sorts of persons to look; and, as individuals do not move easily from one line of work or one place to another, once you have found a cloth seller, weaver, tailor, or saddler (or more often, several of each) in whom you can have some faith and who seems to have some faith in you, he is likely going to be there awhile. One is not constantly faced with new faces in unaccustomed places and the consequent necessity to seek out new clients. Search, in brief, is made accumulative.[156]

In the second place, clientelization itself lends form to the bazaar, rather than merely relying on the form that is already there, for it further partitions the bazaar in directly informational terms, dividing the market into complexly overlapping sub-populations within which more rational estimates of the quality of information, and thus of the appropriate amount and type of search, can be made. Suwwaqs are not projected, as for example tourists are, into foreign settings where everything from the degree of price dispersion and the provenance of goods to the stature of participants and the etiquette of contract are unknown to them. They operate, as they have since the days of the zettata and the qirad, in places where they are very much at home and rarely stray very far from them. (Those places themselves may of course be widely scattered: Moroccans are anything but geographically immobile.)

Below the level of the gross institutional differentiation of the bazaar economy – periodization, localization, specialization, hierarchicalization – and lying athwart it, a fine structure of communication is formed that has a high degree of stability and brings the problem of figuring out what is what within manageable limits. The oft-noted tendency for individuals to frequent particular bazaars when other markets, equally (sometimes even more) accessible, would seem to offer a more competitive environment, a wider variety of goods, or a more efficiently organized setting is but the most obvious indication of the reality of the advantage this fine structure provides for someone who is even peripherally part of it. As Rothschild has remarked, "perfect competition will not protect the imperfect consumer" (or, he might have added, the imperfect seller); but integration into a network of client relations, reducing the imperfection, can, at least to a degree.[157]

The preference of market goers for familiar suqs, however inefficient in terms of some ideal system of distribution, is evidence not of "traditional," "irrational," or "noneconomic" modes of thought, but of a clear understanding of how bazaars really work and what it takes to thrive in one. That an ordinary villager wishing to dispose of a few sheep prefers the arbitrager in his locality-focusing market to the broker in the Sefrou region-focusing one or, a steeper gradient yet, the Sefrou broker to the Fez exporter with whom the broker deals, despite the "obvious" advantages of the more developed settings is a reflex of his realization that those advantages are genuine only for persons with the clientship connections to exploit them.

Indeed, the enormous multiplication, not only of marketplaces and cycles of marketplaces, but of units within marketplaces, and the fractionization of exchange, the elongation of transaction chains, and the intensification of specialization that go with that multiplication ("l'hypertrophie des étalage et des négociants," as Troin, who has a rather overharsh view, puts it " . . . la pénurie . . . diffusée dans l'espace"), are not mere symptoms of "backwardness" or "lack of enterprise." They are related features of a system in which exchange is mediated across a thousand webs of informal personal contract.[158] When relations are so immediate in character, demand so much in nuanced response and detailed attention, the number any one individual can effectively manage is clearly very limited, and the proliferation of small bazaars, shops, traders and exchanges is a natural development. This has long been recognized in the area of credit, where the penalties of not knowing whom you are dealing with take on a peculiar force; but it applies to bazaar exchange all the way across the board.[159] Where the flow of economic transactions runs along channels of mutual knowledge, trust, and loyalty (or supposed such), the fractionization, miniaturization, specialization, and chain linking of trade units are unavoidable if that flow is to maintain any volume at all. Replication is a substitute for scale as direct acquaintance is for public repute; clientelization, complexification, and "*l'hypertrophie des négociants*" are all of a piece.

In the most general terms, clientelization represents an actor-level attempt to counteract, and indeed to profit from, the system-level deficiencies of the bazaar as a communications network – its structural intricateness and irregularity, the absence of certain sorts of signaling systems and the undeveloped state of others, and the imprecision, scattering, and uneven distribution of knowledge concerning economic matters of fact – by improving the richness and reliability of information carried over elementary links within it. The rationality of this on the surface somewhat quixotic effort, rendering the clientship relation dependable as a communications channel, while its functional context remains unimproved, rests in turn on the presence within that relation of just the sort of effective mechanism for information transfer that seems so lacking elsewhere. And as that relation is adversary – men seeking gain at one another's expense – so too is the mechanism: intensive bargaining along virtually every dimension of commercial life. The central paradox of bazaar exchange is that advantage stems from surrounding oneself with relatively superior communications links, links that themselves are forged in a sharply agonistic interaction in which the existence of information imbalances is the driving force and their exploitation the end.

Search: bargaining. The proper understanding of bazaar bargaining has been somewhat hampered by the moral ambivalance that open, unapologetic jockeying for material advantage tends to arouse in the minds of those not habituated to it. The appreciation of its presumedly integrative economic effects – especially in price making, to which it is too often considered to be confined – goes hand in hand with fear and dislike of its supposedly disruptive effects on the social order. When the appreciation dominates, as it does among most economists, the alleged socially disruptive effects are written off as so many unpleasant but unavoidable social costs. When the dislike dominates, as it does among most anthropologists, the presumed economic functions are regarded as being less painfully performed by more cooperative forms of exchange in marketless societies. In either case, bargaining tends to be represented rather negatively – either a necessary evil or an avoidable one, but in any case an evil.[160]

A more positive characterization of bargaining begins and ends with the recognition that it is a particular mode of information search, not a means for integrating prices (which, given the system frailties of bazaar communication, it can hardly do and, by concealing transactions as private deals, may even hinder) or of exercising the instinct of sociability.[161] The relationships that clientelization (the search for vis-à-vis) produces, bargaining (the search for terms) actualizes. Bargaining's function is to provide men who, amid the suspicions that haunt the suq, have managed to develop enough confidence to imagine trading with one another, with a workable means of actually doing so.

As a process exploring the instant possibilities of face-to-face exchange, suq bargaining displays four critical characteristics:

1. Though price setting, in the narrow sense, is the most conspicuous aspect of bargaining, the higgling spirit penetrates the whole of the confrontation: Whatever is alterable is negotiable.
2. The competitors in a bargaining situation are a buyer and a seller – not two or more sellers, as in modern retail markets; two or more suppliers, as in bid-for-contract markets; or two or more buyers as in an auction.
3. Bargaining does not operate in purely pragmatic, utilitarian terms, but is hedged in by deeply felt rules of etiquette, tradition, and moral expectation.
4. The amount of bargaining involved in any one transaction is affected by a wide number of factors, the more important of which include: type and quantity of good, depth of clientelization, frequency of repetitive exchange, degree of information asymmetry, the shadow price of time, and the relative economic strength of the principals.

Regarding the first item, the most obvious method of manipulating the terms of trade, aside from altering (money) price while keeping quantity and quality constant, is to alter quantity and/or quality while keeping price constant; this is an extremely widespread practice in the suq. In some transactions, especially of ordinary foodstuffs, manipulation may simply consist in adding or subtracting items to the pre-priced pile of fruit, vegetables, meats, or whatever. Or, rather commonly in cloth dealings, the buyer may first offer a price and then higgle with the seller over what it will buy.[162] In other transactions – wheat and wool sales, for example – the manipulation may consist in varying the size of supposedly established units, something the imperfect standardization of weights and measures not only facilitates, but actually encourages. A pint may be a pound the world around, but a *medd* (the reigning grain measure) certainly is not.[163] In yet others, it may consist in offering higher (or lower) quality goods from behind or under the counter.[164] Bulking and, much more significantly, bulk breaking – selling kitchen matches by the match, detergent by the cup – provide an important dimension of negotiation flexibility. Even labor contracts are highly manipulable, and highly manipulated, in work-condition terms. And so on. In a system where so little is packaged, not much more is regulated, and almost everything is approximative, it is almost always possible to do a deal in, so to speak, real rather than monetary terms.

Many other matters in the exchange confrontation are capable of manipulation, including aspects of the clientelization relationship itself. (For some examples of these, see Annex D, "The Song of the Baker": "I bring him [the baker] any news or gossip I hear quickly/Yet he has sworn not to give my bread its due.") Probably the most important is credit, all but the most marginal of transactions being conducted in these terms. Despite appearances, the suq is anything but a cash-and-carry affair; the management of credit balances is a high and delicate art through a very large part of it, and the mechanism of such management is inevitably bargaining. The famous remark of Keynes to the effect that if you owe your banker a thousand dollars you are in his power but if you owe him a million he is in yours, applies – if in radically reduced figures – with great force to the bazaar, where the actual terms of trade as often lie hidden in debt relations as exposed in price quotations.[165]

Aside from the sheer amount of credit (the level of credit balance that is to be maintained between any two cliented suwwaqs) several other aspects of credit giving and taking enter into the bargaining sphere. Although the Islamic prohibition of usury normally removes an open interest rate as a possible item of negotiation, it certainly does not remove a concealed one, and the interaction of credit balances and money prices is an intricate matter, subject to a very high level of moral nuance and commercial artfulness.[166]

Similarly, repayment schedules, which can be extremely complicated and adjusted to all sorts of special situations (salary periods, festival rhythms, seasonal variations, personal conjunctures, acts of God), are often a prime object of negotiation. So are partial payment liquidations of debt, a phenomenon rather more common than one might imagine and, even more surprising, one that does not always dissolve clientship ties: *lli fāt māt* ("what is past is dead") the not very injured creditor says and starts the relationship up, on an even more favorable basis to himself, again. And so, too, is the giving of security, almost always in a pawn-type pattern, where the lender holds the collateral (jewelry, grain, rugs), rather than a mortgage-type one, where the borrower does. The role of credit in the exchange process is very great, and every dimension of it – amount, conditions, forms – is subject to higgling of the most thoroughgoing sort, rivaling at least and often actually dwarfing price higgling as such.

The second characteristic of suq bargaining aside from its intricately multidimensional character – higgling along several interactive gradients at once – is that it channels competitive stress across the exchange frontier rather than along it (i.e., between buyer and seller, rather than between seller and seller). This has a number of implications from an information-and-communications view of bazaar exchange, of which the most important is that search more readily takes the form of exploring matters in depth with particular partners than surveying widely through the market, a case approach rather than a sampling one, or what Rees has called an "intensive" as opposed to an "extensive" strategy:

> The search for information in any market has both an extensive and an intensive margin. A buyer can search at the extensive margin by getting a quotation from one more seller. He can search at the intensive margin by getting additional information concerning an offer already received. Where the goods and services sold are highly standardized, the extensive margin is the more important; when there is great variation in quality, the intensive margin moves to the forefront. This point can be illustrated by considering the markets for new and used cars. Since there is relatively little variation in the quality of new cars of the same make and model and since the costs of variation are reduced by factory guarantees, the extensive margin of search is the important one. A rational buyer will get quotations from additional dealers until the probable reduction in price from one additional quotation is less than the cost of obtaining it.
>
> In used cars of the same make, model, and year, much of the variation in asking prices reflects differences in the conditions of the cars, and this calls for a substantial change in the strategy of the rational buyer. He will invest less in obtaining large numbers of offers and much more in examining each car. For example, he may have each car he seriously considers inspected by a mechanic. He may want information on the history of the car as a substitute for the direct assessment of condition and will pass up a used taxi in favor of the car owned by the proverbial little old lady who drives only to church. It will, not be irrational for him to pay a relatively high price for a car owned by a friend if he has favorable information about his friend's habits as a car owner.[167]

The prominence of bargaining is thus a measure of the degree to which the suq is more like a used car than a new car market: one in which the important information problems have to do with determining the realities of the particular case than the general distribution of comparable cases.[168] Further, and more important, bargaining is an expression of the fact that such a market rewards a clinical form of search (one that focuses on the diverging interests of concrete economic actors: individual suwwaqs wrangling an exchange) rather more than it does a survey form (one that focuses on the general interplay of functionally defined economic classes: anonymous crowds of vendors and customers integrating prices).[169] Search is intensive, in Rees's sense, or anyway primarily so, because the sort of information one most has to have cannot be acquired by asking a handful of index questions of a large number of people, but only by asking (and answering) a large number of diagnostic questions of a handful of people. It is this kind of questioning (and counter-questioning), exploring nuances rather than canvassing populations, that, for the most part, suq bargaining represents.

All this is not to say that extensive search plays no role in the bazaar, but rather that it is considered ancillary to intensive search, the true heart of the matter. Suwwaqs, in fact, make a clear distinction between bargaining to test the waters (*sāwem*, from a root meaning "to estimate the value of an object," "to appraise something") and bargaining to conclude an exchange (*tšeṭṭer*, from a root meaning "to divide, split, or share out something") and tend to conduct the two in different places: the first with people with whom they do not have clientship ties (or at most weak ones); the second with people with whom they do. This reduces the value of extensive search even further, of course, for bargaining is not likely to be serious when the participants know exchange is unlikely to eventuate, though the desire of suwwaqs to extend their clientele acts to correct this somewhat, and what begins as *sāwem*, an extensive bargaining relationship between mere acquaintances, can end as *tšeṭṭer*, an intensive one between suq "friends," if things go right. In general, extensive search tends to be desultory and to be considered an activity not worth large investments of time.[170] From the point of view of search (which, trying to sort the real and the reasonable from the lying and the vain in a swirl of news, is the suwwaq's point of view), the truly productive type of bargaining is that of the clientelized buyer and seller exploring the dimensions of a particular, likely-to-be-consummated transaction. Here, as elsewhere in the suq, everything rests finally on a personal confrontation between intimate antagonists.

The whole structure of bargaining as a social institution is determined by this fact: that bargaining is a communications channel evolved to serve the needs of men coupled and opposed at the same time. The rules governing it – some of them technical, some of them merely conventional, and many of them deeply moral – are a response to a situation in which (normally) two persons on opposite sides of some exchange possibility are at once struggling to make that possibility actual and to gain some (usually) very marginal advantage within it. Most bazaar price negotiation takes place to the right of the decimal point, a good deal of it several places to the right; but it is no less keen for that.

The technical rules are more or less given by the situation and thus are essentially universal, the same in Haiti or Oaxaca as in Nigeria or Morocco. "A tug of war between seller and buyer," bargaining as a formal procedure consists in a series of alternating, stepwise approaches toward an agreed price from separated initial offers. The most important variable factors are the spread between the initial offers, the size and number of the approaching steps, the distance each participant can be persuaded or can persuade himself to go, and the amount of time the process takes. Cassady has presented a usefully simple model of the process (Figure 7).[171]

Within this frame, the course of bargaining mainly depends on the size of the settlement region – the overlap between the maximum price the buyer will pay and the minimum price the seller will accept. If the overlap is wide, agreement is virtually certain; if it is narrow, agreement is less so; if it is nonexistent (i.e., the buyer's maximum is below the seller's minimum), accord is impossible. Considered as a communications channel, bargaining consists of a system of conventionalized signals designed to reveal which of these situations obtains. Sluggishness on one side or the other, or on both, in moving toward consensus – long periods between bid changes and/or small magnitudes of change – indicates agreement will be difficult at best and perhaps impossible; the inverse suggests the inverse. Bargaining generates its own dynamic out of its inner temporal rhythm: Rapid and large bid changes accelerate it toward consummation; slow and small ones declerate it toward abortion. It is the way things move that counts.

More precisely, there are three main phases of intensive bargaining: initial bidding, movement toward a settlement region, and, if that region is in fact entered, settlement itself. The absolute separation of initial bids, almost never so great in bargaining between clients as to preclude exchange from the start, suggests how wide the settlement region is likely to be (the greater the separation, the narrower) and the difficulty of

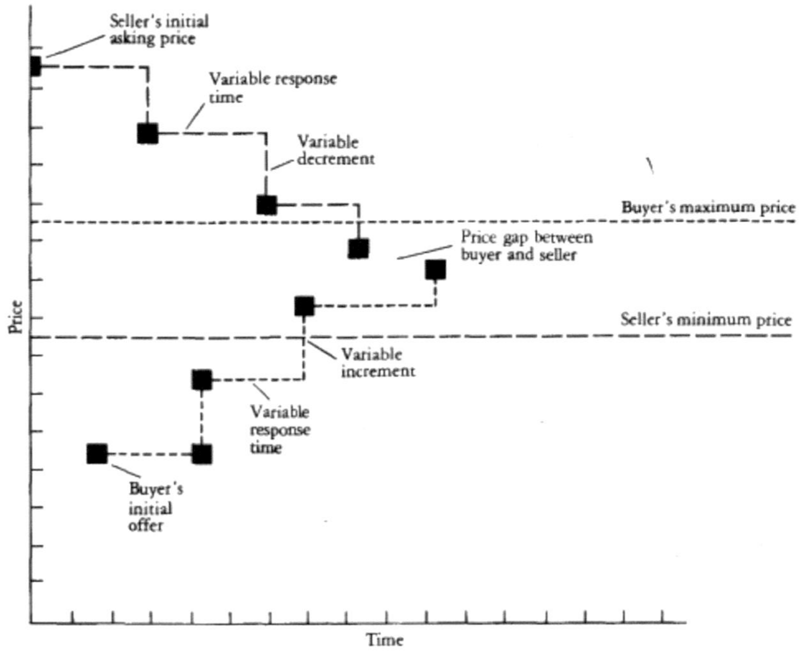

Figure 7. Bargaining: the basic model. (After R. Cassady, "Negotiated Price Making in Mexican Traditional Markets," *America indigena*, 28:51–79, 1968.)

reaching it.[172] The rapidity of movement toward the settlement region further specifies the situation (the faster, the wider). And the settlement itself will be more protracted the wider the region as each participant, more or less assured of exchange, maneuvers to locate final price a few rial closer to his boundary than to his antagonist's. (Where the region is narrow, the final phase, if it is reached, hardly differs from the middle one.) The interaction of these processual signals with price signals as such (i.e., how much is at stake) is, of course, complex, and the variation in the temporal structure of bargaining is consequendy extremely great.[173] But so too, are the capacities of accomplished suwwaqs to discriminate the signals: A sense for the "music" of chaffering is one of the primary (and one of the most unequally distributed) exchange skills in the bazaar.[174]

This formal dimension of bargaining is, of course, supported by a wide range of conventions: that the seller bids first, that bids alternate, that backward moves are forbidden, that accepted bids must be honored, that one ought not break off an interchange that is moving actively ahead, and so on. Like any conventions, these may sometimes be breached – a buyer is sometimes forced to make the initial bid, several consecutive moves are occasionally made by one side or another, a buyer occasionally refuses to purchase at a price he has already offered or walks away from a responsive seller – but hardly ever without complaint from the injured party. The cry Cassady heard from an Oaxaca vendor – "I *palabra* three times and you only *palabra* once" – can be heard now and then (though there the term is *tkellem*) in Sefrou as well, and suwwaqs have been known to strike people who fail to exchange at a price they themselves have offered.[175] The conventions of bargaining thus slip into its etiquette and morality. This is a vast subject, touching on everything from speech styles (which can be very elaborate – the "I will give you kisses, I will give you hugs" rhetoric of bazaar trading those foreign to it consistently misinterpret as hypocrisy) and hospitality patterns (hardly any large-scale exchange in the suq is consummated without drinking tea, and for clients tea may accompany even small-scale deals) to humor, flexibility, and patience. But the main principle animating bargaining is that participants should conduct themselves vis-à-vis one another so as to render the process successful. Both buyer and seller have more than a material desire to triumph over their functional opposition to effect an exchange: They have a moral obligation to do so. For only to the degree that they are able to do this over and over again, able to keep aborted encounters to the absolute minimum of those cases where there is no settlement region, can the bargaining relationship serve them as an effective communications channel, a useful device for intensive search:

> Bargaining . . . serves an economic purpose, that is, to regulate prices in societies where suspicion and uncertainty of the value of commodities dominate. In the Middle East [and North Africa], bargaining is not for fun, nor merely for the sake of bargaining. Through the manipulation of cultural norms and symbols, a bargainer, whether seller or buyer, aims to eliminate suspicion of commodity and price and establish instead an atmosphere of trust often leading to client-relationships, and occasionally to friendship. True . . . "business tricks" . . . are used, but even these tricks cannot be carried out without the initial establishment of trust and through an idiom of trust: kinship terms, polite formulas, observance of good manners. In the Middle Eastern case, the failure of a bargainer to evoke and manipulate this idiom of trust leads eventually to a failure in successfully consummating the intended transaction. As long as the consummation of a

> transaction depends primarily on the establishment of trust in bargaining, trust necessarily takes precedence over the profit motive. Any act of discourtesy . . . inevitably puts an end to the bargain[ing] . . .
>
> In bargaining, the social status of the bargaining partners is at stake. They attempt to neutralize this status by following the strict rules of bargaining etiquette. But bargaining is not used only to neutralize positions, but also to improve them. If either party to the bargain, seller or buyer, is unusually successful in his approach, he earns social recognition among his group by developing the reputation of knowing how to "handle" people and subsequently affect their choice of behavior. Since profit in bargaining is translated into social recognition, seller-bargainers in the Middle East resort to all sorts of polite formulas to affect the economic choice of their partners . . .
>
> In the absence of [fixed prices], as in the sūqs of the Middle East, bargaining becomes essential to . . . sustained economic relationships between buyer and seller. Just as bargaining enables the buyer to distinguish reliable sellers from unreliable ones . . . it also enables the seller to eliminate distrustful buyers . . . and to establish lasting clientship with trustful ones . . . Hence, in a very intricate and sensitive way, bargaining brings order into an otherwise uncontrolled market system.[176]

Bargaining and clientelization are thus not so much two search processes, the one following after the other in the tracks laid down, as reinforcing aspects of a single search process. Through intensive bargaining, enclosed in an established cake of custom, clientship is formed and given substance; clientship, an institutionalized bazaar-friendship relation, with its own rules, obligations, and expectations, directs intensive bargaining and contains its powerful agonistic elements within an organizing moral code. The elaboration and stabilization of the two-person communication link that enables operation in the information cacophony of the suq can be seen equally as a social relationship within which an exchange pattern forms or an exchange pattern around which a social relationship forms. In either case, whether "clientelized bargaining" or "bargainized clientship," it is a good deal more than a war of opposed preferences.

Finally, the amount of bargaining that takes place in any given transaction is itself highly variable. *Ceteris paribus*, which they never are, higher price transactions normally take longer than lower price exchanges, strong clientship ties normally shorten bargaining time, repetitive exchanges (e.g., buying food) are normally completed more rapidly than occasional ones (e.g., buying a cow), and so on. Several even more incidental facts also influence the amount of bargaining: time of day; season of the year; inventory size, composition, and flexibility; the perishability of the goods; the "fullness" of the bazaar; and, not least, the relative social status, experience, astuteness, and the mere temperaments of the participants – the list, if not infinite, is surely very long.

The shadow price of time for a suwwaq may not be as high as for a modern corporation executive, but it is not so low as is often thought. The length of time bargaining takes is an important cost for suwwaqs, who could, after all, be higgling with someone else and who in any case are extremely busy men in their attempts to cumulate a large number of marginal gains into a decent living. Along with the ability to assess the quality of goods and the rationality of their prices, and the capacity to persuade others into profitable agreements, a sense for whether a particular effort to come to terms is worth the candle is a primary attribute of an effective suwwaq. One needs to know not only how to bargain, but how long.[177]

The information game: the large and the small. Looked at from the point of view of the observing ethnographer, *sūq Ṣ-Ṣefrū* is a distended complexity; looked at from the point of view of the acting suwwaq, it is a shrunken one. The individual shopkeeper, artisan, arbitrager, auctioneer, or target seller operates over a very narrow region of what, when it is projected onto the level of a comprehensive description, is a vast and multiplex system ramifying irregularly in diverse dimensions. From within, the whole, as a whole, is but a dim outline. It spreads away from the individual like a sea, its general form perceived in only the most abstract and simplified terms and regarded – the overall behavior of prices, flow of goods, location of marketplaces, distribution of wealth – as so much presented fact. It is the immediate environment, the surround of actual and potential exchange partners, particular men in particular places placing particular prices on particular goods, that is apprehended in concrete and differentiated form and toward which the energies of the struggle for advantage, immense, unremitting, and sensitive to microns, are directed. What in the large is beyond human control is, in the little, malleable to the ambitions of lilliput merchants.

Clearing a small space in the grand cacophony of the suq where one can interpret and evaluate information with at least some minimal confidence is thus the central strategy of any suwwaq. The multiplicity of enterprises, the intensive division of labor, the inhomogeneity of goods, the complexity of the flow of trade, the elaborate structure of religious, ethnic, and moral categorization are overcome, to the degree they are overcome, by constructing around oneself a personal network of exchange relations in which these matters can be given a reasonably determinate, stabilized form. The gross structure of the bazaar, considered as an institution – one of the great social formations of Moroccan (and, beyond it, Mideastern) civilization, on a par, at least, with the city, the state, the family, the clan, the village, or even *ummat l-Islām* – only sets the frame within which the fine structure, a virtual infinity of overlapping suwwaq-to-suwwaq connection clusters, develops. At the heart of the suq system, considered as an information game, lies a seeming paradox dissolved by a familiar principle. The paradox is that comprehensive ignorance promotes local knowledge. The principle is that in the country of the blind, the one-eyed man is king.

This can perhaps be most easily clarified with the aid of what may seem a rather curious model but is actually an apt one: horseracing.

As M. B. Scott has shown, horseracing revolves, like the suq, around the distribution of information, information being "defined simply as what a social actor knows about a situation."[178] Considered formally, horseracing consists of three main parts: the race as such, the betting on the race before it is run, and the payoffs to successful bettors after the race is run. The odds on the individual horses, and thus the payoffs, are pari-mutuel (i.e., they are determined by the distribution of bets: the greater the percentage of the entire pool wagered on a particular horse, the less, dollar for dollar, the return to the bettor if he wins, and vice versa). For the bettor, therefore, the road to maximization consists not just in picking winning horses, but in picking winning horses others do not pick; that is, in possessing (correct) information – knowledge – about a situation with respect to which those from whom he profits are either ignorant or misinformed. "There is," as the racing writer Joe Palmer once said, "nothing better around a track than a well-told lie except a truth that no one will believe."[179]

One has, then, a crowd of bettors out of which the actual race selects a much smaller crowd of winners; the larger crowd of losers is kept more or less in play by the fact that there is, save for those washed out entirely, always another race coming along. Although the role of luck, important in any game where information is less than perfect, plays a role in determining betting success, as does capital, enabling one to engage in more elaborate strategies, the main differentiating factor between the effective and the ineffective horseplayer is, as Scott demonstrates in fine detail, the amount of knowledge (or ignorance) they possess concerning the instant facts:

> What is generated in the world of horse racing is an *information game*. The information game is a game of *strategy*. That is, each player in deciding on a course of action takes into account that other players are engaged in the same sort of accounting. The players in this game are concerned with *strategic information*, which is not shared by the players in interaction; if this information were shared, the nature of the interaction would be radically different. Since information is a crucial feature of this game, much activity will be devoted toward discovering, concealing, and using information. Taken together, these *patterns* of interaction make up the information game, and the *mode* of interaction characteristic of the information game [may] be called *strategic interaction*.
>
> For [the] players, the object of this game is to obtain "reliable information," which will enable them to make winning bets. Each bet may be called a play, and the game generated event where the play occurs is the race. To make a successful play is to "beat the race." A continual pattern of beating the race gives rise to the much sought state of "beating the game" or "beating the system."[180]

Scott goes on to describe both the various sorts of players in this game (owners, trainers, jockeys, stewards, bookies, touts, regular bettors, occasional bettors, hustlers) and the devices they employ (form charts, paddock observation, personal contacts, a great deal of rumor chasing and rumor mongering) in their effort to gain an information edge over their fellows.

There are, obviously, substantial differences between playing horses and operating in the suq (that is why racing is only a model): Rival bettors do not bet against one another directly; the formal aids to search are very much more developed; action is well defined and discontinuous; a mass of unprofessional participants is thrown in together with a much smaller number of professionals. Yet the structure of the information game as such is the same (that is why racing is a model): a set of interest-opposed individuals pursuing the high art of local, intensive, qualitative search so as to capitalize on the ambiguity, scarcity, and maldistribution of knowledge generated by the system as a whole. Beating the game, either in the suq or in horseracing, something rather difficult in both cases, does not turn on how much you know as such. That rarely comes to a great deal anyway. It turns on how much more you know (i.e., how much less ignorant you are) about particular, given cases than others are-how many races (exchanges) you can beat. Whatever their other differences, which are vast, both the horseplayer and the suwwaq live, or fail to, from marginal information asymmetries they first detect and then exploit.

Leaving the model behind, its analogical force already a bit extended, this concept of the bazaar as an information game played out in piddling maneuvers casts a somewhat different light on its general structure. Rather than an ascending hierarchy of broader integrations, each one manned by more and more imposing entrepreneurs, it is a vast field of petty traders and craftsmen, amid which now and then a more consequential individual arises. Success in the bazaar – and there are those who succeed by any standard, though not very many, and usually not for very long – comes from accumulating small-scale advantages, not from coordinating large-scale activities. With modern developments, especially in such fields as construction and transport, a few such large-, or anyway larger-, scale managerial types have begun to appear. But, for the most part, the suq is still populated, indeed overpopulated, by scramblers, some a bit more adroit, a bit more lucky, or a bit more relentless than others.

The extreme difficulty, if not the impossibility, of seeing the suq steadily and whole, of gaining knowledge about its general workings sufficiently circumstantial to enable one to conceive large-scale operations or pursue long-term strategies – to say nothing of exercising any deliberate control over those workings – reduces the suwwaq's life to a continuing string of hand-to-hand combats in particular, intimately known corners of commercial life, a microworld of perfected tactics. The overall structure of the suq, a weakly joined system of multiple divisions, multiple units, multiple signals, and multiple activities, none of them either clearly outlined or well standardized, puts an enormous premium on interpersonal exchange skills, the developed apparatus of practical judgment, informal contract, and intensive search.[181] For all the apparent incoherence, the large and the small in the suq play into one another: The prismatic quality of the first and the focalizing quality of the second are reflexes of one another, aspects of a single, not very elegant, not very efficient, and not very rewarding, but nonetheless ordered, intensely active, and reasonably workable tradesman economy.

Conclusion: suq and society

The large/small question applies, of course, not only to the relation between the Sefrou suq as a system and Sefrou suwwaqs as individual actors within it, but to the relations between the suq as a system and the wider context within which it in turn is set. That wider context is, in the first instance, Moroccan, or, perhaps better, Maghrebian, society; but it stretches beyond to transregional, intercontinental, even global dimensions. One institution, if a formidable one, among others in North African society, the suq is also an element, if a marginal one, among others in the modern world order.

It is neither possible nor appropriate to describe these wider relations, removed or immediate, in any detail here. But much of what has been described here cannot properly be understood if they are not kept at least generally in mind. It is not necessary to comprehend everything to comprehend anything, and the megaanalyses of macrosociology – Marxist, Durkheimian, Spencerian, Weberian, or whatever – are all too often of more rhetorical than cognitive force, ideological efforts to direct the destiny of modern society rather than scientific inquiries into its dynamic. Yet modern society has such a dynamic, and microstudies of contemporary social phenomena that are not conducted with a sense for the nature of that dynamic and directed toward clarifying it are reduced to academic exercises.

Whatever the traditional forms it employs – *nisba*, *ḥabūs*, *ḥenṭa*, *ḥanūt*, *ṣedaqa* – the Sefrou bazaar was born and evolved in the twentieth century and represents as much a response to the social, political, and economic realities of that century as they have appeared on the local scene as it represents an emanation of Morocco's arabesque past. If the development of underdevelopment occurred anywhere, it occurred here, as an increasing number of increasingly marginal traders and artisans tried to crowd themselves into a slowly expanding economic niche, a niche whose size and nature were in good part reflexes of developments elsewhere. The immiseration that accompanies a form of economic change which consists in accentuating the struggle for the leftover rewards that appear at the edge of an industrial system as it connects up with a classical agrarian one – the leitmotif of Asian, African, and Latin American history from about 1870 – appears here in, if anything, hypertrophied form.[182] The development of the Sefrou bazaar from about 1900 to 1970 represents at once the quantitative growth and structural complexification of local commercial activity as the region became peripherally integrated into the modern capitalist system and the parcelization of that activity in such a way that, save for a few fortunate moments (mainly around 1920) and a few well-placed individuals (mainly men with political connections), the gains of the whole, modest in any case, were dispersed in the parts.

This general situation remains intact despite the formal devolution of colonial power: The suq, in Sefrou and elsewhere, is still rather more in the world economy than of it. Changing that fact, assuming one wishes to see it change and the Sefrou economy to "develop" in the nonironic sense of the term, would seem, if what has been written above has any merit, to involve the reconstruction of the bazaar as a communications system, the creation of institutional forms within which the individual suwwaq's access to relevant information would be improved.

Whether such a change is possible at all (to say nothing of whether deliberate policy decisions can do anything to accelerate it) is simply not known, because theoretical understanding of bazaar economies is still so limited and because most development thinking has been concerned with replacing bazaar systems with supposedly more modern (read Western) forms, rather than with perfecting such systems – modernizing, if that is the word, what is already in place and in its own terms.

If "the bazaar economy" is seen as an economic type rather than an evolutionary step toward something more familiar to people used to other ways of doing things, and, more importantly, if a deeper understanding of its nature can be obtained, perhaps, just perhaps, some relevant and practicable suggestions for improving it, for increasing its capacity to inform its participants, might emerge and its power of growth be restored and strengthened. Even such an improvement, assuming it can be done at all, would not be costless and certainly would not lead to radical transformation of the suwwaq standard of living. But given the present levels of collective ignorance and the standard of living that goes with them, the attempt should well be worthwhile:

> Ignorance is like subzero weather: by a sufficient expenditure its effects upon people can be kept within tolerable or even comfortable bounds, but it would be wholly uneconomic entirely to eliminate all its effects. And, just as an analysis of man's shelter and apparel would be somewhat incomplete if cold weather is ignored, so also our understanding of economic life will be incomplete if we do not systematically take account of the cold winds of ignorance.[183]

However that may be, the suq is also of importance in understanding Moroccan – Maghrebian, even, to an extent, Mideastern – society generally. Drawing on anthropological traditions of analysis, students of Moroccan social organization have tended to apply a kinship-derived model, the so-called segmentary system theory, to it.[184] That such a model fits the North African situation very well has been questioned with increasing frequency.[185] The pyramiding of corporate lineages into larger and larger solidary unilineal units, each in complementary opposition to one another at the appropriate level of organization, not only fails to account for the great part of Moroccan society, now and in the past, that cannot in any reasonable reading be called "tribal," but is not much more effective with respect to the section of society that, a bit more reasonably, can. And although no one model is adequate to such broad purposes, it is at least arguable that a model constructed out of an analysis of the bazaar will fit the surface facts better and reveal more accurately some of the deeper processes underlying them. Imperfect communication may be a better key to the distinctive features of Maghrebian social organization than lineage fission and recombination; information bargaining, than complementary opposition; clientship, than consanguinity.

Looking at the Moroccan sultanate, the social organization of Fez or Marrakech, or the nature of Berber "tribalism" (to say nothing of Algerian religious life or Tunisian village structure) in such terms lies in the future as but a beckoning possibility. But the great social formations of the Maghreb do bear a family resemblance to one another that the suq, as one of the most formidable and most distinctive of them, can, when properly understood, throw into more exact relief. This is not to suggest that Maghrebian society is a big bazaar, any more than it is a big tribe. Nevertheless, in the details of bazaar life something of the spirit that animates that society – an odd mixture of restlessness, practicality, contentiousness, eloquence, inclemency, and moralism – can be seen with a particular and revelatory vividness.

Notes

1. Goitein, S. D., *A Mediterranean Society,* Vol. I; *Economic Foundations*, Berkeley, 1967, p. 70.
2. For some other good ones, see Le Tourneau, R., *Fès avant le Protectorat*, Casablanca, 1949, pp. 271–452; Massignon, L., "Enquête sur les corporations musulmanes d'Artisans et Commerçants au Maroc," *Revue du Monde Musulman*, 58:1–250 (1924); Waterbury, J., *North for the Trade*, Berkeley, 1972; Skinner, G. W., "Marketing and Social Structure in Rural China," *Journal of Asian Studies*, 24:2–43 (1964), 195–228 (1965); Davis, W. G., *Social Relations in a Philippine Market*, Berkeley, 1973; Dewey, A. G., *Peasant Marketing in Java*, Glencoe (IL.), 1962; Bohannan, P. J., and G. Dalton (eds.), *Markets in Africa*, Evanston, 1962; Mintz, S., *Caribbean Transformations*, Chicago, 1974; Beals, R. L., *The Peasant Marketing System of Oaxaca, Mexico*, Berkeley, 1975; Tax, S., *Penny Capitalism*, Washington, D.C., 1953; Oster, A. "A Bazaar Narrated," (Bengal), forthcoming. Cornelius Osgood's Hong Kong study (*The Chinese, A Study of a Hongkong Community*, Tucson, 1975) is perhaps the fullest description of a developed bazaar economy but lacks much analytical interest. For an interesting series of studies from a central place theory point of view, see Smith, C. A. (ed.), *Regional Analysis*, Vol. I., New York, 1976. For a general descriptive review of Mideastern city bazaars from an urban geography point of view, see Wirth, E., "Zum Problem des Bazaars (Suq, Çarsi)," *Der Islam*, 52:1–46, 204–61 (1975). Cf. my earlier attempt for Indonesia, *Peddlers and Princes*, Chicago, 1963.

   After the present study was essentially completed, a major work on Moroccan suqs from the point of view of economic geography appeared: Troin, J. F., *Les Souks Marocains*, Aix-en-Provence, 1975, 2 vols. Troin's study, conceived on entirely different lines than the present one, relies on government statistics, survey methods, computer manipulations, and mapping techniques to produce an essentially quantitative analysis of 384 bazaars in the northern half of Morocco. (The southernmost points of his dividing line are Skhirat, Tounfite, Midelt, Missour, and Berquent. Sefrou is thus included.) B. G. Hoffman's brief and inadequate treatment (*The Structure of Traditional Moroccan Rural Society*, The Hague, 1967, pp. 79–84) is, like the book as a whole, useful mainly for its references. A brief description of market activity in a town (Azemmour) about the size of Sefrou can be found in Le Coeur, C., *Le Rite et l'outil*, Paris, 1939, pp. 129–50; an extended investigation of a single bazaar trade, tanners, in Marrakech, is presented in Jamma, D., *Les Tanneurs de Marrakech*, Algiers, 1971; and some interesting remarks about rural markets in northeastern Morocco can be found in Hart, D. M., *The Aith Waryaghar of the Moroccan Rif*, Tucson, 1976, pp. 69–88. A brief, general "state of the art" review of Mideastern bazaar studies appears in Bonine, M., "Urban Studies in the Middle East," *Middle East Studies Association Bulletin*, 10(3):1-37 (Oct. 1976). Other particular studies of Moroccan markets will be cited, as occasioned, below.

3. For nonmarket economies, see Polanyi, K., C. Arensberg, and H. Pearson, *Trade and Markets in the Early Empires*, Glencoe (IL), 1957; Mauss, M., *The Gift: Forms and Functions of Exchange in Archaic Societies*, London, 1954; Firth, R., *Primitive Polynesian Economy*, London, 1939; Sahlins, M., *Stone Age Economics*, Chicago and New York, 1972; Dalton, G. (ed.), *Tribal and Peasant Economies: Readings in Economic Anthropology*, Garden City (N.Y.), 1967; Dalton, G., "Aboriginal Economies in Stateless Societies," in *Exchange Systems in Prehistory*, New York, 1977, pp. 191–212; Belshaw, C. S., *Traditional Exchange and Modern Markets*, Englewood Cliffs (NJ), 1965. For information mechanisms in modern economies, see Lamberton, D. H. (ed.), *Economics of Information and Knowledge*, Middlesex (UK), 1971; Spence, M., *Market Signalling*, Cambridge (MA), 1974. As the sequel will make clear, these matters are quite relative, and virtually any developed economy, and many not so developed ones, will display all three types of "information pattern" in one context or another. A contrast similar to the one drawn here is made briefly in Khuri, F., "The Etiquette of Bargaining in the Middle East," *American Anthropologist*, 70:698–706 (1968).

4. According to the 1960 census, bazaar-connected occupations accounted for about 64% of the employed labor force, as against about 16% for professionals, white-collar workers, government officials, etc., and about 20% for farmers and farmworkers (see Table 2). It is difficult, of course, to distribute these "bazaar workers" among the three realms because so many of them participate in more than one. But that the permanent bazaar is far and away the main occupational sector in the town economy, so far as numbers employed are concerned, is beyond all doubt.

5. There are some markets that meet twice a week and a few that meet three times. The very largest cities have only traditional peak days in what has become by now a more or less continuous meeting pattern. There are no periodic markets now that meet on Friday, the Muslim day of collective prayer, but this has not always been the case. Troin (*op. cit.*, t. 2, pl. 2) gives a total figure (excluding the very smallest markets) of about 850 markets in Morocco in 1968. There are actually some hiatuses in the market scatter across the countryside (*ibid.*, p. 361).
6. For a general discussion of market cycle patterns in northern Morocco, see Troin, *op. cit.*, t. I, pp. 81ff. A market cycle sketch for a region in north Morocco is given in Hart, *op. cit.*, p. 75. The simple division of market centers into two levels is something of a simplification. Both locality-focusing markets within a region and region-focusing markets within a section of the country differ among themselves in size and range. On this problem, see Berry, B. L., *Geography of Market Centers*, Englewood Cliffs (NJ), 1967.
7. My figures for animals are from the Sefrou Cercle office. Troin (*op. cit.*, t. 2, pl. 10, p. 9) gives the following approximate figures (I have estimated them from his graphs) for the Sefrou periodic market, per year:

Sheep	32,000	head
Goats	5,000	head
Cattle	10,000	head
Mules, donkeys, etc.	2,500	head
Cereals, beans	4,000	metric tons
Fruits, vegetables	2,000	metric tons

These figures, gathered in a formal questionnaire survey with "autorités locales" by Troin and two young officials from the Ministries of Agriculture and Agrarian Reform sometime between 1963 and 1968, ought not, as Troin himself emphasizes, to be taken too exactly; but they seem the proper order of magnitude. Train's estimate (t. 2, pl. 12) of the weekly value of goods and services of just under Dh 400,000 for Sefrou (Fez, Dh 1,610,000) is even more tremulously based (for the method, see 1.1, p. 133), but again the order of magnitude – it puts Sefrou in about the sixtieth percentile of the markets surveyed – appears about right.
8. The Tafilalt, a very large (about 311 square kilometers) "Mesopotamian"-type alluvial oasis lying between the Gheris and Ziz rivers at the edge of the Sahara, was the major entrepôt of the Moroccan trans-Saharan trade – both south toward Timbuctoo and east toward Kairouan, Cairo, and Mecca – from the tenth century forward. Until the end of the fifteenth century, the oasis was the site of the famous city of Sijilmasa, the capital of "the golden trade of the Moors" and most especially of the slave trade north from the Sudan. After the sixteenth century, trans-Saharan trade gradually declined, essentially disappearing by 1894, the year the French

finally took Timbuctoo, but the Tafilalt (whence, in the seventeenth century, the present Moroccan dynasty – the Alawites – arose and moved north to capture Fez) remained an important trade center, and caravans to and from Fez continued, if with diminished frequency and shrunken size, up to the eve of World War I. For an excellent description of the Tafilalt in the nineteenth century (when there was, in fact, something of a brief recovery of the trans-Saharan trade), see Dunn, R., "The Trade of the Tafilalt," *African Historical Studies*, 4:271–302 (1971), and the same author's *Resistance in the Desert*, Madison (WI), 1977. On Sijilmasa, see George Colin's entry under that title in *The Encyclopaedia of Islam*, and Brignon, J., et al., *Histoire du Maroc*, Paris and Casablanca, 1967, pp. 78, 83, 88–9, 121ff., 155, 190–1, 218–21, 236, 239. For the Fez end of things, see Le Tourneau, *op. cit.*, pp. 405–37. On the North African caravan trade generally, see Bovill, E. W., *The Golden Trade of the Moors*, London, 1958.

9. During the nine months or so the route was passable, perhaps twenty-five or thirty caravans (*qwāfel;* sg. *qāfla*), some as large as a 100 mules, came through Sefrou each year in the first decades of this century. Toward the Tafilalt (whose population, ca. 1900, was some 100,000), they carried cotton goods, sugar, tea, firearms, cannabis, and various sorts of craftwork; toward Fez, dates, skins, leather, figs, raisins, perfume, and henna. Sefrouis also called this trail s-sb' *l-ᶜaqabi* ("the seven climbs upward"). See also Le Tourneau, *op. cit.*, p. 471. Stopovers varied in length and number, but six or seven hours was considered a fair day's travel. An itinerary of caravans between the Tafilalt and Fez can be found in *Renseignements coloniaux, supplément au "bulletin du comité de l'Afrique française" de Juin 1905*, 6:220 (1905).

10. *Ḥabus* (pl. *ḥubus*) is the Malikite term; elsewhere the institution is known as *waqf.* See Schacht, J., *An Introduction to Islamic Law*, Oxford, 1964; and entry under *waqf* in *The Shorter Encyclopedia of Islam*. Cf. Stillman, N. A., "Charity and Social Service in Medieval Islam," *Societas*, 5:105–15 (1975).

11. Sefrou's Jewish population, which had risen steadily since at least 1880, and especialy readily in the French period, dropped 40% between 1947 and 1960 (see Voinot, L., *Pèlerinages judeo-musulmans du Maroc*, Paris, 1940, pp. 9–10). Voinot's estimate for the Sefrou Jewish population in 1900 – 1,000 – is, however, almost certainly much too low. *La Vie juive au Maroc* [in Hebrew], Jerusalem, 1973, p. 18, gives 2,500 for 1904; 4,046 for 1931; 5,757 for 1947; and 3,118 for 1960. Since 1960 the decline has been even more precipitous. By 1972 less than 200 out of a community that by 1947 was approaching 6,000 remained (Stillman, N., "The Sefrou Remnant," *Jewish Social Studies*, 35:255–63 [1973]); by 1976, less than 50. In 1960, the Muslim population of Sefrou was 0.7% of the total Moroccan Muslim population; the Jewish was 2.3% of the total Moroccan Jewish population (Benyoussef, A., *Populations du Maghreb*, Paris, 1967, p. 111).

The foreign – largely French – population was 0.1% of the whole foreign population.

12. Roughly "long distance trader." The term is never used in Sefrou for ordinary merchants, no matter how large. (It also means "rich," plain and simple.) The estimate of a dozen Muslims and two dozen Jews is derived from interview material, obtained from aged informants, which is particularly circumstantial in this regard.
13. Again, it is impossible to say anything very exact, or even very positive, about the situation prior to 1900; but what evidence exists suggests that this entrance by Sefrouis into the body of the caravan trade is quite recent. Al-Bakri in the eleventh century, al-Idrisi in the twelfth, Leo Africanus in the sixteenth, and Charles de Foucauld in the nineteenth all remark that, though a stop on the caravan trail, Sefrou is essentially an agricultural, not a commercial, town. Al-Bakrī, *Description de l'Afrique septentrionale*, de Slane (ed. and trans.), 2 vols., Algiers, 1911–13, Vol. 1, p. 146; al-Idrīsī, *Description de l'Afrique et de l'Espagne*, R. Dozy and M. J. de Goeje (eds. and trans.), Leiden, 1866, p. 87; Leo Africanus, *Description de l'Afrique*, Ch. Schefer, ed. and annotated, 2 vols., Paris, 1896–8, Vol. 2, p. 359; de Foucauld, C, *Reconnaissance du Maroc*, 2 vols., Paris, 1888, Vol. 1, pp. 37ff. Scattered but interesting descriptions of bazaar and caravan activities in and around Sefrou during the first decade of the present century can be found in *The Gospel Message*, the publication of the Gospel Missionary Union in London, from 1904 to 1912, which had (and still has) a mission station in Sefrou (see especially Apr. 1904, Jan. 1906, Feb. 1906, Mar. 1906, Feb. 1907, Dec. 1908, Aug. 1909, Nov. 1909, Dec. 1909, June 1912).
14. Udovitch, A. L., "At the Origins of the Western *Commenda:* Islam, Israel, Byzantium?" *Speculum*, 37:198–207 (1962). Udovitch traces the various forms of this sort of contract in the Jewish, Byzantine, and Islamic traditions, concluding that the Islamic and the European (i.e., Italian Renaissance) forms are virtually identical. Cf. Udovitch, A. L., *Partnership and Profit in Medieval Islam*, Princeton, 1970. For the operation of the qirad in medieval Egypt, see Goitein, *op. cit.*, pp. 171ff.
15. Regarding amounts advanced, the terms of agreement, and so on, qirad contracts seem to have always been written and officially witnessed, but their operation clearly depended most heavily on the personal relation between the parties, and especially on the confidence of the financier (*muqriḍ*) in the trader (*muqāriḍ*). Such contracts were often, however, not between individuals, but between groups of capital suppliers and/or groups of traders, operating, each on his own side of the line, in genuine partnerships. The highest development of the qirad was in maritime rather than caravan trade, but the similarities between the two sorts of long-distance commerce – including the dangers faced, the goods carried, and the organization required – made the institution equally suitable to both. For

the qirad in North African maritime trade, mainly that going in and out of Kairouan, see Idris, H. R., "Commerce maritime et Kirād en Berberie orientale," *Journal of the Economic and Social History of the Orient*, 4:225–39 (1961). For its probable origins in Meccan overland trade, see Udovitch, *Partnership and Profit*, pp. 170–6.

16. In intra-Jewish contracts, Talmudic commercial forms, setting a two-thirds/one-third, agent/investor return and saddling the agent with a certain degree of liability, seem mainly to have been used; in Jewish-Muslim contracts, the liability-free and normally half/half qirad pattern was employed. On the Jewish form, called *ʿisqa*, and its similarities to and differences from the Muslim qirad, see Udovitch, "At the Origins." For the *ʿisqa* in Morocco, see Zafrani, H., *Les Juifs du Maroc*, Paris, 1972, pp. 181–88.
17. Dunn (*Resistance*, p. 87) estimates the Jewish community in the Tafilalt as ca. 6,000 in 1900, which would make it about three times the size of Sefrou's, three-quarters the size of Fez's (Dunn, *Morocco's Crisis*, p. 159). There seems to have been a fairly sizable group of Tafilalt Jews (informants' estimates run as high as a fifth of the whole) in Sefrou itself around the turn of the century.
18. One other element, Fez merchants temporarily resident in Sefrou (about a dozen of them rented one of Sefrou's larger funduqs, number 2 in Figure 3, for a while toward the end of the nineteenth century as a base for their cloth trade operations), should be mentioned in connection with qirad operations. But they were never numerous and their relations to the Sefrouis were always quite distant, not to say hostile. Fez-Sefrou commercial alliances were (and are) extremely rare, and this was as true for the Jews – whose connections with the Meknes Jewish community, about 80 kilometers away, were always closer than with the Fez, only 40 kilometers distant – as for the Muslims.
19. The gun trade developed with increasing intensity after the fall of Mulay Hasan in 1894 and the rise of various self-promoted claimants to the throne, the most important one in the Sefrou region being Bou Hamara. On this whole period, see Burke, E., III, *Prelude to Protectorate in Morocco*, Chicago, 1976, and Dunn, *Resistance*. The guns were made in Fez, Meknes, Marrakech, or Tetuan or, increasingly, brought into the country from Europe. They were mostly single-shot muzzle loaders, though some German and Italian craftsmen produced some breach loaders in the royal workshop, the famous *makina* in Fez (see Le Tourneau, *op. cit.*, pp. 353–5).
20. Funduq number 5 was the center of trade concerning animals, but there most of the activity was in the area surrounding it, rather than the funduq itself: blacksmiths, saddlemakers, sellers of animal feed, and animal brokers all collected around it. (Owner-to-owner selling of animals was virtually nonexistent then; both seller and purchaser were represented by brokers. This tended to be the pattern in the lumber and olive-oil trades as

well.) Funduqs 3, 8, and 10 seem to have remained in the more traditional pattern – mere caravanserais rather than commodity houses. For Sefrou markets around 1910 and the funduq role in them, see Annex B.

21. Only Funduqs 2, 3, 4, 5, 7, 8, and 9 still stand (1969), and they are either reduced to parking lots for donkeys and mules or house various craft workplaces, in either case but faint images of what they once were. For their present uses, see Annex A.
22. For more ethnographic detail (and there is a great deal) on all this than can be given here, see Westermarck, E. A., *Ritual and Belief in Morocco*, London, 1926, Vol. I, pp. 518–69; Brunot, H., and G.-H. Bousquet, "Contribution a 1'étude des pactes de protection et d alliance chez les Berbères du Maroc central," *Hespéris*, 33:353–70 (1946). The latter paper, however, formulates the matter in "tribe-and-territory" terms rather than as here, in "person-to-person" ones. A (rather schematized) summary of types of "alliance-relationships" is given in Hoffman, *op. cit.*, p. 101. For some brief comments on these pacts among Berber groups at the southern end of the caravan trail, see Hammoudi, A., "Segmentarité, stratification sociale, pouvoir politique et sainteté: réflexions sur les thèses de Gellner," *Hespéris*, 15:147–80 (1974).
23. How many links the chains contained is difficult to determine, but it can hardly have been fewer than the number of days involved in the journey. Also the chains were not necessarily identical for all the caravan chiefs, for there were normally alternative local powers among whom one could bargain. Nor did a caravan sheikh's zettat relations in one area have to be confined to a single man, and such relations were not insusceptible of shifting, dissolving, broadening, and so on. To attempt to formalize the zettata pattern in some systematic way – by tribe, by territory, by institutionalized political role – is inevitably to misrepresent it, for power relationships in the Berber highlands were neither stable nor clear-cut. Rather, a constantly rearranging kaleidoscope of political constellations centering around rising and falling strong men was the pattern, and to this sort of mobile complexity the caravan sheikhs (whose own positions were not all that fixed) had to adjust as best they could. For all that, the zettata system seems, from all reports, to have worked exceedingly well. Actual attacks upon caravans, even in the more than usually disordered period after 1894, seem to have been rare. At the same time, the zettata system is not entirely responsible for that: The caravaners themselves were well enough armed.
24. This is not to deny that there were such connections earlier, but merely that they were very developed or played a very important role in either town or countryside. The tendency to assume that a system of social relationships (which, like the caravan economy before it, is what the bazaar economy is) that operates in terms of traditional forms is, historically

speaking, old is based on the mistaken premise that traditional societies are incapable of reorganizing their institutions into novel patterns, that persistence of cultural forms implies fixity in their social use. Though most "development" theorizing in the social sciences is based on this premise, nothing could be further from the truth – and not only in Morocco.

25. The usual practice was for the Jew to make the first sacrifice, binding "the man who knew how to shoot" (the Berber) under the "conditional curse" (*ʿar*) pattern (for this, see Westermarck, *op. cit.*, pp. 518–69), though the actual relationship had been personally negotiated before all this ritual sealing took place. The Berber word most often used in this context was *amur* ("neck") in the sense of "by my neck, I will protect you." But the (probably) Arabic term, *mezrag*, seems, despite the fact that virtually all riding Jews spoke Berber, to have been far more common.
26. For some specific examples of vigorous reactions to breaches of mezrag protection (which, in themselves, seem again to have been quite rare), see Geertz, C., *The Interpretation of Cultures*, New York, 1973, pp. 6–30.
27. Another important factor was the increasing involvement after 1900 of Sefroui merchants, especially Muslims, in the caravan trade to the north-east – Tetouan, Tangiers, Ksar El Kebir, Ceuta – with which previously the town, away from its main routes, had not been directly connected. The northward caravans, which carried mainly wool outbound and pepper, tea, cannabis, and Spanish cloth inbound, differed from the Saharan ones in that they (1) were more frequent; (2) had much shorter and less arduous routes to traverse; (3) were not composed of professional Berber porters but of Arabic (and some Jewish) traders grouping themselves into ad hoc bands of five or six for company and security (which, as there were towns more or less all along the route, was much less of a problem here); (4) were financed either by the traders involved or by other traders on a simple consignment-and-commission basis (qirad arrangements occurred, but they were rare). All in all, the northeast trade – which continued to flourish well into the Protectorate period, when the creation of an international border just north of Fez turned it into a contraband operation – was more like itinerant trading than it was like the classical Atlas and Saharan type of caravaning. Indeed it gradually evolved into such itinerant trading.
28. On the general question of the role of endogenous and exogenous economic factors in the development of bazaar systems, see Schwimmer, B., "Periodic Markets and Urban Development in Southern Ghana," in Smith, *op. cit.*, pp. 123–44.
29. For a comparable microsociological attempt to discuss a bazaar economy in its cultural setting – the Islamic/Javanese – see Geertz, *Peddlers and Princes*.
30. In addition to ethnic-like diversity, another "demographic" characteristic of the Sefrou (and the Moroccan) bazaar sets it apart from most such

economies in Asia, Black Africa, the Caribbean, etc.: the virtual absence of women in it. For Morocco as a whole the number of men in "commerce" (i.e., merchants) in 1950 was about 62,000: the number of women, 1,400 (i.e., about 45:1). Though there is a noticeably higher degree of female participation in the Jewish than in the Muslim community (about 15:1 vs. about 70:1), the male predominance is overwhelming in both cases (Bensimon-Donath, D., *Evolution du Judaisme marocain*, Paris and The Hague, 1968, p. 134). For Sefrou (1960) the comparable proportions were Muslims 46:1, Jews 10:1, overall 29:1, suggesting either (or, more likely, both) that Sefrou is not at the extreme in these matters and that the situation evolved somewhat between 1950 and 1960. There are some specialized, and not unimportant, modes of participation of women in the bazaar, which will be touched on below; cf. Troin, *op. cit.*, 1.1, pp. 113–88. But overall, the bazaar is an emphatically male realm, and so far as Sefrou is concerned there is not a single woman of any real importance in either the trade or artisan worlds (see Annex A). Though the pattern is changing, even most of the everyday household shopping in the bazaar is still done by men. Elsewhere in Morocco, especially in the Northwest, female participation in market activities has apparently become much more significant in recent years (see Troin, *op. cit.*, 1.1, pp. 63–4). For some brief and generalized comments about women (or paucity thereof) in rural markets in Morocco, see Fogg, W., "Changes in the Layout. Characteristics, and Function of a Moroccan Tribal Market, Consequent on European Control," *Man*, 72:104–8 (1941), and "A Tribal Market in Spanish Morocco," *Africa*, 11:428–58 (1938). Cf. Montagne, R., *Les Berberes et le makhzen dans le sud du Maroc*, Paris, 1930, pp. 251ff. Hart, *op. cit.*, pp. 86–8, briefly describes some of the few rural women's markets in Morocco. For useful discussion of women's economic role overall in a Middle Atlas region south of Sefrou, see Maher, V., *Women and Property in Morocco*, Cambridge (Eng.), 1974. For the generally very great prominence of women in bazaar activities, amounting occasionally to outright dominance, outside the Middle East, see Mintz, S., "Men, Women and Trade," *Comparative Studies in Society and History*, 13:247–69 (1971).

31. Today (1972), when there are perhaps only forty or fifty Jews still active in the bazaar, it is no longer of much importance at all. In describing the bazaar as a cultural form, the sixty-year period, 1910–70, a line in time not a point, will be treated as a unit. Changes occurring during (and, in a few cases, after) that time which it would be misleading to ignore will, of course, be remarked on as well. But unless otherwise specified, present tense references refer in a general way to the period as a whole.
32. These figures, which should have the appropriate *approximatelys* and *abouts* prefixed to them, are drawn from a systematic census of all permanent bazaar establishments carried out during 1968–9 in the course of

fieldwork (see Annex A). This census, which we shall refer to as the bazaar survey, is, along with the computer analysis of the 1960 government census of Sefrou, the source of all the quantitative material – and much of the qualitative – on the Sefrou bazaar that follows. For some brief and highly general impressions of ethnic division of labor in other Moroccan towns ca. 1924, see Massignon, *Enquête*, pp. 25ff.

33. To survey the periodic bazaar, especially that of Sefrou town, in the same manner as the permanent would be a bit like trying to census a swarm of bees. Theoretically it could be done, but practically it is beyond a lone ethnographer's power, at least if he is going to do anything else. A census of one rural periodic suq (Aioun Senam in Figure 1; see Annex B) found that, in sixty-one in-place traders (as opposed to the general populace moving as casual buyers and sellers through the bazaar), twenty-one locally recognized ethnic-like categorizations were represented.

34. The nisba is not confined to the above more or less straightforward "ethnicizing" uses, but is employed in a wide range of domains to attribute relational properties to persons: e.g., occupational role (*ḥrār*/silks – *ḥrārī*/ silk merchant); religious sect membership (*Darqāwa/*a Sufi brotherhood – *Darqāwī/*a member of that brotherhood); abstract relations (*madīna/* city – *madanī/*civil, civilized, civic; cf. *sūq/sūwwāqī*, above); even ad hoc characteristics (Ben Barka/a martyred political leader – *Barkāwī/*a follower of his). The effect of this extensive use of nisba (apparently more extensive than elsewhere in the Arab world, though it is common everywhere) is to turn all sorts of social statuses into ethnic-like properties and extend this way of perceiving people as carrying their backgrounds with them through the whole of life. But a discussion of this, crucial to an understanding of Moroccan culture generally, and Moroccan concepts of personhood particularly, would take us too far afield. For the beginnings of such a discussion, see Geertz, C., "'From the Native's Point of View,' On the Nature of Anthropological Understanding," in Basso, K., and H. Selby (eds.), *Meaning in Anthropology*, Albuquerque, 1976, pp. 221–37.

35. The causal language should not mislead. The non-randomness could as easily be said to derive from the view as the view from the non-randomness. What is being defined here is not a sequence of products, *A* determines *B*, and *B*, *C*. but a culturally conventional way of looking at things: *A* implies *B*, *B* implies *C*, and *C* implies *A – for Moroccans*. For the general methodological position, which derives from Weber's concept of *sinnzusammenhang*, see Geertz, *Interpretation of Cultures*, pp. 3–30.

36. For a full discussion of the construction of these categories (which are not themselves those of the census), their methodological basis, and their sociological import, see H. Geertz's "Appendix: A Statistical Profile of the Population of the Town of Sefrou in 1960," in the original hardcover edition of this volume. For a simpler (twofold) classification of traders

of this same sort for a coastal city, see Brown, K., *People of Salé: Tradition and Change in a Moroccan City, 1830–1930*, Cambridge (MA), 1976, pp. 152–3.

37. Adluni and Meghrawi are old Sefrou names. Yazghi and Bhaluli refer to nearby rural places; Zaikumi and Zgani refer to certain Berber-speaking villages; Tobali and Robini are Sefrou Jewish names.
38. Unemployment figures (which here include those merely "inactive") reinforce the picture: Sefrou-born Arabs, 19% (of men over fifteen years of age); Jews, 15%; rural Arabs, 37%; Berbers, 35%. This contrast is even greater than it looks, because if one takes the critical age group (thirty-one to forty-five) alone, the figures are 15%, 3%, 34%, and 37%. That socio-ethnic category, however externally constructed and inadequately named, is a genuine variable is further supported by the fact that breakdowns according to length of time in town (i.e., for in-migrants) show no clear pattern, either for employment categorization or unemployment rate.
39. The measure is quite conservative, for two reasons. First, no within-trade divisions, by size, type, scale, technical development (e.g., hand tailors vs. machine tailors), etc., have been made. Narrowing the universe to the larger, more substantial enterprises would, in any of the trades, markedly raise the degree of compactness. This is especially important for such categories as grocers, ready-made clothes sellers, tailors, shoemakers, and café keepers, all of which are surely underrated in comparison with other trades in Table 3 because of the larger number of marginal operators in them. Second, the measure was constructed by using not all the nisbas that could possibly be represented in the trade (i.e., all those found in Sefrou, weighted by their proportion in the population – a parameter whose value is not known), but merely those actually represented. This, of course, eliminates the zeros and so greatly reduces the deviation sum and with it the index.

    In short, the degree of nisba concentration is, from a stricter null hypothesis point of view, even higher than here displayed, and the range of the scale is somewhat exaggerated on the downward end. Also, it should be noted that this survey is, in the nature of the case, only of men with fixed permanent-bazaar places of work (and thus is much more complete for occupations like miller, barber, grocer, tobacconist, or blacksmith, than for ready-to-eat-food seller, odds-and-ends seller, or even silk merchant); includes only the owners among them, not apprentices, employees, and assistants (surely more than half the whole); and includes only traditional trades, not "modern" ones. The modern trades are also strongly nisba-bound, but the number of people in any one trade, like plumber or radio seller, is too small for statistical handling.
40. The terms *tribe*, *fraction*, *subfraction* are used here merely for momentary convenience. It should not be assumed that they, and the nisbas deriving

from them, point to an underlying segmentary type of social organization. Though it is not possible to go into the problem here, they do not.

41. The two exceptions, the Alawi sherifs and the residents of a separate walled quarter in the town, the Qlawis, are included in Table 5. All other nisbas fall below ten. After the Alawis and Qlawis, the next eight nisbas (the so-called, and like tribal, miscalled, family categories) yield only 35 cases, or an average of 4.4 per nisba. Beyond them the mosaic gets differentiated indeed: For the entire "all other Sefroui" category, the average number of persons per nisba *in the survey* is 3.8.

42. These data come from the records of the Sefrou habus office. There are two basic compilations, one of separate deeds of gift (*ḥawāla*, literally "transfer of obligation") stretching from the mid-seventeenth to the early nineteenth centuries, and one (*l-mujallad l-mubarak*, "the blessed bound book") a systematization of these, produced in the early nineteenth century at the behest of Sultan Mulay Sliman, who, in response to the reform movement in Islam, wished a more rational ordering. The original habus gifts seem to have been essentially completed by the time of the *Mujallad*, the overwhelming proportion of later additions to the habus being purchased out of profits, though there is an original gift recorded as late as 1920. In the late nineteenth century, another reforming Sultan, Mulay Hassan, unified the Sefrou habus, which had previously been scattered among a large number of nadirs (i.e., habus stewards) according to the particular mosque, Quranic school, or whatever concerned, under the nadir in Fez. After the establishment of the Protectorate, which set up a central Direction des Habous, a separate nadir was placed in Sefrou. Since Independence, he has been transformed into a civil service official under the minister of habus in Rabat, but for all intents and purposes he still operates autonomously.

43. The extent of the agricultural property the habus owns could only be recovered from an exhaustive examination of the records mentioned in note 42. The largest single parcel, now exploited as a modern olive-tree plantation, runs 170 hectares, and it is not the only sizable holding. The percentage of the town's shops and ateliers owned by the habus is also difficult to determine because of multiple occupancy (running to a dozen or more in the funduqs), but I would estimate that about a third, including a majority of those in the heart of the old city, are habus-owned. If habus-owned sites on which individuals have erected their own shops are added, the total goes even higher. The situation is further complicated by the fact that habus holdings – agricultural or urban – take a variety of rather elaborate legal forms, many of which give the habus a part share in an individual property, rights to shares of output, fixed payments, and so on. Finally, a distinction must be made between the "public habus" discussed in the text, called in Sefrou *ḥabus kubra* ("greater habus"), and habus properties

whose income goes to private groups, mainly families and religious brotherhoods, and which is not under the nadir's control, called *ḥabus ṣuḡrā* ("lesser habus"). So far as its bazaar role goes, however, the "lesser" habus acted about as the "greater," if on not so broad a scale (see note 54).

44. Gibb, H. A. R., and H. Bowen, *Islamic Society and the West in the XVIIIth Century*, 2 vols., London, 1950–7.
45. In the 1965 budget mentioned above, about 80% of the $17,000 or so expenditure went for personnel costs and about 20% for property maintenance. It is more difficult to determine the proportion of the total spent in the town, but, given the generally low level of activity of the habus in the countryside, it is probable that more than three-quarters is spent in the town. Indeed, it seems likely that the activities of the habus provide a subsidy of several thousand dollars a year to the bazaar economy from the agricultural. This is certainly the rural view of the matter and the reason for the limited spread of the institution beyond the town. Berber groups, in particular, almost never make use of the habus.
46. There have been *some* increases, both through new auctions and in the course of running leases, but they are extremely rare. Of a large number of habus rents for different trades checked through interview in 1965, only a handful were found to have changed at all, and they quite moderately, in thirty or forty years, and the general opinion was that such rents not only would not, but should not, change in the future. The practice also keeps government taxes on commercial property low, of course. There is no significant trade in subleases because it is considered immoral to earn a profit on habus properties, and one can lose one's right to a habus property for doing so. If a habus property is improved by its holder, the improvements are the private property of the lessee and can be added to the price of a sublease. If an improved habus is surrendered, the improvements are charged to the habus institution. The whole system is thus arranged for the benefit of the lessee, the market trader, not the lessor, the community.
47. This applies especially to fixed enterprises in what has been called above the permanent bazaar (the *sūq l-medīna*). "Rent" in the Thursday bazaar (the *sūq l-ḵemīs*) and the periodic markets connected with it comes in the form of tickets purchased (from the government market administration) for a onetime right to sell goods. These tickets (which can be resold, so that there is something of a brokerage trade in them) are more responsive to market changes, but still tend to remain, for political reasons, fairly low. Stores and sites in the *sūq l-betrina* (the business district bazaar) rent on a more or less free-market basis and are thus, comparatively, both high and unstable.
48. On varieties of Islam in Morocco, see Geertz, C., *Islam Observed*, New Haven, 1968.

49. On zawias in Morocco, see Drague, G., *Esquisse d'histoire religieuse du Maroc, confréries et zaouias*, Paris, 1951; Michaux-Bellaire, E., *Essai sur l'histoire du confréries marocaines*, Paris, 1921; Brunel, R., *Essai sur la confrérie des aissaoua au Maroc*, Paris, 1926; Abun-Nasser, J. M., *The Tijaniyya*, London, 1965; Crapanzano, V., *The Hamadsha*, Berkeley, 1973; Gellner, E., *The Saints of the Atlas*, London, 1961; Eickelman, D., *Moroccan Islam*, Austin, 1976; Depont, O. and X. Coppolani, *Les confréries religieuses musulmanes*, Algiers, 1897, and the article under that title in *Shorter Encyclopaedia of Islam*. For a general sociological view of their role, see Geertz, *Islam Observed*, pp. 48–54. A good bibliographical review is given in Hoffman, *op. cit.*, pp. 120–9, whose own comments should be ignored.
50. At entry, Ṭarika, in *Shorter Encyclopaedia of Islam*. The real problem in censusing brotherhoods is deciding which are properly branches of others and which autonomous entities, something even their members do not always agree upon. Overall brotherhood integration is commonly quite weak in any case.
51. The size figures (surely far too low, as Moroccans did not like to admit zawia membership to French authorities) are from Drague, *op. cit.*, p. 121, who estimates about 4% (also too low) of the entire Moroccan population ca. 1939 belonged to zawias. (For the city of Fez, the estimated rate was 13%, the highest in the country.) In Sefrou, the leading zawias ca. 1920 seem to have been, also in roughly estimated order of size, the following (I give the names they were colloquially known by, usually names of famous sheikhs or founders, with their general, all-Morocco tariqa affiliations in parentheses): B-l-Khadira (Darqawa); Mulay Abdelqader l-Jillali (Qadariyya); Mohammed ben Nasser (Nasiriyya); Sidi ben Aissa (Aissawa); Sidi Ahmad l-Tijani (Tijaniyya); Mohammed b-1 Larbi (Darqawa); Malin Dalil (Malin Dalil); Abdelhayy l-Kittani (Kittaniyya); Sidi Hamid b-l-Abdelsadeq (Sadqiyya); Sidi l-Ghazi (Darqawa); Mulay Ali Sherif (Alawiyya); Sidi Lahcen Yusi (Nasiriyya); and Sidi Ali Hamdush (Hamadsha). This list, too, is incomplete, for a number of small, often evanescent zawias also existed. For another list, for the whole Sefrou region and dating from 1952, see Si Bekkai ben Embarek Lahbib, "Sefrou," *Bulletin économique et social du Maroc*, 15:230–42 (1952).

    Similarly membership sizes are very hard to estimate. The largest, the "green turban" Darqawa of Zawia B-l-Khadira, had upward of seventy members at its peak (i.e., men: many of the zawias also had "women's auxiliaries" that met in members' houses, not in the zawia proper); but size estimates of the others vary too widely to report. A significant number of individuals in the town also belonged to zawias located elsewhere, most especially in Fez. All the zawias, save the one in the Qlaᶜa, were in the medina, in the heart of the permanent bazaar areas. For the ten still (1969) functioning, at a much reduced level, see Annex A. There was also a large number of, generally very small, zawias in the countryside, entirely separate from the urban ones and functioning quite differently, though often affiliated with the same tariqas (Nasiriyya, Kittaniyya, Qadariyya, Aissawa, and so on). Unconnected to the bazaar economy – they played no role in the periodic market system – they are not considered here. Zawia membership ca. 1939 for all Morocco is summarized in Hoffman, *op. cit.*, pp. 127–9.

52. Hard statistics are again hard to establish, but in a series of detailed interviews with older informants I could not find a leading trader or artisan of the interwar period not known to have been a zawia member, and most minor ones seen to have belonged also. Not very many nonbazaar types were involved, at least in the Sefrou town zawias. Partial exceptions were the Tijaniyya, which, founded by the son of Qaid Umar al-Yusi, himself later qaid under the French, attracted a number of civil servants, and the Kittaniyya, which was closely connected in Sefrou with one of the town's leading families, the Adluns, only some of whom were traders.

53. The main studies of Moroccan "guilds" (called, in even less suitable terminology, *corporations*) are Massignon, "Enquête" (cf. his "Complément à l'enquête de 1923–1924, sur les corporations musulmanes," *Revue des études islamiques*, 2:273–93 (1928), and Le Tourneau, *op. cit.*, pp. 295–306. Unlike Massignon, whose study was conducted by an officially circulated questionnaire, Le Tourneau seems well aware of the problem, even if he does little more than throw up his hands at it:

"Ce mot [corporations – *ḥnaṭi*, plural of *ḥenṭa*\ évoque aussitôt, dans nos esprits européens, des souvenirs de notre Moyen Age; nous songeons à des groupements de travailleurs d'un même métier étroitment réglementés, fortement hiérarchisés, jalousement fermés à l'étranger, où l'on ne peut pénétrer que grâce à des répondants et où l'on ne peut faire un chemin que dans la mesure où a donné la preuve de solides capacités professionelles. Peut-être cette représentation ne traduit-elle pas très fidèlement la réalité à laquelle elle s'appliquait jadis; en tout cas, elle n'a que peu de rapports avec l'organisation corporative de Fès.

"Quand on examine la corporation fasie, on est étonné d'y trouver si peu de cohésion, si peu d'efficience. Certes, l'institution, telle qu'il m'a été donné de l'étudier à partir de 1934, avait perdu de sa vigueur depuis l'établissement du Protectorate, mais tous les témoignages que j'ai recueillis auprès de vieux artisans qui avaient connu l'ancien régime me permettent d'affirmer quelle n'en avait pas tellement plus au temps des Sultans indépendants. Cette organisation apparente recouvrait un réalité très anarchique: la corporation fasie n'était pas un faisceau de forces solidement cordonnées, mais bien plutôt un agglomérat de forces seulement juxtaposées et qui répugnaient à s'appuyer les unes sur les autres" [*ibid.*, p. 295].

That the perception of exotic social arrangements as "anarchie" is almost always the result of the analyst's misconception of their nature is perhaps the one proposition anthropology can confidently be said to have established. The reason "la corporation fasie" seemed to Le Tourneau, who was a thorough, careful, and honest, if somewhat flat-footed, observer, a mere "agglomérat de forces seulement juxtaposées" was, or at least so on the basis of the Sefrou evidence one could argue, that it did not exist. The sense of disorder arises from aggregating separate social institutions into a supposedly unitary one; discovering the order that in fact was there demands disaggregating the imaginary "corporation" back into the particular institutions and reconceptualizing their relationships to one another. This is especially evident in Massignon, where simple headings his market officials gave their "corporation lists" display it: *Bayān al ḥiraf wal ṣanā'i bi Fās* [Fez]; *Taqyīd iḥsā arbāb al tijara wal ḥanātī wal ḥiraf bi hadhihi'l hadrat al Marrākoshiya* [Marrakech]; *Bayān asmā al ḥiraf* [Rabat]; *Fihrist konnāshat al ḥisba* [Salé]; *Taqyid al omani* [Taroudant] (transcriptions Massignon's). For a brief, rather generalized, recent discussion of Moroccan "guilds" (*ḥanṭa*) closer to the present one, see Brown, *op. cit.*, pp. 135–49.

On the absence of guilds in medieval Egypt, see Goitein, *op. cit.*, pp. 82–3. For an excellent survey of corporate trade organization in ancien régime France, see Sewell, W., Jr., *Work and Revolution in France: The Language of Labor from the Old Regime to 1848*, Cambridge (UK), 1980, especially Chap. 2.

54. Zawia habus, some of which was considerable in scope, was considered lesser habus, not greater, and thus was not under the town nadir's control but was managed independently by a nadir of the zawia itself. The general policies of management were, however, about the same. Zawia muqqadems were usually elected by the local group, though occasionally appointed by the tariqa sheikh.
55. The principles upon which trades were ranked from clean to dirty are even less precise than for the sects. In general, dealing in cloth or clothing, commercial trading (mainly in wool or wheat) on a "large" scale, and light artisanry were cleaner than ordinary peddling, heavy artisanry, and manual labor, with common grocering, café keeping, etc. in between. Certain behavioral traits (e.g., hashish consumption, considered by many of the heavier trades as essential to their work) also were involved. Cf. Jamma, *op. cit.*, pp. 83–5. A ranking of traditional occupations in Salé in "noble/ignoble" terms by a single older trader is given in Brown, *op. cit.*, pp. 140–8.
56. Massignon (*Enquête*, pp. 140ff) gives a series of brief and unsystematic lists of trade – zawia "affiliations" (ca. 1924) in various Moroccan towns and cities, though he says nothing about the basis of rationale of the affiliations. Jamma (*op. cit.*, pp. 92–5) discusses the role of zawias among the

Marrakech tanners, most of them belonging, as would be expected, to the hyperecstatic Hamadsha and Gnawa sects.

57. There were nearly 100 herfas (see Annex A) in Sefrou, but only a minority were involved in the henta system, the most important being (in no particular order): blacksmiths, carpenters, weavers, butchers, silk merchants, cloth merchants, cafe keepers, bakers, barbers, wheat traders, wool traders, tailors, shoemakers, vegetable and fruit sellers, grocers, saddlepack makers, masons, porters.
58. There could be more than one henta in a zawia (e.g., blacksmiths, butchers, and porters in Aissawa; tailors, wool sellers, and cafe keepers in b-l-Larbi), but not, apparently, more than one in a trade. This is one of the reasons the guild image has sometimes seemed to apply, though there does not, in fact, seem to have been a henta in Sefrou to which all members of the trade concerned belonged. Also it should be remarked that there were not hentas in all zawias: There were apparently none in Tijaniya, Kittani, or Sidi Lahcen Yusi, for example.
59. That is, among members. Some hentas also indulged in a certain amount of general "charity" (*ṣadaqa*) work for the population at large (orphans, poor, sick), but this seems generally to have been minor.
60. In particular, neither the zawias nor the herfas were in themselves such groups. The zawias were very loosely organized: a small crowd of adepts clustered around a spiritual leader, the whole representing a religious "path" to be followed, whether in company or alone, by each person individually. The herfas were somewhat less invertebrate, but were not groups at all or even composed of groups, but categories of men (butchers, grocers) composed of subcategories of them (masters, apprentices; suppliers, peddlers) multiply connected in an involuted network. The internal organization of the trades – including the so-called *amīn* system, usually conflated with the henta in the guild interpretation – will be discussed below in the context of the role structure of the bazaar, where it properly belongs.
61. For example, by Le Tourneau, *op. cit.*, pp. 301–4. For descriptions of saints' festivals, see Brunel, *op. cit.*; Rabinow, P., *Symbolic Domination*, Chicago, 1975. On saints and saint worship generally, see Bel, A., *La Religion musulman en Berbérie*, Paris, 1938; and Geertz, *Islam Observed*.
62. This was just the most prominent of a number of local saints, not a patron saint in the Christian sense. The use of Christian vocabulary – "saint" (*siyyid*, *sīd*); "shrine," "sect," one even sees "cathedral mosque" for *l-jam*ᶜ *l-kebir* – is unfortunate, but not always avoidable. Hentas played no role in the Aids (i.e., the Day of the Sacrifice and the Day of the Breaking of the Fast), which involved mass open-air praying, a public sermon "from the throne" by the Khatib, official sheep sacrifice by the qadi, etc. On the French suppression of the musim, see later in this essay.

63. Of emerging modern occupations actually very few have been absorbed into the herfa system, mainly because they tend to be represented by only two or three occupants each. Only those brought into being by the automobile have grown large enough to develop an apprentice system, elect amins, and so on.
64. For a review of the religious (and some of the political) factors leading to the enfeeblement of the zawias in Morocco generally, see the discussion of "scripturalism" in Geertz, *Islam Observed*, Chap. 3. Cf., 'Alāl al-Fāsi, *Independence Movements in North Africa*, New York, 1970, pp. 111–18; Eickelman, *op. cit.*
65. The entire cult was not banned, only the musim, the collective side of it. Individual worship at the shrine continued, but the social heart was cut out of it by prohibiting henta participation. At first, people stayed away altogether, fearful of French reprisals, but in time they drifted back. Today, the shrine is moderately important again, but the worship pattern is almost wholly individual, and the cult appeals mainly to women, countrymen, and the poor. The bazaar class as such no longer has anything particular to do with it.
66. Latifs are an old tradition in Morocco, considered to be very powerful, even dangerous, and so invoked only in times of great public calamity – droughts, earthquakes, locust plagues. In Sefrou, hentas participated as units in these too. For the latif movement generally, see Halstead, J. P., *Rebirth of a Nation: The Origins and Rise of Moroccan Nationalism, 1912–1944*, Cambridge (MA), 1967, pp. 181–4; Brown, *op. cit.*, pp. 198–205. On the Berber decree, see Halstead, *op. cit.*, pp. 178ff; Al-Fāsi, *op. cit.*, pp. 118ff; and Berque, J., *Le Maghreb entre deux guerres*, Paris, 1962.
67. For a general description of the rise of Moroccan nationalism and the formation of the Istiqlal, see Ashford, D. C., *Political Change in Morocco*, Princeton, 1961; Halstead, *op. cit.*; Rézette, R., *Les Partis politiques marocains*, Paris, 1955. An adequate history of the role of the zawias in the rise and triumph of the nationalist movement has yet to be written. When, aided perhaps by in-depth local studies such as this and Eickelman's (*op. cit.*), one is finally written, the now-standard view (e.g., Bidwell, R., *Morocco Under Colonial Rule*, London, 1973, pp. 144–52) of a "good guys/bad guys" opposition between "progressive" nationalists and "reactionary" brotherhoods is in for serious revision. Bidwell's straight-faced quotation (*ibid.*, p. 146) of a French captain's report that the number of Derqawis in Sefrou had declined from 750 to 10 between 1921 and 1937 only demonstrates the naiveté of both of them.
68. The specific occupations were as follows: grocers, 4; barbers, 2; periodic market sellers, 2; hardware/spice sellers, 2; masons, 2; coffeeshop keeper, 1; porter, 1; bathhouse keeper, 1; tobacco seller, 1; cloth seller, 1; wool trader, 1; clerk in the religious (qadi) court, 1; farmer, 1; soldier, 1. This material

and that in the text derive mainly from interviews with two of these men, the coffeeshop keeper and the wool trader, the first a participant in the movement from the latif days, the second a younger man who emerged as the main leader of Istiqlal in Sefrou during the revolution.

69. The stores were set up mainly at the other region-focusing markets in the area, such as Guigou, Enjil, Marmoucha (see Figure 1), plus a few other small towns (e.g., El Menzel, Boulemane, Bhalil). In the 1963 elections, the last reasonably free ones held in Morocco, Sefrou was one of the twelve circumscriptions (out of 144) in the country in which the Istiqlal vote exceeded 35% (national Istiqlal average, 21%), electing an Istiqlal candidate over one of the king's closest, best known, and most vigorously promoted aides. See Marais, O. [R. Leveau], "L'élection de la Chambre des Représentants du Maroc," *Annuaire d'Afrique du Nord*, 2:85–106 (1963); cf. Leveau, R., *Le Fellah marocain défenseur du trône*, Paris, 1976, pp. 150–1. For a description of similar activities among tradesmen in Casablanca during the revolution, see Waterbury, *op. cit.*, pp. 68, 122–31.

70. On the role of Abdel Hayy Al-Kittani, whose hostility to both the royal family and that of Al-Fassi was of very long standing, in the revolutionary period, see Le Tourneau, R., *Evolution politique de l'Afrique du Nord musulmane, 1920–1961*, Paris, 1962, pp. 180–1, 225–6, 234–5, 246; Burke, E., III, *Prelude to Protectorate in Morocco*, Chicago, 1976, pp. 121–2, 129–30, 133–5.

71. In the following discussion I am concerned with the Jewish community only so far as it relates to understanding the bazaar economy and shall describe just so much of it as seems essential to that end. For general discussions of the Sefrou Jewish community, see Rosen, L., "North African Jewish Studies," *Judaism*, 17:425–29 (1968); Rosen, L., "A Moroccan Jewish Community During the Middle Eastern Crisis," *American Scholar*, 37:435–51 (1968); Stillman, "The Sefrou Remnant." The last Rabbi of Sefrou, David Ovadiah, has compiled a collection of documents relating to the Jewish community there: *The Community of Sefrou*, Jerusalem, 1974–5, 3 vols., in Hebrew.

Some material on Jewish economic activities in 1938 in Sefrou, which rather exaggerates them, can be found in Le Tourneau, R., "L'activité économique de Sefrou," *Hespéris*, 25:269–86 (1938).

The main works on Jewish life in Morocco include: Zafrani, H., *Les Juifs du Maroc*, Paris, 1972; Bénech, J., *Essai d'explication d'un mellah*, Baden-Baden, 1949; Bensimon-Donath, D., *Evolution du Judaisme marocain sous le Protectorat français, 1912–1956*, Paris and The Hague, 1968; Chouraqui, A., *La Condition juridique de l'Israélite marocain*, Paris, 1950; Chouraqui, A., *Between East and West: A History of the Jews of North Africa*, Philadelphia, 1968; Chouraqui, A., *La Saga des Juifs en Afrique du Nord*, Paris, 1972; Flamand, P., *Un Mellah en pays berbère: Demnate*, Paris,

1952; Flamand, P., *Diaspora en terre Islam*, Casablanca, n.d. (ca. 1948–58); Slouschz, N., "Etude sur l'histoire des Juifs et du Judaisme au Maroc," *Archives marocaines*, Paris, 1905–6; Slouschz, N., *Travels in North Africa*, Philadelphia, 1927; Voinot, *op. cit.*; Brunot, L., and E. Malka, *Textes judéo-arabes de Fès*, Rabat, 1939; Foucauld, *op. cit.*; Marty, P., "Les Institutions israélites au Maroc," *Revue des études islamiques*, 4:297–302 (1930); Goulvin, J., *Les Mellahs de Rabat-Salé*, Paris, 1927; *La Vie juive au Maroc*, Jerusalem, 1973, in Hebrew. For a full bibliography, see Attal, R., *Les Juifs d'Afrique du Nord, bibliographie*, Jerusalem, 1972, pp. 145–222. For the earlier history of the Jewish community in North Africa, see Hirschberg, H. Z., *A History of the Jews in North Africa*, Vol. I, *From Antiquity to the Sixteenth Century*, Leiden, 1974. Some remarks on Jewish-Muslim relations in traditional Salé are given in Brown, *op. cit.*, esp. pp. 151ff.

72. All this refers to the urban setting, for there were, unlike the case in many parts of Morocco, virtually no permanent Jewish settlements in the countryside in the immediate Sefrou region. (The 1960 census does not list a single Jew as living outside the town, and 90% of the town's Jewish population – as against 56% of the Muslim – was born there.) The role of the itinerant Jew was rather another matter. Sefrou has long had a general reputation in Morocco of being a place where Muslim-Jewish relations were unusually good, a reputation it seems to deserve. Though there have been occasional raids on the Jewish community by rural tribesmen during periods of political turmoil, there seems never to have been an urban pogrom of any sort – at least there is no memory of one in either community. Since the foundation of Israel, and especially since the Six Day and the Yom Kippur (or Ramadhan) wars, relations have, of course, worsened, but even then they have been marked by a surprisingly high level of civility and a complete lack of violence. (On Sefrou during the Six Day War, see Rosen, "A Moroccan Jewish Community.")

    It is worth noting, in accord with the argument in the text, that Muslim negative stereotypes of Jews in Sefrou are largely not economic in content (cheats, misers, usurers, etc.) but social (they don't take care of their old people; they marry their nieces; even, they aren't circumcized). Comments about Jewish commercial abilities tend to be positive and admiring, their fairness more affirmed than doubted.

73. The origin of the word *mellāḥ* is disputed, but the most common folk theory is that it derives from *milḥ* ("salt") because it was the duty of the Jews in the old imperial capitals to salt the heads of the king's fallen enemies and hang them on the city gates. In the 1920s and 1930s, when almost all Jews still lived in the mellah, its density (about 4,000 persons per hectare) was more than twice that of the surrounding Muslim quarters and was the densest by far of any in Morocco (Stillman, "The Sefrou Remnant"). Despite the Protectorate's abolition of obligatory residence, in 1960, 55%

of the Sefrou community (i.e., about 1,600 people) was still living there; by 1965, none of the 400 or 500 Jews still in the town resided in the mellah. Except for soap making and a couple of kosher butcher shops and grocery stores, the Sefrou mellah was entirely residential; Jewish bazaar activities, both commercial and artisinal, took place outside it, scattered more or less randomly among the Muslims. This virtual absence of bazaar activities in the mellah is not general for Morocco, however (for the suq section in the Fez mellah, which was quite elaborate, see Le Tourneau, *Fès avant*, pp. 379–80). One final peculiarity of the Sefrou mellah should be noted: The overwhelming proportion of residential land and housing was Muslim-owned (much of it in habus) and rented to the Jews. The reason for this seems to have been not a Muslim regulation but a Jewish preference, a disinclination to hold capital in the form of land or buildings.

74. On the *maʿamad*, detailed references to which are found in responsa at least as early as the mid-sixteenth century, more generally, see Zafrani, *op. cit.*, pp. 104ff; Bensimon-Donath, *op. cit.*, pp. 87–8; cf. Chouraqui, *La Condition juridique*, pp. 180ff. After the French arrival, the more common term for it in Sefrou generally was *l-komiṭi*.

75. Le Tourneau, *Fès avant*, p. 369. Virtually every work on Moroccan Jewish communities, including those by Moroccan Jews, stresses their near total domination by rich merchants. Zafrani (*op. cit.*, p. 105): "Les notables qui peuvent être, eux aussi, de fins lettrés, représentent, en quelque sorte, une oligarchie ploutocratique qui, en règle générale, sert le bien public avec zèle et dévouement mais il lui arrive aussi parfoir de se prévaloir de sa fortune et de son influence pour 'régenter durement la communauté' pour réclamer des privilèges et commettre des abus que le rabbinat est obligé de condamner." Bénech (*op. cit.*, p. 71): "Cependant il existe dans le mellah une classe riche et puissante. Elle est formé par le petit nombre de Juifs 'indispensables' auquels les [Muslim] puissants réservent leurs faveurs." Bensimon-Donath (*op. cit.*, p. 19): "Ainsi s'est créée une caste qui, sans être vraiment riche au sens occidental du terme, vivait à l'aise et jouissait d'une certain influence auprès des [Muslim] pouvoirs. Son aisance était d'autant plus remarquée que la masse du peuple végétait dans une indescriptible misère." Le Tourneau (*Fès avant*, p. 369): "[The committee's] membres étaient théoriquement élus, mais dans la réalité le recrutement se faisait par cooptation; les membres du conseil appartenaient tous à l'aristocratie d'argent du Mellah et la communauté était soumise à une petite oligarchie." Even as late as 1953, Flamand refers (*Un Mellah*, p. 229), for Demnate, to an "oligarchie ploutocratique."

Of course, there were rich Muslims too, but they did not form a solidary class, much less a committee. They were, rather, a collection of mutually rivalrous and antagonistic big men connected personally to the less rich by ad hoc patron-client arrangements, and they did not concern themselves much with issues of community welfare.

76. There were, of course, the *dimmī* (cl. *ḏimmī*) ("protection" rules): the capitation tax; the obligation to wear distinctive clothing (in Morocco, black), live in the mellah, and remove one's shoes when passing a mosque; the prohibition against carrying guns and riding horses, some of which persisted, as custom if not law, even after French rule. There were also obligatory gifts to the sultan and various local officials of his, raised by the committee from the community generally on the same sliding scale described for charity, on Muslim holidays, royal entries, and so on. Though symbolically important in defining the dominance of Islam over Judaism in the society and thus Jews as wards of a state not their own, the rules do not seem (certainly not in Sefrou) to have led to either Jewish or Muslim communalism beyond the domains of the religious and the domestic, where it was absolute. (No record of an interfaith marriage was uncovered in either the statistical or the qualitative data.)

77. The role of the sheikh l-Yahud varied somewhat from community to community, though his power has, in my opinion, tended to be much overestimated by external observers anxious to find "someone in charge" and unaware of the strong checks upon him by the plutocrats whose creature he was. For a Marrakech sheikh l-Yahud who does seem to have achieved a certain independent power (though more on his own than as a result of his role) in the early part of this century, see, but with a good deal of caution, Benech, *op. cit.*, pp. 256–70. For a situation where a sheikh is claimed (by his grandson!) to have acted as a protector of the populace against the "aristocratie de 1'argent," see Zafrani, *op. cit.*, p. 106, note 23.

78. When Jews quarreled with Muslims – almost inevitably in the bazaar context – regulation took place through the same mechanisms as intra-Muslim disputes, the so-called amin system or, for some matters, the qadi and, later, French courts. Intra-Jewish disputes occasionally were also taken to Muslim (or French) authorities, but this was generally considered something assiduously to be avoided. The authorities usually sent the disputes back to the committee anyway for resolution. On the Sefrou rebaas, see Ovadiah, *op. cit.* (UK), 1974, pp. 102–8, who gives the formal name of the Simaun rebaa as *Ḥevrat Gomele Ḥasādīm*. I am grateful to Professor Norman Stillman for this information.

79. Synagogues (at one time there were as many as sixteen) were built by rich men, whose names they usually bore, and membership, though theoretically voluntary, was in fact more or less fixed: Men joined the synagogue of their fathers; women (who, in any case, were less involved) could choose that of either their fathers or their husbands. The school system was equally complex, including both religious and secular schools of various sorts. The intrusion of the Alliance Israelite, which founded a modern French-type

elementary school in 1911, further complicated the situation, for it tended to divide the community, at times quite bitterly, along traditionalist vs. modernist lines. On the Jewish educational system in Morocco in general, see Bensimon-Donath, *op. cit.*, pp. 21–40.

Another division found in many Moroccan Jewish communities – that between descendants of exiles from fifteenth-century Andalusia (Heb. *megorāshīm*) and supposed "autochthons" (Heb. *toshābīm*) – was, however, absent in Sefrou, as, a few odd cases aside, there were no Andalusians. Until the 1940s, when a large number of rural Jews from southeast Morocco moved into Sefrou (by the 1960s most had moved out again, either to Israel or the Atlantic coast), to the intense displeasure of the Sefroui Jews, the meghrarba/fillali ("citified"/"rustic") distinction mentioned above as critical in the caravan period was reflected in the town population composition, only, so to speak, retrospectively. Nor were there more than a handful (less than 1% in 1960) of meghrarba Jews immigrant from other urban communities. In general, the Sefrou community seems to have been one of the more culturally homogeneous internally, in Morocco, as well as dating back to at least the thirteenth century (Stillman, "The Sefrou Remnant"), one of the oldest and the most stable. Except for Tangiers, a rather special case, the Sefrou Jewish population fluctuated less than that of any urban Jewish community in Morocco between 1904 and 1960 (*La Vie juive*, p. 18).

80. All these public properties – synagogues, religious schools, orphanages, funds for charity or holiday celebrations, sacred objects, the Jewish graveyard, the cave shrine – were part of what the Jews called *heqdeš* (from Heb. Ha-qodeš, "the Holy"). Usually compared to the Muslim habus (e.g., Zafrani, *op. cit.*, p. 127; Le Tourneau, *Fès avant*, p. 269), the heqdesh was, in fact, a somewhat different institution. Aside from the fact that, in Sefrou anyway, only a handful of secular properties (stores, ateliers) seem to have been involved, the institution was conceived more in terms of a "community chest" public appeal notion than a mortmain "church foundation" one – a continuing religious-cum-moral obligation of the community to itself (not of individuals to the community), an obligation defined, organized, and administered by the committee. On Jewish philanthropy in medieval (950–1250) Cairo, see Goitein, *op. cit.*, Vol. II, pp. 99ff; in twentieth-century Marrakech, Benech, *op. cit.*, pp. 207–17. Cf., Gil M., *Documents of the Jewish Pious Foundations from the Cairo Geniza*, Leiden, 1976.
81. As with the qadi court for Muslims, commercial disputes (i.e., intra-Jewish ones) could be submitted to the court for advisory opinions. But, as with the qadi court, this seems to have been very infrequently done.
82. The data in Table 7 are for 1960. As emigration from the Sefrou Jewish community has generally been from the bottom up – the poor leaving first, the rich last – these figures may slightly exaggerate the Jewish advantage

over the half century or so considered here, whereas increased upward Muslim mobility in the bazaar sector since Independence may slightly obscure it. All in all, there is no reason to believe the 1960 picture much different (except in numbers) from the pre-war one, a view supported by Sefroui informants, Jewish and Muslim alike, who say that *so far as the bazaar is concerned* there has never been sharp economic stratification between the two groups. On the other hand, it must also be remembered that until quite recently an enormously greater proportion of Jews than of Muslims was traders and artisans (see Table 1), so that *so far as the society as a whole was concerned*, the Jews did form, and were perceived as, a relatively advantaged group. For the country as a whole, of every 10,000 Jews in the all-Morocco labor force in 1951, about 9,100 were in bazaar-type occupations; of every 10,000 Muslims, about 2,600 were (Bensimon-Donath, *op. cit.*, p. 138). Even here, however, one should keep in mind that a great many Jewish peddlers and craftsmen were indescribably poor, and at least a certain number of Muslim farmers were spectacularly wealthy. For some assorted data on Jewish bazaar occupations in various Moroccan towns ca. 1924, see Massignon, *Enquête*, pp. 149–58 (Sefrou, p. 154).

83. Another, and sociologically more precise, way of putting the general point is to narrow the universe to only "traditional commerce" and "traditional craft" occupations, and to the "old urban" social groups, town-born Arabs and Jews, as defining the heart of the permanent bazaar, in which case the phenomenon is even more striking. The proportion of bazaar workers in traditional commerce and in traditional craft occupations is, respectively, 24% and 76% for Sefrou-born Arabs (N = 1,074) and 52% and 48% for Jews (N = 441).

84. In 1960, after a significant post-war migration of Berbers from the countryside to the town was well underway, the town was still about 85% Arab speaking, the countryside about 60% Berber speaking. If the two main Arab concentrations – Bhalil, a small town-village just north of Sefrou and something of a satellite to it, and the Beni Yazgha, the main Arab-speaking tribe in the region – are put aside (and Jews have played virtually no role among either group), the countryside was nearly 80% Berber speaking. In the 1920s and 1930s there were only a few dozen Berbers living permanently in the town, and urban Arabs (except for a few religious figures, government officials, and large land owners) scarcely ventured into the countryside.

85. Though a fact any Sefroui trader will quite spontaneously affirm (it is almost always the first distinction between traditional Muslim and Jewish trade one is offered, and quite commonly the last), this is very hard to measure precisely. Census categories are not readily disaggregated along such lines, and the effect was much more pronounced in the period preceding World War II, for which there are no exact figures, than for that

following, for which there are. However, even in 1960, when the pattern was coming to an end (by 1969 it had virtually disappeared), about 70% of the Jewish traditional craft workers were in tailoring and shoemaking – both largely of the cheap rural product sort – alone. Only about 15% of the Muslim traditional craft workers were in these occupations, and they concentrated on the better-made, urban product side. In contrast, if one takes only the very clearly urban-oriented crafts – masonry, carpentry, baking, butchering, barbering – about 50% of the Muslim craft workers were in them as against about 10% of the Jewish.

The commercial side is even harder to divide into urban- and rural-oriented components on the basis of census data. But even under very weak assumptions, only about a fifth, if that, of the traditional Muslim merchants of the town were predominantly rural-oriented in 1960 (and they to rural Arab, rather than rural Berber, settlements), whereas more than three-fifths of the Jewish were. For 1938, Le Tourneau reports ("L'Activité économique") the Jews as extremely prominent in the animal, hides, wool, and wheat trades.

Of the major traditional crafts in Sefrou, the only one in which the Jews were not represented was the masons, though there were very few Jews among the weavers and bakers. Gold- and silver-smithing (always small trades in Sefrou), tinsmithing (a trade hard to classify in rural-urban terms), and soap making (a home industry wholly directed to the rural market) were entirely Jewish.

Yet another index of the Jews' rural orientation is language: Virtually no urban Arabs were bilingual in Berber (and until the 1940s, very few Berbers in Arabic); the majority of male Jews seem to have spoken Berber as well as their native Arabic.

86. Other terms for such ambulant traders were *sefārin* (sg. *sāfer;* "traveler," "stranger," "guest") and *duwwāsa* (sg. *duwwās*, apparently from a Hebrew root meaning "to walk about"): cf. Zafrani, *op. cit.*, p. 160; Stillman (personal communication) regards the word as properly *duwwāz*, from an Arabic, not a Hebrew, root, meaning "to go about." The sitting Jews, sometimes called *škā'ir* (sg. *škāra*, a kind of "purse," "moneybag"), provided capital on the two-thirds/one-third, agent/investor *ʿisqa* pattern prescribed by Jewish law, though, as always, circumstances were altered to fit cases. Numbers here are hard to recover, but the largest Jewish financier of Sefrou – head of one of the Simaun sections – in the 1930s was said by informants, perhaps exaggeratedly, to have "about a hundred" riding Jews connected to him. For some comments on Jewish activities in a rural market in northern Morocco ca. 1937, see Fogg, W., "A Tribal Market in the Spanish Zone of Morocco," *Africa*, 11:428–58 (1938).

87. The usual pattern was for the riding Jews to leave town on the morrow of Passover, return the eve of Rosh Hashanah, leave again immediately after

Succoth, and return on the eve of Passover. For the same pattern in a rural south Moroccan settlement, see Zafrani, *op. cit.*, p. 215.

88. The siting Jews were, of course, the apex of only the local hierarchy and dealt in turn with even more formidable figures, Jewish and Muslim both, higher up at the city levels. However, it was mainly in tying the locality-focusing levels of the central place structure that the Jews seem to have been especially critical; Sefrou-Fez commercial ties were as much mediated by Arabs as by Jews, or more exactly, by Arabs and Jews intermixed (see, in this regard, Le Tourneau, "L'Activité économique"). Indeed, the ties between the Jewish communities of Sefrou and Fez seem not to have been especially close, even somewhat antagonistic. As mentioned earlier, their pole was Meknes.

89. There were some European stores – French and Spanish – as well by the mid-1930s. Again, language – or more specifically literacy – is an excellent, if indirect, index of the greater involvement of Jews than Muslims in this sector of the bazaar. If one takes, from the 1960 census, men over forty-five years of age (i.e., those who would have been at least twenty years old in 1935), 5% of the Muslims were literate in French, 14% of the Jews.

90. For this view, see the (otherwise quite useful) series of papers by Walter Fogg: "Villages and *Suqs* in the High Atlas Mountains of Morocco," *Scottish Geographical Magazine*, 51:144–51 (1935); "The Economic Revolution in the Countryside of French Morocco," *Journal of the Royal African Society*, 35:123–39 (1936); "The Importance of Tribal Markets in the Commercial Life of the Countryside of North-West Morocco," *Africa*, 12:445–79 (1939); "A Tribal Market in the Spanish Zone of Morocco," *Africa*, 11:428–58 (1938); "Beliefs and Practices at, or in Relation to a Moroccan Tribal Market," *Folklore*, 51:132–8 (1940); "Villages Tribal Markets, and Towns: Some Considerations Concerning Urban Development in the Spanish and International Zones of Morocco," *Sociological Review*, 32:85–107 (1940); "A Moroccan Tribal Shrine and Its Relation to a Nearby Tribal Market," *Man*, 124:100–4 (1940); "Changes in the Lay-Out, Characteristics, and Functions of a Moroccan Tribal Market, Consequent on European Control," *Man*, 72:104–8 (1941); "The Organization of a Moroccan Tribal Market," *American Anthropologist*, 44:47–61 (1942). A similar view can be found in Mikesell, M. W., "The Role of Tribal Markets in Morocco," *Geographical Review*, 48:494–511 (1958), and, much less critically, in Benet, F., "Explosive Markets: The Berber Highlands," in Polanyi, K., et al. (eds.), *Trade and Market in the Early Empires*, Glencoe (IL.), 1957, pp. 188–217.

For a view closer to mine (though one that still seems to regard the suq as an essentially rural phenomenon – "une ville à la campagne et pour la campagne . . . enraciné au plus profond de la vie rurale marocain"), see

Troin, *op. cit.*, 1.1, pp. 38–9: "Néanmoins, malgré la variété de ses visages, le souk conserve dans son principe son fonctionnement, son organisation interne, son rôle, une réele unité. Qu'ils soient situés en pays bebérophone ou arabophone, en plaine ou en montagne, dans des zones céréalières, fruitières ou pastorales, près des villes ou loin d'elles, les souks du Nord Marocain connaissent le même déroulement, semaine après semaine, et ont les mêmes fonctions." Except that it is as profoundly enraciné in la vie urbaine marocaine as in la vie rurale and that the gulf between ville and campagne is (and from Ibn Khaldun forward, characteristically has been) easily exaggerated for Morocco, this seems exact.

91. Rural markets may not only be larger and more complex than urban ones, but as high or higher in any central place hierarchy one might want to fit to the Moroccan situation. One of Walter Fogg's Spanish Zone "tribal markets" contained (1930–5) no less than 1,100 regular suwwaqs (thirty of them Jews) representing, in Fogg's classification, about 100 occupational categories ("A Tribal Market"). Dwarfing urban markets in Asilah, Larache, and Ksar Al-Kebir, it was the commercial hub of the whole western sector of the northern zone, frequented by individuals from more than twenty different major tribal groups spread over some 3,000 square kilometers. Rural markets in the immediate Sefrou region (i.e., those within the hexagon of Figure 1) are not very large, ranging from 50 to 250 regular suwwaqs (and 300 to 1,500 visitors – also suwwaqs, but not purchasing tickets giving rights to a particular selling place) per market day, but the region-focusing markets in the Atlas to the south (Guigou, Marmoucha, Enjil) run upward of 500 or 600 regular suwwaqs (and 3,000 to 4,000 visitors) (Records, Bureau de Cercle, Sefrou, 1968). The population, regular and visitor, of any particular marketplace varies importantly with season, current economic situation, and various other matters, including the state of local political stability (for the latter, see, though rather overdrawn, Benet, *op. cit.*). For a map and census of a small rural market near Sefrou, see Annex C. Plans of large, medium, and small rural markets are given inTroin, *op. cit.*, t. 2, pl. 3; see also t. l, pp. 355–9. Hart (*op. cit.*, pp. 72–86) describes some rural markets in northeast Morocco.

92. Figure 4 should be compared with Figure 3, showing the funduq distribution ca. 1900; with Figure B.l (in Annex B), showing the layout of markets in immediate pre-Protectorate Sefrou; and especially with Figures A.l, A. 13, and A. 19 (in Annex A), depicting the present (i.e., 1968–9) pattern. A very schematized map of Sefrou's extramural markets, apparently ca. 1964, can be found in Troin, *op. cit.*, t. l, p. 415. The easy sociological generalizations appended to Troin's map – the product apparently of a few elite interviews and a walk around the town – need to be taken with a very large grain of salt. The most recent (1976) disposition of Sefrou's markets can be found in Annex E. For another cultural setting in which an indigenous

distinction is made between a permanent "shop" market (*mercado*) and an open-air periodic (*plaza*), see Beals, *op. cit.*, pp. 8–9.

93. Le Tourneau, "L'Activité économique."
94. Si Bekkai, *op. cit.* The third staple of the Sefrou region, olives, had already by Le Tourneau's time become, as now, a crop sold on site (i.e., in the groves surrounding the town and in the countryside) and carted away to mills by truck; there was no longer a specific olive bazaar in Sefrou. Except for local consumption milling, oil sold retail in grocery shops, and the auctioning of habus-owned trees for harvest, the olive trade in Sefrou no longer passes through either the periodic or the permanent bazaar; the crop is bought up (ostensibly at prices fixed by the government, which, as noted, also establishes the opening of harvest season) directly by agents of largescale entrepreneurs, almost all of them from Fez. (There are four motor-driven oilmills in Sefrou town, only one of them of any size.) As Annex B indicates, olives is not the only trade to have disappeared from the Sefrou bazaar in the last half century: Tanning is another. Cord making, goldsmithing, and plow-making also used to be more important than their few scattered remnants now indicate, and shoemaking – mainly by Jews, of *belḡa*, a form of leather slipper once the almost universal footware – was in the 1920s and 1930s the largest craft. On the other hand, neither potting nor dyeing, important trades elsewhere, seems ever to have been significant in Sefrou. For a salutary warning against the easy assumption that all commodities flow through a given hierarchy in similar ways, see Jones, W. O., "Some Economic Dimensions of Agricultural Marketing Research," in Smith, *op. cit.*, pp. 303–26.
95. In the mid-1970s (after the completion of our fieldwork) a process of spatial unification of the Thursday markets in a government-built suq area at the southern edge of town was begun, which by 1976 was nearing completion. For this, see Annex E.
96. About 56% of the adult Muslims living in the medina in 1960 were rural-born (non-medina quarters; 40%), as against virtually none (certainly well under 5%) before 1930. Well over 80% of these in-migrants derive from the immediate countryside around Sefrou.
97. The distribution described in these tables is based on the data in Annex A plus informants' judgments about the location of the various suqs. This involves a certain amount of judgment concerning boundaries, but the general pattern is beyond question. If only the more well-established enterprises in each trade were taken into account, the effect would be markedly stronger. Permanent markets remain in the old city, shoemakers and carpenters being the major exceptions (for their original locations, see Annex B). The shoemaker trade shifted to the new quarter as Muslims began to replace Jews in it; the carpenters, as increased mechanization

(motor-driven saws, lathes, grinders) became important. For some general comments on trade localization in other Moroccan towns, see Massignon, *Enquête*.

98. Virtually no one in Sefrou lives in, above, or behind his shop or workplace or, in general, anywhere near it. As Figure 4 (and the figures of Annex A on which it is based) clearly shows, residential and commercial areas are sharply discriminated, and Weber's supposedly modern separation of "home" and "office" is, in line with the "mosaic pattern" of integration discussed earlier, as complete here, and not just spatially, as perhaps anywhere in the world.

99. As always, usage varies, and there is no simple consensus on such matters. I have merely given the distinctions and the terms for them that seem in most common use in Sefrou. Also, it must be understood that the tree form of the diagram is intended solely as a presentational device: It depicts the distinctions – and connections – Sefrouis make, but not their concept (so far as I can discover, they don't have one) of how the total system of such distinctions should be abstractly represented. A Venn diagram could probably catch the suwwaq overall image better than a tree (though Sefrouis don't draw those either), but I do not feel certain enough of the nuances involved – how large to make the circles, how to overlap or space them – to construct one.

100. The total number of terms, or modifications of terms, for commercial and craft occupations in the raw data of the bazaar survey is over 150, and I could doubtless have gathered more were my patience for fine detail equal to the task. This extraordinarily intensive division of labor (remembering a total bazaar labor force of slightly over 2,000) is apparently characteristic of Middle Eastern bazaars everywhere and always: "While scanning the Geniza records [of tenth- to twelfth-century Cairo] for the arts and crafts mentioned in them, the modern observer is impressed by the great number of occupations and by the high degree of specialization and division of labor apparent in them. The terms for about 265 manual occupations have been identified thus far, as against 90 types of persons engaged in commerce and banking and approximately the same number of professionals, officials, religious functionaries, and educators. With this total of about 450 professions compare the 150 or so professional corporations traced in ancient Rome by J. T. Waltzing . . . and the 278 *corporations de métier* listed by André Raymond for Cairo in 1801 . . . The collection of 435 colorful descriptions of Damascene occupations begun by Muhammad Sa'îd Qâsimi . . . also includes agricultural laborers of different types, long lists of shopkeepers selling specialties, as well as musicians and other persons engaged in the entertainment business" (Goitein, *op. cit.*, p. 99). On the intense division of labor in other Moroccan towns, see, with caution, Massignon, *Enquête*; cf. Brown, *op. cit.*, pp. 152–3.

101. The nearest exception is prewar Jewish shoemaking, whose practitioners were under the thumb of one or another of the large sitting merchants. But even those in fact wholly dependent craftsmen were conceived of as formally independent, their output being merely more or less completely engrossed. The modern furniture enterprises, in which a single entrepreneur presides over both the craft and sales aspects, are also Jewish. For a counter-example of a bazaar economy in which integrated craft-commercial enterprises are of importance, see Geertz, *Peddlers and Princes*, pp. 28–81.
102. The wholesale/retail contrast in English has two meanings – gross vs. detail selling and intratrade sale vs. sale to the general public. This produces a great deal of confusion when the terms are used with respect to bazaar economies. Though the first, scale-based opposition (in fact, more a gradation than an opposition) exists and is of importance, the second, functionally based opposition, by and large does not. Thus, though there are Moroccan expressions for selling *en gros* (*b-ž-žumla*) as against *au détail* (*b-t-tefrād*), they are not applied to merchant-merchant, as opposed to merchant-consumer, trade, a distinction that is simply not made. On the difficulty of consistently applying the wholesaler/retailer distinction in eleventh-century Egypt, see Goitein, *op. cit.*, pp. 150–2. On the complementary meaning relations of *biʿ* and *šri* (the first originally means "to shake hands," the latter the "busy activity of the market"), see under *baiʿ* in *Shorter Encyclopaedia of Islam*, p. 56. For a popular proverb expressing the equivalence ("O buyer, remember the day when you will sell"), see Westermarck, E., *Wit and Wisdom in Morocco*, London, 1930, p. 170.
103. On the importance of the *dellāl* (an occupation mentioned by Ibn Khaldun) in traditional Fez, where there were 140 of them in hides and 70 in cloth alone (they were, as in Sefrou, specialized by market area), see Le Tourneau, *Fès avant*, pp. 310–14, 347, 349. and Bousquet, G. G., and J. Berque, "La Criée publique à Fès," *Revue d'économie*, pp. 320–45, May 1940. Popular critical proverbs concerning them (that they are friendless, thieves, shameless, etc.) can be found in Westermarck, *op. cit.*, p. 174. For a theoretical-empirical treatment of auctioneering in general, see Cassady, R., Jr., *Auctions and Auctioneering*, Berkeley and Los Angeles, 1967.
104. The dellal pattern was especially used for rural crafts, such as rugs, blankets, and baskets; certain secondary rural products, such as rock salt, eggs, hides, and firewood; secondhand goods of all sorts; and certain urban light manufactures, such as cloth, shoes, rope, and farm implements, and because of the women's role in it, yarn. Smaller quantities of grain, wool, and even vegetables were occasionally sold this way, and a certain number of live animals were "dellal-ed" in the animal market rather than sold directly. Dellals were particularly active on the day of the periodic market, though permanent market traders – shopkeepers and place sellers – would give

them goods to hawk about the various appropriate market areas as well. A few dellals could also be found, and still can, in the country markets, but the gap between the suwwaq and the non-suwwaq being less formidable there, they were never as important in the town. Finally, in the pre-war period there was a handful of female auctioneers who went about from house to house in town taking bids from women on household items. This practice has now virtually disappeared.

105. On "target marketers," see Bohannan and Dalton, *op. cit.*, p. 7, and, in the same volume, E. Colson, "Trade and Wealth Among the Tonga," p. 615. Bohannan and Dalton tie target selling to target buying more closely than I, or the Moroccans, do ("'target marketers' engage in marketing sporadically to acquire a specific amount of cash income for a specific expenditure, such as a bicycle or tax payment") and seem to think they are confined to minor, "peripheral" markets, and minor, peripheral transactions. Whatever the case in sub-Saharan Africa this surely does not hold for Morocco. But the essential notion (which can apply as well to labor – e.g., in South Africa) of seeking a more or less discrete and immediate economic end, rather than engaging in a continuous, cumulative enterprise, is the same.

106. The *bāyeᶜ* pattern is not confined to grain and animals. Among the Berbers especially, rugs, blankets, and cloak material, woven by the women and carried to market by the men, serve as a reserve to be drawn on as the need arises. In many Berber farmhouses one sees piles of rugs, fluctuating in size, to be used for target selling and quite explicitly regarded as a home-made bank account, as well as, like animal herds and granary stocks, prime public symbols of family wealth and status. To a lesser extent, wickerwork and rock salt, as well as minor farm products (chickens, condiments) serve in the same way. In the market described in Annex C, a rather small one, upward of 80% of those present (excluding target buyers, who, as they neither rent spaces nor purchase tickets, cannot readily be counted) were target sellers. Even most of the fruit and vegetable sellers were *bāyeᶜ* – i.e., people selling their own produce (and only in this market) in occasional fashion – rather than regular *ḵeḍḍāra* greengrocers. Town artisans, on the other hand, now sell most of their products via client systems (including putting out contracts from merchants) of one sort or another, and almost never target sell.

107. It should be understood that "sitting" is applied not just to sellers but to buyers as well, so that even what we would call a customer is regarded as sitting in the market he customarily buys in. This too is, apparently, a very old and widespread pattern: "The term 'sitting' applied [in Medieval Egypt] to both the vendor and the buyer. I arrived in Alexandria on the Muslim holiday and did not find him 'sitting' that is, his store was closed. 'I shall sit with these goods in a store,' that is, sell them locally, 'or travel with them to Syria.' 'Let there be no other business to you on Sunday

morning except sitting in the bazaar of the clothiers and picking up all you need,' that is, while shopping the buyer would sit down in the stores where he intended to make his purchase" (Goitein, *op. cit.*, Vol. I, p. 192). Unless the essential identity in Moroccan eyes of the buyer and the seller functions and the precise, rather than apparent, meaning of the sitting (fixed)/ riding (traveling, ambulant) contrast are grasped, the suq division of labor cannot be properly understood.

108. There *are* some fixed merchants who are established in two different settings, and some target sellers and buyers operate equally in more than one nearby market. In fact, and rather in opposition to the appearance of fluidity and randomness the bazaar often gives to foreign observers, this is quite rare.

109. In the Protectorate period such door-to-door countryside peddling, of household implements, spices, cosmetics, medicines, charms was mainly a Jewish specialty, because only a Jew could approach a Muslim woman easily. The trade was mostly barter, the peddler (called a *duwwās*, "trudger," a term used only for Jews) receiving eggs, secondhand clothes, sheep skins, and so on in exchange for his goods. This sort of trade has now entirely disappeared, though a few Muslim peddlers (called, to distinguish them from the Jews, *ʿaṭṭar*; see Annex B) and knife sharpeners are still occasionally seen in villages. Even in Protectorate times, however, most Jewish riding merchants operated in or at the edge of marketplaces, and in 1936 the French, pressured by pious town Muslims, actually forbade duw- was trading in the Sefrou region as exploitative of rural female credulity and contrary to local mores (Le Tourneau, "L'Activité économique"). In the countryside, as in the town, trade and women – or anyway, trade and decent women – do not mix (but see, for the exception proving the rule, note 116), and the home and business realms are sharply separated. Aside from the marginal and carefully insulated exceptions already mentioned, no bazaar activities take place (and, at least for the proximate past, apparently never have) in the villages, and suqs are always located a significant distance from the nearest settlement. This too is general in the Maghreb (see Benet, *op. cit.*, p. 196). For some general remarks on the role of itinerant peddlers in laying the groundwork for the development of periodic markets, see Plattner, S. M., "Periodic Trade in Developing Areas Without Markets," in Smith, *op. cit.*, pp. 69–88.

110. Only a minority of Sefrou-based sebaibis limit themselves to the locality-focusing markets of the immediate Sefrou area (for which see Figure 1). Of those who roam more widely, the largest number moves southward toward Almis du Guigou, Enjil des Ikhatarn, Ksabi, and even Boumia and Midelt. But significant numbers go southeastward toward Imouzzer des Marmoucha, Outat Oulad el Haj, and Missour; eastward toward El

Menzel, Ahermoumou, and Sidi Brahim; northeastward toward Arhbalou Arkane, Ras Tabouda, and Outa Bouabane; northward toward Ain Aicha, Taounate, and Sidi El Mokhfi; northwestward toward Ain Cheggag, Sebaa Aioun, Ain Chkef, and Mikkes; westward toward Immouzer du Kandar, El Hajeb, and Agourai; and southwestward toward Ifrane, Azrou, Timhadite, and even Khenifra – thus more or less boxing the compass so far as Sefrou is concerned. Very few go to Fez (though some Fez sebaibis come to Sefrou) or any other large cities, or indeed to higher-order markets than Sefrou of any sort. I am at a loss how to estimate the numbers of sebaibis working out of Sefrou or the number of markets in which they are to be found, save to say that both numbers are quite large. Even in the small (and, when the census was taken, but moderately active) rural market of Annex C, there were ten sebaibis, two of them residents of nearby villages, one from Fez, and seven from Sefrou town; and Sefrou sebaibis may be encountered in rural and small town markets almost anywhere within the rough hexagon formed by Midelt, Khemmiset, Ouezzane, Ketama, Taourirt, and Outat Oulad el Haj. For the locations of these various markets and places, see Troin, *op. cit.*, t. 2, pl. 1.

111. Today, most sebaibis travel by bus between suqs, which are well served by lines. (For the suq-related bus network centered on Sefrou – from which about 1,000 "bus places" to other suqs are available per week – see Troin, *op. cit.*, t. 2, pl. 22.) Some of the more substantial sebaibis own or hire (often in groups of two or three) automobiles or trucks, space in which they often sell or lease to others. Though sebaibis may remain several days at a time on the road (and earlier, when transport was less rapid, somewhat longer), they do not engage in the extensive stays in distant markets described earlier for the riding Jews, and most return to Sefrou weekly, or at the very least biweekly. Sebaibi itineraries do not require, and the larger ones preclude, attendance at any particular market every week; some markets are visited only every three, four, or even five weeks. As in everything else, much depends upon season, the state of the market in various commodities, the ceremonial calendar, and so on, including, not least, the condition of the sebaibi's personal finances.

112. As noted above, the bulk of semsar buying of olives is conducted in the groves at harvest time, and the olives are immediately carted away to non-Sefroui processers, so that the trade really does not pass through the local suq system.

113. Le Tourneau, «L'Activité économique." Le Tourneau (who, it should be noted, has an excessively Fez-eye view of Sefrou) mentions semsars as important in the hide, charcoal, wool, and rug trades. There are also semsars for Sefrou town merchants operating, usually on a quite moderate scale, in the country markets about. The term more often used for them, however, is *mulāqī* (a word that also means "pimp") rather than semsar.

114. Which occupations are considered by Sefrouis to fall on the artisan side and which on the buyer-seller side (something not entirely predictable on the basis of Western conceptions) is indicated in Annex A. Some remarks on masters, workers, and apprentices in Moroccan towns generally can be found in Massignon, *Enquête*, pp. 80–1, where the term for journeyman is given as "*sonnàᶜ*" (i.e., *ṣunnaᶜ;* sg. *ṣānᶜ*), a term also common in Sefrou. Cf. Jamma, *op. cit.*, pp. 79–80; Brown, *op. cit.*, p. 136.

115. Goitein, *op. cit.*, Vol. I, p. 172, remarks with respect to medieval Egypt, that although "muslim lawyers usually envisage partnerships only between two persons, . . . this should be viewed merely as legal idiom." Even on his own evidence (*ibid.*, pp. 87ff.) this seems too constricted a view; and so far as Sefrou is concerned, the radically dyadic concept of the nature of contract is a popular, virtually universal one, not a property of the jurists. The "idiom" is thus a powerful and pervasive cultural, not a narrowly legal, one.

116. The organization of one rather special craft-special, in that it is the only one that significantly involves women and that it takes a household industry form not otherwise developed in Sefrou-may be briefly described, both for its intrinsic interest and for its usefulness in indicating the limits of the artisan work structure. It is the yarn trade.

Yarn is made by women, called *ḡezzāla*, in their homes. Most of these women are urban, though some are found in Arabic-speaking villages as well, in a sort of complementary contrast to the rug, blanket, and cloak-cloth weaving of the Berber-speaking women mentioned earlier. The woman's husband may buy the wool and market the yarn, but this is quite uncommon and indeed is felt as a male intrusion into female affairs. Instead, professional entrepreneurs (also called *ḡezzāla*), themselves women, commonly take the wool on consignment from a wool trader, more often than not a relative, and then, having washed and carded it, put it out to anywhere from a half dozen to thirty or forty women to twine in the privacy of their homes. (The latter may put the work out furthep to various relatives and neighbors.) When the yarn is finished, the entrepreneurs, of whom there are perhaps a dozen of any significance in Sefrou, carry it to the "yarn market" (*sūq l-ḡzal*), which is held very early in the morning in front of the Funduq L-Habus L-Kebir in the Bradᶜaiya (see Figure A. 11 of Annex A) on Wednesdays and Sundays, where they consign it to déliais to sell. The dellals walk about the market taking bids in the usual manner and the women leave the scene. (The purchasers are town weavers, sebaibis intending to resell in rural markets to the husbands of those Berber rug and blanket makers, and semsars representing Fez yarn merchants.) The yarn sold, the entrepreneur collects from the dellal and gives him his commission, distributes their shares to the workers, returns to the wool merchant his price, and retains what is left, enough in some cases to make her markedly well-off by Sefrou standards.

The only other, and much less important, putting-out craft of any note is the making of knotted silk buttons *ᶜuqad;* sg. *ᶜuqda*), also by women at home. In this case, the silk merchants/spinners are the putter-outers and engross the product directly, but the yarn entrepreneurs act, on a commission basis, as go-betweens here as well.

117. For the Arabic names of the trades, see Table A.2, Annex A. Both Le Tourneau (*Fès avant*, esp. pp. 299–301) and Massignon (*Enquête*, esp. pp. 99ff.) treat extensively of amins, though both discussions, and particularly the latter, which wobbles factually besides, are seriously marred by the earlier mentioned confusion of socio-religious organizations, occupational categories, and dispute settlement arrangements under the single, unexamined, but nonetheless reified, rubric of "corporation." (Most of Massignon's diversely organized lists seem – that for Taroudant, by far the shortest, notably aside – to be of occupational types, *ḥerfa*, not of amins. His Sefrou list [pp. 48–49] more confusedly presented than most, seems to indicate 43 amins in 1924, almost certainly much too low a figure.) Leo Africanus's references to amins as "consuls" and his insistence on their purely economic role (quoted, quizzically, in Le Tourneau, *Fès avant*, pp. 78, 294) was closer to the mark than later descriptions of them as diffuse, multifunctional *chefs de corporation*. Le Tourneau says the *umana* plural is used for certain state officials (fiscal officers, etc.) and the *amīnāt* one for the commercial figures here being discussed, but that is not true in Sefrou, where the *umanā* plural is the usual one in all contexts. Cf. Brown, *op. cit.*, p. 137.
118. ᶜArif is probably the most general term applied to this class (or, more strictly, paradigmatic set) of roles; each term, including *amin*, is sometimes denoted by it, as is the class as a whole. For similar "expert" roles (the French derivative, *ekspir*, is now often applied to them as well) in the countryside, see Hoffman, *op. cit.*, p. 141.
119. It would be incorrect, however, or at the very least premature, to see in this any intrinsic evolutionary development rather than the most recent state of a very long-term, and as yet unended, bargaining relationship between *ahl s-sūq* ("people of the market") and *ahl l-maḵzen* ("people of the state") eventuating in the usual mixture of *sība* ("fractiousness," "recalcitrance," "dissidence") and *ṭaᶜa* ("submissiveness," "compliance," "obedience"). In medieval Cairo, "the *ᶜarīf*, or head of a profession – as far as such an office existed – was not a leader elected by members of his group, but a supervisor appointed by the market police in order to assist it in its fight against fraudulent practices" (Goitein, *op. cit.*, p. 84). The porters of Fez, following Berber models, traditionally elected four amins for six-month terms whom the government automatically recognized (Le Tourneau, *Fès avant*, p. 196). There have been, and are, certain amins, those of the prostitutes for example (called *ᶜarīfa*, the feminine of *ᶜarīf*), with no official standing

at all but nonetheless of some significance. Even more "non-immoral" but unofficial amins exist in Sefrou – those of mule skinners (*ḫammāra*, *ḫammāla*), hornblowers (*ğiyyāta*), and soup dispensers (*mwālin l-ḥarīra*), for example. Nisba-based amins such as Le Tourneau found in Fez (*ibid.*, p. 193) – Soussi cooks, Touat charcoal sellers, and the like – do not, the Jewish case and conceivably (the facts are unclear) Fassi cloth sellers in the 1920s aside, seem to have existed in Sefrou. It should also be noted that it is possible, though uncommon (the only cases I know of for Sefrou involve porters and wheat sellers, and no longer obtain), for there to be more than one amin in a profession.

120. Massignon (*Enquête*, pp. 129–30) gives a few casebook-type examples of the application of hisba principles in Sefrou during the 1920s, which, save that more tailors and carpenters are involved than millers or bakers, reflect as well present practice. Three examples are:

1. A man gives a quantity of wheat over to a miller to be milled. After delivery, the man claims the flour is impure. The amin of the millers examines the stock of wheat from which that given to the miller was drawn to see if it is of good quality. If it is [not], the miller is responsible and must reimburse the plaintiff.
2. A man buys a loaf of bread from a baker. He claims the merchandise is of inferior quality and does not attain the asserted weight. The amin of the bakers determines the weight question, for which the baker is held responsible. The amin of the millers then examines the flour from which the loaf was made to see if it is adulterated, in which case the miller who milled it is responsible to the baker.
3. Two butchers buy a sheep in partnership. The purchase effected, one of the butchers wishes to slaughter the sheep immediately; the other wishes to grow it for a month first. The amin of the butchers auctions the animal between the two. The higher bidder gains the sheep to slaughter or conserve as he will, the other collects from him the bid price.

Massignon also has (*ibid.*, pp. 192–224) a set of governmental documents detailing formal cases of muhtaseb decisions from the same period, but none, alas, are from Sefrou. For a poem addressing a complaint to the amin of the bakers, see Annex D. The notion of *ʿurf* is further discussed below.

Aside from dispute settlement (*ṣulḥ*), for which they usually receive a small gift from the winner, the amins, backed when need be by the muhtaseb, are responsible for collecting ceremonial presents (sg. *hedia*) offered to the king on behalf of the trades on various royal occasions, though this custom, once powerful, is now much less so. The amins also witness the guarantors (sg. *ḍāmen*) who swear to make good any defaults of entrants (usually apprentices of theirs or in-migrants from elsewhere with whom they are acquainted or otherwise connected) into certain trades – especially butchers, bathhouse keepers, porters, and bakers, but often tailors, carpenters, coffeeshop keepers, and shoemakers as well – though the amins have no actual control of entry as such. In some cases, for example, goldsmiths (who are usually moneylenders as well) and auctioneers, the guarantee takes the form of a cash bond (also called *dāmen*), which the amin holds. Finally, in an attempt to control speculation and fraud, the muhtaseb, with the assistance of the relevant amins, posts "official" maximum price lists (sg. *sʿar*) at irregular intervals for certain basic necessities, especially flour, sugar, charcoal, and meat, an effort fitfully effective at best.

121. The phrase is Le Tourneau's (*Fès avant*, p. 211) and pertains to pre-Protectorate Fez. He also calls the muhtaseb (p. 214), reflecting on his powers (he could order traders fined, whipped, imprisoned, or merely paraded about the market with their crime loudly proclaimed) and his possibilities for graft, "un personnage redouté et impopulaire." And elsewhere (*ibid.*, p. 294) he says of the muhtaseb, with a subtle accuracy missing from accounts that represent him as an administrator rather than a judge, "il ne donnait pas d'impulsion à la machine économique de Fès, il n'était pas le cerveau qui s'efforce de prévoir et de diriger; il apparaissait surtout comme une force d'inertie qui fixait au sol l'échafaudage de l'économie fasie et l'emphêchait de vaciller et de se désagréger." For a general review of the hisba and the muhtaseb role, see Massignon (*Enquête*, pp. 107–10), who sees strong Andalusian influence on its formation in Morocco (cf. Cahen, C., and M. Taibi, "Hisba," *Enyclopaedia of Islam*, Vol. III, pp. 486–9, London, 1971; Chalmata, P., *El Señor del Zoco*, Madrid, 1973). In 1917, the muhtaseb was formally made a state official by the French with the result that "actuellement le Mohtassib n'est plus qu'un fonctionnaire municipal chargé de la surveillance des corporations de métiers et de celles qui vivent du commerce" (Massignon, *Enquête*, p. 110). Some of the aura of his former eminence still clings to him, however, at least in Sefrou. On the decline of the muhtaseb role in Salé, see Brown, *op. cit.*, p. 138.

122. Benet, *op. cit.* Benet's pioneering essay relies too heavily on the "Land of Government" (*Bled l-Makzen*) vs. "Land of Insolence (*Bled s-Sība*) dichotomy so favored by French colonial ethnographers, anxious, for romantic reasons or political, to contrast Arabs and Berbers, and treats the subject too briefly and in too unshaded a manner to be of more than suggestive value. But his central point, that keeping the suq safe for trade and society safe from the suq has long been a central concern, amounting indeed to something of an obsession, of Maghrebian (not just Berber) social, political, and even religious organization, is beyond question.

123. The internal quotation is from Benet, *ibid.*, who remarks: "It is not surprising that the *nefra'a* breeds xenophobia. Strangers and foreigners are sometimes inclined to take the law into their own hands; they have no

part in the policing of the market and do not suffer from the long-range consequences of a *nefra'a*. *Nefra'as* will discredit a *sūq* and people will stop coming to it. Besides, if a murder has been committed in the suq, the market is closed for a period of purification, generally one year." *Nefra* derives from the root "to bolt," "stampede," "run away." The importance in the popular mind of the peace of the market can be seen in two proverbs given by Hart (*op. cit.*, p. 71): "market day is a day of respect (*ḥurma*)" and "market day is a day of peace (*sulḥ*)."

124. The internal quotations are from Benet, *op. cit.*; stress original. Cf. Montagne, R., *Les Berbènes et le makhzen dans le sud du Maroc*, pp. 252ff, and "Une Tribu berbère du Sud-Marocaine: Massat," *Hespéris*, 4:357–403 (1924). On the insulation of the market and village spheres in another part of North Africa, see Bourdieu P., *Outline of a Theory of Practice*, Cambridge (UK), 1977, pp. 185–6.
125. For the first approach, see Tax, *op. cit.*; for the second, Polanyi et al., *op. cit.*; for the third, Beals, *op. cit.*
126. For a (rather schematic) discussion of imperfect competition in a bazaar, see Swetnam, J., "Oligopolistic Prices in a Free Market-Antigua, Guatemala," *American Anthropologist*, 75:1504–10 (1973).
127. For some acute comments on the limitations of Shannon-type, quantitative communication approaches to economic issues, see Marshak, J., "Economics of Inquiring, Communicating, Deciding," in Lamberton, D. M., (ed.), *Economics of Information and Knowledge*, Harmondsworth (UK), 1971, pp. 37–58; cf. Lamberton, D. M., "Introduction," *ibid.*, pp. 7–15, and Arrow, K. J., *The Limits of Organization*, New York, 1974, esp. Chap. 2.
128. Whether one sees the clouds as local crystallizations of the atmosphere or the atmosphere as the summary resultant of the clouds, is, as in all field conceptualizations, more or less a matter of convenience. What is very difficult for a speaker of English, where roots are buried and etymology all too often a notional archeology for digging them up, fully to appreciate, and what most needs to be so appreciated, however, is the degree to which, for a speaker of Arabic, pure, lexically unrealized roots, mere clusters of paradigm consonants, trail with them a palpable aura of meaning, an aura that in turn envelops, more obviously or less, any actually generated lexical item. As Arabic writing, which normally omits most of the vocalic elements, further accentuates the roots (which, of course, here are not buried, but available to immediate perception), the effect is quite pervasive, extending to some of the most developed dimensions of Arab thought. On this, see (with caution), Massignon, L., *Essai sur les engines du Lexique technique de la mystique musulmane*, Paris, 1954. Cf. Izutsu, T., *Ethico-Religious Concepts in the Qur'an*, Montreal, 1966.
129. I have given only derivations that seem to appear (and as they appear) in Moroccan colloquial, though with no claim that these are all that do so.

The full classical list can be found in Wehr, H., *A Dictionary of Modern Written Arabic*, ed. by J. M. Cowan, Ithaca (NY), 1961, pp. 508–9, where it covers two full-page columns, and upward of thirty entries, including *miṣdāq* – "touchstone," "criterion"; *taṣadūq* – "legalization," "authentication"; and *muṣādaqa* – consent," "assent," "concurrence." For a fascinating discussion of the religious meaning of *ṣdiq*, and some of the other words discussed below, to which the following analysis is much indebted, see Smith, W. C., "Orientalism and Truth," The T. Cuyler Young Lecture, Program in Near Eastern Studies, Princeton, 1969; and Smith, W. C., "A Human View of Truth," *Studies in Religion*, 1:6–24 (1971).

130. For this concept of "culture," see Geertz *Interpretation of Cultures*. Of course, and as will become, at least in passing, evident, these words play roles in other rhetorics and meta-languages – moral, political, domestic, aesthetic, religious – than those connected with bazaar exchange. It is impossible not to requote here yet once more the old wheeze: "Every Arabic word has five meanings – its proper meaning, the opposite of its proper meaning, a poetic meaning, an obscene meaning, and the name for a part of a camel."
131. As noted above, *sūwwāqa*, the plural of *sūwwāq*, itself has "mob" and "rabble" as part of its meaning. An active, and thus prosperous and attractive, suq is said to be *ʿāmer* ("populous," "peopled," "full"); the opposite, *ḵāwi* ("desolate," "deserted," "empty").
132. For a brief discussion of the Moroccan concept of the role of speech in social life and the connection of that concept with their religious and aesthetic views, see Geertz, C., "Art as a Cultural System," *MLN*, 91:1473–99 (1976). On the *k-l-m* root in higher Islamic thought, see Wolfson, H. *The Philosophy of the Kalam*, Cambridge (MA), 1976, esp. pp. 1–111.
133. Smith, "Orientalism and Truth."
134. *Ibid.* Some quotation marks have been added for clarification; brackets indicate interpolations. The syntax of "*ṣaddaqa al-khabara al-khabru*," which might most literally be translated "the (further) news (or experience) caused to be regarded as true (the previous) news (or experience)," is: causative verb, object, subject. *Taṣdīq* is, of course, not a verb; its gloss as one is merely a stylistic convenience of Smith's. For a similar discussion of *ṣdiq* as it appears in the Quran which comes to similar conclusions ("*Sdiq* [possesses] obvious implications of sincerity, steadfastness, honesty, and trustworthyness . . . For a given statement to be *ṣdiq* . . . it is not enough that the words used conform to reality; they should also conform to the idea of reality in the mind of the speaker. It is the existence of the intention or determination to be true that constitutes the most decisive element in the semantic structure of *ṣdiq*"), see Izutsu, *op. cit.*, pp. 89–94, who also adverts (p. 91) to the Quran as eternal Divine Speech side of all this, quoting VI, 115 ("Perfect are the words of thy Lord in *ṣdiq* and *ʿad!*

[justice]. Naught can change His words") and remarking: "Here we see *ṣdiq* used in reference to the words of God. This means simply that God as an active participant in the 'covenant' remains true to His own words. And this is nothing other than a particular way of expressing the thought that God's words once uttered cannot be changed with fickleness, that, in other words, they are absolutely trustworthy." And, it needs be added, absolutely powerful.

135. Smith's representation of *ṣiddīq* as someone held to be "an habitual teller of truth by moral character" may seem to count against this argument. But Smith here is perhaps a bit misled by his own "inner light," Protestant conscience view of things, for the term *siddiq* is applied to someone whose specific reputations for honesty, normally attested by a string of concrete examples (the paradigmatic one being Abu Bakr's response to Mohammed's account of the night journey), are, so to speak, very many. It points to a history of social encounters, not a settled, much less "habitual," psychic state. On the relational nature of Moroccan conceptions of selfhood and personal identity, see Geertz, "'From the Native's Point of View,'" *Islam Observed*, and above.

136. As with the other appraisal terms, *ṣdiq* has no true antonym. Its opposite is indicated by its negation, *ma-ši-ṣdiq* ("not *ṣdiq*"). The normal, mixed situation is indicated by the addition of that all-purpose skepticising term, without which no Moroccan could talk at all, *šwiya* ("somewhat," "a little bit," "to a certain extent," "yes and no") to either the positive or the negated form.

137. The connection is developed across the whole field: *ʿaref* is "to perceive," "to distinguish," "to be aware of," "to discover"; *maʿrifa* is "learning," "lore," "knowledge," "gnosis"; *tʿāref* is "to become mutually acquainted," "to get to know one another," "to associate with one another"; *ʿurfī* is "correct," "conventional," "socially acceptable." The quranic antonym for *mifrif*, *munkar* ("unacknowledged," "denied," "evil," "forbidden" – from a root having to do with "ignorance," "obliviousness," "estrangement," "foreignness," "deviance," "rejection") does not seem to appear in the bazaar context, or indeed in any secular contexts at all, where the opposite of *maʿrūf* is, again, merely its negation. On *maʿrūf* in the Quran, see Izutsu, *op. cit.*, pp. 213–17.

138. Descriptions of bazaar *ʿurf*, even for as limited a field as Sefrou, could run to volumes. For some typical examples concerning everything from tailors' thread and dyers' dyes to masters' responsibility for the insulting language of their apprentices and the rights of perfumers to sell the work of braidmakers (*majādlīya*), see Massignon, *Enquête*. For a popular poem that projects the "generally accepted" expectations surrounding an important trade – baking – with some vividness, see Annex D.

139. Cited in Waterbury, *op. cit.*, p. 35. A J'ha trickster tale Waterbury quotes also communicates well the bazaar mentality to which the *ṣḥīḥ* (or, better,

ṣḥīḥ??) concern for whether things are what they seem to be is appropriate. J'ha was dying. He promised his neighbors that if they prayed for him and he recuperated he would sell his donkey and divide the proceeds among them. They did, and he did. He then went to the bazaar and said, "who wants to buy my donkey for a dirham and my stick for 500 dirham?" The two sold for 501 dirham, he returned and gave one dirham to his neighbors: "May peace be on you. Know that the donkey was sold for one dirham. As for the rest, it is not yours; it is the price of the stick." As Waterbury well remarks, "the people have been had, but they curse their own stupidity [better, their unwariness] rather than the man who had them" (*ibid.*, p. 95). In Sefrou, similar stories, all with the same moral – think about what is really being "said" – are legion: A man wants to borrow four dirham from a moneylender, but has no security. But he is carrying another man's purse for him. The moneylender takes the purse for security and lends four dirham of the fifty in it.

140. Westermarck, *op. cit.*, p. 267. The transcription has been altered.
141. For an excellent discussion of the constraining function of *ʿaql* ("reason," "the faculty by which one knows God's commands") over *nafs* ("everything that arises from within man – hunger and sexual yearning, as well as love for the world") and the relation of such a concept of things to bazaar trading ("each successful act of exchange maintains the dominance of *aql* over *nafs* and affirms the rationality of the trader" in a Muslim society (Acheh), physically very distant from Morocco, but in this regard at least, spiritually very close, see Siegel, J., *The Rope of God*, Berkeley and Los Angeles, 1969, pp. 98–133, 242–50.
142. Smith, "Orientalism, and Truth." Cf. Izutsu, *op. cit.*, pp. 89, 97–9.
143. These constructions can, of course, take any object-pronoun ending: *ʿandu l-ḥaqq* ("he is right"); *fi-hum l-ḥaqq* ("they are in the wrong"); *ḥaqq ʿalina* ("it is our duty").
144. Wehr, *op. cit.*, pp. 191–3. Others include "essence"; "real meaning"; "to test, verify, check"; "to make come true, implement, realize"; "worthy"; "deserving"; "legal"; "assertion, affirmation"; "conviction, certitude"; and "legitimate exploiter of a habus property."
145. Cited in Izutsu, *op. cit.*, pp. 40, 101. There are dozens of examples. The classical root is *k-ḏ-b*, but the *ḏ* changes to *d* in colloquial Moroccan. *Kdūb*, a verbal noun, can mean either "lying" or, in the abstract collective sense, "lies."
146. Westermarck, *op. cit.*, p. 53. Some examples, from among many: "Truth [*l-ḥaqq*] is a lion and lies [*l-kdūb*] are a hyena." "Lies are a stinking dead worm and truth is a clean thing." "Lies are the weapon of the rascal." 'The liar is cursed, even though he is a learned man he is cast off by God." "Everything is useful, except that lies and slander bring no profit." "The breaking of wind will not save [a liar] from death." "The cause of death

in the world is lies and fornication" (*ibid.*, pp. 264–5). Cf. comments on oaths and perjury – "the most dangerous form of falsehood" (*ibid.*, pp. 26971). For a fascinating discussion of the concept of falsehood – there rendered as *kzib* – in an Arabic-speaking community in North Lebanon, see Gilsenan, M., "Lying, Honor, and Contradiction," in Kapferer, B. (ed.), *Transactions and Meaning*, Philadelphia, 1976, pp. 191–219.

147. Izutsu, *op. cit.*, p. 99. It should perhaps be added that as *tasdiq* means "faith," the same form built on *k-ḏ-b* means "skepticism". "*Takdhīb* . . . is a flat denial of the divine revelation, refusal to accept the Truth when it is sent down, with an additional element of mockery and scorn. In other words, *takdhīb* in the Qur'anic context denotes the characteristic attitude of those stubborn unbelievers who persist in their refusal to accept the revelation as really coming from God, and never cease to laugh at it as mere old folks' tales" (*ibid.*, p. 100).

148. As the imagery suggests, this view of what thinking is and where it takes place descends from Ryle, G., *The Concept of Mind*, New York, 1959; for a discussion of its implications for anthropological analysis, see Geertz, *Interpretation of Cultures*, pp. 32–54, 55–83, 360–1.

149. It should be unnecessary, but alas probably is not, to note that the table is, however primitive, a model, and that "of course" there *are* some standardized goods, some impersonal exchanges, some bureaucratized relationships, some demarcation of vendor roles from purchasing ones, etc. The suq is no more a perfect "bazaar" than it is a perfect "market."

150. In the course of the research period a decree by the muhtaseb lowering advisory meat prices led to a spontaneous one-day work stoppage by most of the butchers. This led, in turn – more because of the fear of violence than the solidarity of the butchers, which had already begun to dissolve – to the withdrawal of the decree.

151. Insofar as it has any meaning at all (and it has very little), this is what the supposed Islamic fatalism comes to: the conviction that the equations governing human life are "written," and what maneuvers are possible must take place within the space these equations define. The maneuvers, however, are, at least in Morocco, manifold, and most individuals, men and women alike, are about as far from being passive as one can get and not expire from nervous exhaustion. So far as the suq is concerned, this ultimately metaphysical view of how things "really" are does not in itself prevent a collective policy approach to economic matters; it merely prevents the absence of one from seeming conspicuous, worrisome, unnatural, or scandalous. On the nature of the relation of religious concepts and social practices generally, see Geertz, *Interpretation of Cultures*, pp. 126–41, and *Islam Observed*, pp. 90–117.

152. On search in general, see Stigler, G., "The Economics of Information," in Lamberton, *op. cit.*, pp. 61–82, upon which much of the following rather

unrigorously depends. Cf. Akerlof, G. A., "'The Market for Lemons': Quality, Uncertainty and the Market Mechanism," *Quarterly Journal of Economics*, 84:488–500 (1970); Spence, A. M., "Time and Communication in Economic and Social Interaction," *Quarterly Journal of Economics*, 87:651–60 (1973); and, for a general review, Rothschild, M., "Models of Market Organization with Imperfect Information," *Journal of Political Economy*, 81:1283–1308 (1973). The usual automatic "and services" should, of course, be appended to all general references to "goods" in this discussion.

153. The internal quotation is from Rothschild, *op. cit.* Cf. Stigler, *op. cit.*: "Price dispersion is a manifestation – and indeed, it is a measure – of ignorance in the market."

154. The quotation is from Cohen, S., *Labor in the United States*, as given in Rees, A., "Information Networks in Labor Markets," in Lamberton, *op. cit.*, pp. 109–18. Rees goes on to deny the applicability of such an image to industrial labor markets, commenting: "The effectiveness and advantages of informal networks of information [in labor markets] have been too little appreciated." In bazaar economies, where they are of paramount importance throughout, they have been perhaps a bit more appreciated, but that's about all. Clientelization has been more often ascribed to the supposed greater "embedding" of economic life in the wider society in traditional cultures – the hedging in of narrowly "material" concerns by more broadly "humane" ones – than to the characteristics of bazaar-type exchange as such. For exceptions, see Mintz, S., "Pratik: Haitian Personal Economic Relations," *Proceedings, American Ethnological Society*, Seattle, 1961, pp. 54–63; cf. Davis, *op. cit.*, pp. 211–59; and for the Middle East, Khuri, *op. cit.*; for India, Oster, *op. cit.*

155. Though clearly recognized, and even celebrated, there is, in line with its informal nature, no firmly established term for clientship. The word probably most often used to refer to the relation is, again, an *ṣ-d-q* derivative, *ṣedāqa* ("friendship," "loyalty"; see above). Given the oppositional, even agonistic quality of such ties, this may seem odd, but the oddness arises from the highly un-Moroccan assumption that friendship and loyalty (as opposed to "love," *ḥubb*, a wholly other thing) have mainly to do with affection and absence of conflict rather than veracity and straightforwardness in necessarily conflictual relationships. The Euro-American and North African conceptions of what "friendship" (*ṣedāqa*) is (a sublimated form of romantic attachment, "warmth," on the one side, and a generalized form of contractual probity, "trustworthiness" on the other) simply do not match very well; and nowhere is this clearer than in the suq. Finally, it must be explicitly noted that, in itself, clientship is a wholly economic, functionally specific tie. Broadly social, functionally diffuse relationships may, of course, form around it once it has been created or may precede and

lay the basis for it; but this is not normally, or even very commonly, the case. Khuri (*op. cit.*) argues that diffuse ties are often consciously avoided in Middle Eastern bazaars because of the fear they will be used exploitatively – to delay delivery, pass off shoddy goods, pressure terms, etc. An excellent general discussion of Moroccan conceptions of interpersonal ties under the general rubric of "closeness" (*qarāba*) can be found in Eickelman, *op. cit.*, pp. 95–105, 206–10.

156. Reliable statistics on interoccupation mobility are hard to come by, but several dozen occupational history interviews with representatives of the major categories of trader in the bazaar survey revealed almost no occupational shifts, except at the very beginnings of careers. Once a man has his stall in the cloth market or his blacksmith forge, he tends to stay there. This even holds in the periodic markets, where some suwwaqs return to the same spot over extended periods of time, and arbitrager itineraries tend, as mentioned, to be highly fixed. It is less true, of course, for marginal figures; but even among them stability of occupation and even of place seems to be high. On accumulative search, and its relation to market localization and repetitive exchange generally, see Stigler, *op. cit.*

157. Rothschild, *op. cit.*

158. The quotations are from Troin, *op. cit.*, 1.1, pp. 219, 222. That transport costs and "the friction of distance" have precious little to do with all this is evidenced by the fact that the radical improvement in transport in the past fifty years has not reversed this involutional pattern and has not even slowed its growth. Improved transport spreads out the webs somewhat, but it does not simplify them or change their nature.

159. "There is no doubt that . . . the numbers of small-scale middlemen in the societies under consideration [Sarawak, Hong Kong, Malaya, Uganda, Ghana] are large. So are those of retailers . . . My suggestion is that such a state of affairs is at least partly to be accounted for by the fact that...a large proportion of the everyday commercial transactions . . . is carried on by means of some form of credit arrangement. In the vast majority of cases the creditor parties to such arrangements themselves have very little capital, the number of debtors they can serve is closely restricted. Furthermore, these are nearly always arrangements of personal trust made between individuals who are well acquainted with each other, and there is a limit to the number of individuals any one creditor can know well enough to trust in this way. . . . If credit is to be advanced only to personal acquaintances, then there is a limit – and a fairly low limit – to the number of clients any one creditor can have . . . [and there must be] a large number of creditors" (Ward, B. E., "Cash or Credit Crops? An Examination of Some Implications of Peasant Commercial Production with Special Reference to the Multiplicity of Traders and Middlemen," *Economic Development and Cultural Change*, 8:148–63 [1960]). It is not, however, the amount of capital

one has that limits the number of clients one can service, but, for the most part anyway, the number of clients one can service that limits the capital one can effectively deploy. This, too, is true for bazaar trade generally, not just for the credit market: Fixed costs are low because scale is small, not (or not mainly) the other way around. My own earlier discussion of the bazaar economy (*Peddlers and Princes*) now seems to me to have underestimated the importance of clientelization outside the area of credit manipulation and overemphasized what I there called (pp. 35–6) "an essentially speculative, *carpe diem*, approach to commerce." For a more balanced view, cf. Waterbury, *op. cit.*, pp. 178–9.

160. For a general discussion of this problem, to which the present one is much indebted, despite a somewhat different tack in avoiding it, see Khuri, *op. cit.*

161. For an interesting, if rather formal, discussion of the maintenance of "perpetual price variability" in information-imperfect markets, see Rothschild, *op. cit.* Cf. Shalop, S., "Information and Monopolistic Competition," *American Economic Review*, 66:2, 240–5 (1976). For a balanced judgment on the oft-invoked "social enjoyment" aspect of bargaining – that it is real, but secondary – see Cassady R., Jr., "Negotiated Price-Making in Mexican Traditional Markets: A Conceptual Analysis," *America indigena*, 28:51–79 (1968).

162. Such bargaining modes as these give rise to what may be called "fixed-price illusion" with respect to certain bazaars that sometimes appears in the literature. This is especially common with respect to perishables, where price negotiation is hidden beneath delicate manipulations, invisible to the innocent observer, of the great inhomogeneity of goods. It also occurs with respect to the apparently take-it-or-leave-it approach of modern, or anyway modern-looking, businessmen, such as those of Sefrou's show-window bazaar, where the fact that money prices are not, or not usually, bargained does not in itself imply that real ones are not. In fact, totally unbargained exchange, though it occurs, remains quite rare in any part of the suq. For goods bargaining of the add-a-radish, subtract-a-radish sort in Mexican bazaars, see Beals, *op. cit.*, pp. 194–5, who discusses it under the rubric of "quasi-negotiated prices," though just what is "quasi" about it – especially from the point of view of those who engage in it – is not clear. For the "packaged to price" approach in Philippine bazaars, see Davis, *op. cit.*, p. 166.

163. For a discussion of bazaar weights and measures and their variability in both Fez and Sefrou, see Le Tourneau, *Fès avant*, pp. 276–82. In addition to facilitating goods bargaining, variable weight and measure systems also function to control entry into trades (because one cannot learn to operate as a cloth trader or a carpenter until, through apprenticeship, one has learned how to use the particular scales involved) and, of course, to

increase information asymmetry between those inside a trade and those outside.

164. Lowering quality often includes rather frank adulteration, which can on occasion be dangerous. In 1959, a number of grocers, including prominently a number from Sefrou, mixed surplus fuel oil bought from American authorities closing down a Casablanca airbase with cooking oil, leading to paralysis and even death for a large number of people. (Some also mixed it with hair tonic, causing baldness.) Most of the grocers, who were eventually brought to trial, claimed they did not know the adulteration would be dangerous in any serious way and were merely following normal practice in adjusting quality to price. This view – that they had made an honest, if serious, technological mistake in the pursuit of a quite legitimate, pervasive, and indeed often quite open activity – seems to have been rather general; and in fact the king eventually pardoned them all. For a description of this event and some characteristic suwwaq attitudes toward it, see Waterbury, *op. cit.*, pp. 99–102. Cf. Feruel, J., "Etude sur une intoxication par l'huile frelatée au Maroc," CHEAM, 1960, pp. 3372ff. Most adulteration procedures (e.g., of coffee, spices, construction materials, metals) are more careful, tested, and undramatic.

165. I have quoted this remark of Keynes's before (another version of the same idea is the aphorism attributed to a Zurich gnome: "once you owe enough you own the bank") in the course of a fuller discussion of the maintenance of credit balances in a bazaar economy than can be given here (see *Peddlers and Princes*, pp. 36–40). For a fine empirical study of the phenomenon, see Ju-Kang T'ien, *The Chinese of Sarawak*, London School of Economics and Political Science Monographs on Social Anthropology, No. 12, London, n.d. Cf. Firth, R., and B. S. Yamey (eds.), *Capital, Saving and Credit in Peasant Societies*, London, 1964. For medieval Egyptian practices, see Goitein, *op. cit.*, pp. 197–200, 250–62.

166. Simple money lending, still (in 1968) mostly by Jews, is also frequently disguised as goods transaction. Commercial borrowing from banks and elaborated legal instruments with respect to credit are virtually absent in the bazaar – even the qirad has largely disappeared, though something like it is sometimes found in arbitrager activities. Some small intrafamilial loans aside (and even those are rare), the advancement of credit for direct investment purposes – to finance someone else's enterprise – seems to be rather uncommon. The role of credit is confined to more or less direct exchange processes.

167. Rees, *op. cit.* I have discussed this matter, too, in *Peddlers and Princes* (pp. 33–5), if in less technical terms. Cf. Spence, M., "Job Market Signaling," *Quarterly Journal of Economics*, August 1973, pp. 355–74.

168. The new and used car markets are far from the only examples of the contrast in our economy: "Organized commodity and security exchanges deal

in highly standardized or perfectly uniform contracts, where the intensive margin of search is effectively eliminated. One is entirely indifferent as to whether one buys a hundred shares of General Motors from a taxi company, a little old lady, or Alfred P. Sloan, though much search may enter into the decision to buy General Motors rather than some other security. Organized exchanges perform a highly effective job of widening the extensive margin of search and need to transmit only a few bits of information (the name of the contract, the quantity, and the price) to conclude a transaction. Labor markets lie as far from this pole as used car markets, and a grain exchange for labor is about as possible as a contract on the Chicago Board of Trade for 1960 Chevrolet sedans" (Rees, *op. cit.*). Rees then goes on to describe the elaborated institutions for intensive search in labor markets. All this merely demonstrates once again that, as used here, "bazaar" is an analytic notion, and indeed one that fits some of our so-called markets rather better (domestic housing is perhaps another example) than the neoclassical concept of market does. Cf. Khouri, *op. cit.*

169. Cf. Cassady, *op. cit.*: "[Inter-vendor] competition in a negotiated price market is not likely to be as sharp as that found in a one-price market . . . The main reason for this is that knowledge of competitors' prices is much more difficult to obtain, and indeed to interpret, in a market where prices for each sale are individually negotiated. Price warfare, for example, which occasionally develops out of [vigorous] price competitive efforts in a fixed price system, would be inconceivable in a negotiated price situation.

170. "Many buyers test prices (bargain) in one shop and buy their goods in another [and] this behavior is repeated so frequently . . . that shops situated at the entrance of a market [area] are considered less profitable than those situated in the center. These shops, a shopkeeper in Rabat . . . complained, are 'rich in bargaining but poor in selling'" (Khuri, *op. cit.*). Actually, outsiders often overestimate the amount of price testing that goes on, confounding it with genuine bargaining. There are other modes of extensive search in the market as well, of course – exchange of information along various sorts of seller and buyer grapevines, mere overhearing of the higgling of other suwwaqs, etc. – but their importance also can easily be overestimated. Even extensive (*sāwem*) bargaining tends to be confined to suwwaqs one at least knows, rather than conducted with strangers; true sample shopping is, in Sefrou anyway, quite rare. Indeed, asking the price of something from someone you have no acquaintance with at all may not even bring a response. If you don't know anyone in a particular trade, you usually will find someone who does to introduce you before discussing prices, etc. with him.

The terms for bargaining in Sefrou are actually interrelated along a gradient of markedness, rather than categorically, as the text may seem to suggest. The most general, unmarked, term is again merely *biʿ u šri* ("to buy and sell"). *Sāwem* is a somewhat more marked form, perhaps best glossed as "looking at prices" (*kayšuf t-tamanat*); and *tšetter* is the most marked: well-launched, "four-eyes" bargaining with intent to commit an exchange. Thus even intensive bargaining may be generally described merely as *biʿ u šri* or even (especially the opening phases) as *sāwem*; the inverse (use of the more specific terms more generally) rarely, if ever, occurs.

171. Cassady, *op. cit.*, from which the "tug- of-war" quotation also comes. Cassady goes on to complicate the model for situations of unequal vendor-buyer strength, aborted transactions where the price gap is not closed and either vendor or buyer withdraws, and so on. It must be remembered that money price bargaining is but the most straightforward example of the process, not the whole of it, and though Cassady's model represents the general form of buyer-seller interaction well enough, it does so at the usual expense of realism.
172. Normally, and especially in significant exchanges, initial bidding includes not just the very first offers, but the first several, as the buyer and seller maneuver to establish starting positions, and thus has an internal temporal structure of its own. How suwwaqs determine their initial bids is a complex and ill-understood subject involving a wide variety of factors: whether the seller has a prior price to guide him (as is usually not the case for artisans or target sellers), the social characteristics of the bargainers, the time of day, the nature of the good or service at issue, inventory sizes, the distance the buyer (or seller) has come, the depth of clientship, and so on almost *ad infinitum*. But, for all this, and for all their importance, initial offers are usually quite quickly established and the movement toward consensus promptly begun. A systematic study of this matter – a difficult and delicate enterprise – would reveal a very great deal about the structure of bazaar judgments and expectations in general.
173. For a general discussion of the relations between price and time signaling, see Spence, "Time and Communication." Cf. Khuri (*op. cit.*), who for Beirut found the average bargaining time for very expensive carpets was about 54 minutes (range 100–9); for cheaper, but still expensive carpets, 36 minutes (range 45–10); for clothes, 5 minutes (range 7–2); and for everyday foodstuffs, 40 seconds (range 3 minutes–12 seconds).
174. For an interesting distinction between "adventurous" and "nonadventurous" bargaining, depending upon whether, after having reached their seller-minimum or buyer-maximum price, exchangers tend immediately to settle or to press on beyond it to wrangle the price gap – a matter depending, *inter alia*, on the durability and homogeneity of the good (or service) at issue, amount of markup, relative economic strength of the participants, and individual variations in willingness to be perceived as hard traders, see Swetnam, *op. cit.*, some of whose other comments on bazaar price formation are less persuasive.

175. Cassady, *op. cit.* There are also many conventions for special trades and markets: the palm-to-palm hand touch to conclude a deal in the animal market, provision of eleven pieces of fruit when the bargaining has been for ten, and so on. Also conventions may differ with situations: A professional wool trader bargaining with a rural target seller is expected to bid first.
176. Khuri, *op. cit.* Again, to deny that bargaining is for fun is not to deny that proficient practitioners do not hugely enjoy it; merely that enjoyment is not the central motivation for bargaining.
177. In addition to a cost (and *because* it is a cost) time is also, of course, a signal, indicating how serious the intensive bargainer really is: "The value of time as a signal is its unavoidable cost. It is difficult to counterfeit" (Spence, "Time and Communication"). The notion that the supply elasticities of time are very high in the bazaar – that suwwaqs' willingness to bargain is a result of the fact that they are sitting around with time on their hands, or lacking wristwatches, have no sense of its value – could hardly be more wrong. A suq is not a scene of limp indolence but of high impatience.
178. Scott, M. B., *The Racing Game*, Chicago, 1968, p. 1. What follows is stimulated by and depends heavily on Scott's fascinating study, but I have added some formulations of my own and simplified a good many of his. Of these latter, the most important are that I assume the betting pool is wholly distributed to bettors (ignoring track takeout, taxes, etc.) and that there is one payoff horse, not three.
179. Formally, the difference between being ignorant and misinformed (or for that matter irrational) is trivial, because it does not matter why people bet on the wrong horse so long as they do so. Practically, however, because misinformation may be a positive stimulus to wrong bets, it is not trivial. The matter is not very different in the suq.
180. Scott, *op. cit.*, p. 4; italics original. On the concept of "strategic interaction," see Goffman, E., *Strategic Interaction*, Philadelphia, 1969.
181. This is as true for artisans as for buyer/sellers. The craftsman's ascendancy comes but marginally at best from any edge he may have in technique. The range of variation in such matters is minute in the plebian artisanry of a suq such as Sefrou's, and what there is goes largely unappreciated. (The one exception, and that partial, is rugs.) Nor does industriousness differentiate much, being uniformly high. It is in their ability to handle the commercial ties – the acquisition of materials, the disposal of products, the contracting of labor – in which their activity is set that separates the more successful artisans in any trade from the less successful.
182. For an extended discussion of this general thesis concerning the Europe and non-Europe confrontation in the late nineteenth and early twentieth centuries, but for agriculture and Indonesia, see Geertz, C., *Agricultural Involution*, Berkeley, 1963. An economic geography study based, on 1970

census materials, of Sefrou which appeared while this book was in press, and so could not be utilized, Benhalima, H., "Sefrou, de la tradition du dir à l'intégration economique – Etude de géographie urbaine," Thesis, Université Paul Valery, Montpelier, 1977, develops this point further. Cf. Chaoui, M., "Sefrou: de la tradition a 1'integration, ce quest un petit centre d'aujourd'hui," *Lamalif*, July–August, 1978, pp. 32–39.

183. Stigler, *op. cit.* Cf. Demsetz, H., "Information and Efficiency: Another Viewpoint," in Lamberton, *op. cit.*, pp. 160–86: "The view that now pervades much public policy economics implicitly presents the relevant choice as between an ideal norm and an existing 'imperfect' institutional arrangement. This *nirvana* approach differs considerably from a comparative institution approach in which the relevant choice is between alternative real institutional arrangements. In practice, those who adopt the nirvana viewpoint seek to discover discrepancies between the ideal and the real and if discrepancies are found, they deduce that the real is inefficient. Users of the comparative institution approach attempt to assess which alternative real institutional arrangement seems best able to cope with the economic problem; practitioners of this approach may use an ideal norm to provide standards from which divergences are assessed for all practical alternatives of interest and select as efficient that alternative which seems most likely to minimize the divergence." If the primary (but not, of course, the sole) "economic problem" of the bazaar is socially organized ignorance, then a comparative institution approach will judge proposed reforms in terms of the relation between their cost, broadly conceived, and their capacity to reduce it.

184. For an all-out effort in this direction with respect to a southeast Moroccan group, see Gellner, E., *The Saints of the Atlas*, London, 1969; cf., more carefully and circumstantially, Vinogradov, A. *The Ait Ndhir of Morocco*, Ann Arbor, 1974.

For a (rather strained) attempt to extend this sort of analysis to the level of the national polity, see Vinogradov, A., and J. Waterbury, "Situations of Contested Legitimacy: Morocco – An Alternative Framework," *Comparative Studies in Society and History*, 13:1 (Jan. 1971). For a fine discussion of the problem in general, see Meeker, M., *Literature and Violence in North Arabia*, Cambridge (UK), 1979.

185. See, for example, Peters, E., "Some Structural Aspects of the Feud Among the Camel-Herding Bedouin of Cyrenaica," *Africa*, 32:261–82 (1967); Hammoudi, *op. cit.*; Eickelman, *op. cit.*; Rabinow, *op. cit.*; Geertz, C., "In Search of North Africa," *New York Review of Books*, April 22, 1971, pp. 20–4; and Meeker, *op. cit.*

Annex A: The bazaar survey, 1968–9

The bazaar survey was conducted during 1968–9, in several stages, by a single investigator – the author of the present study. First a mapping of each suq area was undertaken, with the assistance of several market people, according to trade or craft, the name of the owner or manager, his nisba, and (less reliably) his place of origin and approximate length of time in Sefrou. This was done first through the agency of a knowledgeable informant overall; then separately with such an informant in each identified area and sometimes subarea. Finally the information was checked directly door to door, at least in regard to trade or craft type and nisba. Very little failure to cooperate was encountered, and in the few cases where it was a neighboring suwwaq could always be found to check the material. Finally, several responsive informants in each of the major trades were interviewed at some length, in part to recheck the survey data, but more particularly to investigate the nature and organization of the trade and various matters concerning the bazaar in general.

For all that, the methodological difficulties of this sort of work should not be underestimated: Kinship, language, political process, even art and religion, are, in a practical sense, much easier to research in a non-Western society than is the bazaar because, given the fractioning quality of the suq discussed in the text, no single person can inform you about more than a very small aspect of it.

Beyond the general difficulties, some specific limitations of the survey must be kept in mind in interpreting it:

1. It is concerned only with the owners of the stores (*mwālīn l-ḥawānut*) or the masters of the ateliers (*mᶜällemin ṣ-ṣnaīᶜ*), not with all those at

work in them, which would simply have been too great a task for a lone investigator to carry out.
2. It includes only sitting merchants or craftsmen (i.e., those with established stores or ateliers). Completely ambulant suwwaqs, those selling only in the Thursday markets, and craftsmen working out of their homes on a contract basis – masons, tile layers, prostitutes – are not included. The survey thus represents the heart of the Sefrou suq, but far from the whole of it. Certain critical sorts of suwwaqs discussed in the text (e.g., auctioneers and arbitragers) do not enter into it at all, nor do mere handymen, marginal peddlers, colporteurs, and so on.
3. The maps, although generally in proportion within themselves, are not to exact scale and are not all on the same approximate scale (the medina ones are magnified with respect to the extra-medina ones, for clarity's sake, because the medina is enormously more crowded than the new quarters). This is why the illustrations are called figures rather than maps. Nor is variation in size of establishment (of which there is, in fact, not all that much) indicated. Major institutions relative to the market, but not themselves commercial or craft enterprises (e.g., zawias, administrative offices), are indicated.
4. The results of the bazaar survey and of the census study compiled by Hildred Geertz and presented as the Appendix to the original hardcover edition of this volume are, though mutually reinforcing in their implications, incapable of direct comparison. Not only do they refer to different times (1960 vs. 1968–9), but one is a census of the whole population, the other of only the more established merchants and craftsmen within it, and different sorts of characteristics (e.g., birth place vs. nisbas, employment vs. trade type) are counted.

This presentation of the bazaar survey is organized into four tables and twenty-four figures.

Table A.1 is a general key to the symbols used in the figures to indicate physical features, regional designations, and market elements.

Table A.2 lists the Arabic terms and English glosses for the various trades found in the Sefrou market, together with the abbreviations for these terms that are used in the keys to the figures.

Table A.3 lists the nisba classes of the various owners and masters of bazaar enterprises, together with the abbreviations of these nisba classes that are used in the keys to the figures. For the purposes of the bazaar survey, the nisbas are classified into general types because actual nisbas are meaningless to anyone unfamiliar with the detailed structure of Moroccan, or anyway Sefrou, society. Personal names (three-fourths would be some variation on Mohammed, Umar, or Ali) are not given because they are not significant in the context. Only two women, both widows whose sons operated their enterprises, appeared in the bazaar survey. It is important to note that these are nisba classifications, *not* birth-place classifications.

Table A.4 lists each public bath and public oven in the Sefrou market area, together with the number of the figure that shows its location, the nisba class of the bathhouse keeper or baker, and, where relevant, a descriptive comment.

Figures A.1 through A.24 chart the establishments that make up the Sefrou market areas surveyed. The areas are divided into three main sections: the extra-medina area, the southern half (right bank) of the medina, and the northern half (left bank) of the medina. Figures A.13 and A.19 show the general layout of, respectively, the southern and northern halves of the medina. Figures A.1, A.14, and A.20 show the disposition of the areas charted in the remaining figures in the three main sections of the bazaar area.

In Figures A.2 to A.12, A.15 to A.18, and A.21 to A.24 the location of each of the establishments is indicated by an identifying number, and the accompanying key explains for each establishment the nisba class of the owner and the type of trade practiced. For example, in the legend to Figure A.21, the entry *30 SRA hrr* should be interpreted as follows: *30* indicates the number locating the shop (i.e., on the right side of the street, just inside Mkam Gate): *SRA* (Sefrou Rural Arab) indicates the owner's nisba is one connecting him to an Arabic-speaking group within the immediate area around Sefrou; *hrr* indicates this person's trade (silk merchant, *ḥarrār*).

Table A.1 *General key to symbols in figures A.1–A.24*

Major physical features	
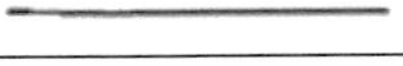	Street (*ṭriq*)
	Alley (*derb*)
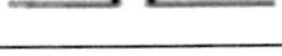	Gate (*bab*)
	City wall (*ṣoṛ*)

	Public space
	River (*wad*)
	Bridge (*qenṭra*)
Other physical features	
□	Point of interest (e.g., Semarin mosque)
	Public fountain (*seqqāya*)
○	Traffic circle
	Stairs
Regional designations	
EL MENZEL	Town or distant area
ZEMGHILA	Quarter or neighborhood (*ḥūma*)
Qisariya	Specialized market area (*sūq*)
Market elements	
1, 2, 3	Shops and ateliers (*ḥānūt*)
	Public baths (*ḥammām*)[a]
	Traditional public ovens (*ferrān*)[a]
①, ②, ③	Modern public ovens (*ferrān jdid*)[a]
Incidental market elements	
×××××	Pottery sellers
○○○○○	Sellers of chickens, eggs, etc.
	Basket sellers
□□□□□	Melon sellers
△△△△△	Sellers of secondhand items

[a] For a brief description of each public bath and public oven, see Table A.4.

Table A.2. *Trades (ḥerfa) found in Sefrou market*

Abbreviation	Approximate English gloss	Arabic term
asa	† Watchman	*ʿAssās*
ashb	† Herbalist[a]	*ʿAššāb*
art	* Small grocer[b]	*ʿAṭṭār* (see bql)
awd	* Wood seller	*ʿAuuād*
awwd	† Curer[c]	*ʿAwwūḍ*
bgr	* Cattle raiser/seller	*Mūl l-bger*
big	† Slipper maker[d]	*Blāġī* (see trf, krz)
bny	† Mason	*Bennāy*
bql	* Grocer[e]	*Beqqāl*
brd	† Saddle make[f]	*Bradʿī* (see smr)
dll	* Auctioneer	*Dellāl*
drz	† Weaver	*Derrāz*
dwa	† Pharmacist	*Mūl d-dwā*
epc	* Modern grocer	*Plserī* (*see* bql)
fkkr	† Potter	*Fekḵār*
fkr	* Charcoal seller	*Mūl l-fāḵer*
fndq	† Funduq keeper	*Fnādqī, mūl l-funduq*
fqh	† Quranic school teacher[a]	*Fqīh*
frn	† Baker	*Mūl l-ferrān, frārnī, ḵebbāz*
ful	* Bean trader	*Mūl l-fūl*
gbl	* Seller of grain-sifting screens	*Mūl l-ġorbāl*
grj	† Garage mechanic/autoparts seller	*Garājīst*
gss	† Floor layer/excavator	*Gessās*
gyt	† Horn blower	*Giyyāta*
gzr	† Butcher	*Gezzār*
hdd	† Blacksmith	*Haddād*
hdid	* Hardware/spice seller[h]	*Mūl l-ḥadīd*
hjm	† Barber/cupper[i]	*Hajjām*
hjr	† Stone cutter/quarry worker	*Hejjār, maʿden d-l-ḥjer*
hlb	* Milk seller	*Mūl l-halīb*

Abbreviation	Approximate English gloss	Arabic term
hlf	* Esparto grass seller	*Mūl l-ħelfa* (see mkn dum)
hlw	* Candy seller	*Mūl l-ḥelwa*
hml	† Porter	*Hammäl* (see zrz, hmr)
hmm	† Bathhouse keeper[j]	*Mūl l-ḥammām, ħmaīmī*
hmr	† Mule skinner	*Hammār, ḥammāl* (see zrz, hml)
hri	*Mūl l-ħerī* (see bql)	* Large wholesale retail grocer[k]
hrir	† Soup dispenser	*Mūl l-ḥarīra*
hrr	† Silk merchant/spinner	*Harrār, ħrārī*
Hut	* Fish seller	*Mūl l-ḥūt*
hwj	* Ready-made clothes seller	*Hwaijī*
jib	* Ready-made jellaba seller[l]	*Mūl j-jlāleb*
jld	* Hide seller	*Mūl j-jild*
kar	† Bus owner/driver	*Mūl l-kār*
kbz	* Bread seller[m]	*Mūl l-ḵubz*
kdr	* Vegetable/fruit seller	*Keḍḍār*
kft	† Cooked ground-meat seller	*Kefaitī* (see tyb)
khb	† Radio (and other electrical appliances) repairman	*Kahrabī*
kif	* Hashish seller	*Mūl l-kīf*
kmn	† Truck owner/driver	*Mūl l-kamiūn*
krd	* Odds-and-ends seller	*Ḵordāwi*
krz	† Shoemaker	*Ḵerrazī* (see trf, big)
Ktb	† Scribe	*Kātib*
ktb mkn	† Typing teacher, typist	*Kātib b-l-makina*
ktn	* Cloth seller	*Mūl l-kettān* (see tub)
kwf	† Modern barber	*Kwāfūr*
kyt	† Tailor[n]	*Ḵiyyāt*
kyt hwj	Tailor of ready-made Western clothes	*Ḵiyyāt ḥwaīj*
kyt jib	Tailor of cloaks (jellabas and seihams[l])	*Ḵiyyāt jlāleb*

Abbreviation	Approximate English gloss	Arabic term
kyt mkn	Sewing machine tailor	*Ḵiyyāt makina*
kyt qft	Kaftan tailor	*Ḵiyyāt qfāṭan*
kzn	Storage place[o]	*Ḵzīn*
ktn	* Cloth seller	*Mūl l-kettān* (see tub)
kwf	† Modern barber	*Kwāfūr*
kyt	† Tailor[n]	*Ḵiyyāt*
kyt hwj	Tailor of ready-made Western clothes	*Ḵiyyāt ḥwaīj*
kyt jib	Tailor of cloaks (jellabas and seihams[l])	*Ḵiyyāt jlāleb*
kyt mkn	Sewing machine tailor	*Ḵiyyāt makina*
kyt qft	Kaftan tailor	*Ḵiyyāt qfāṭan*
kzn	Storage place[o]	*Ḵzīn*
kzn suf	Wool warehouse	*Ḵzīn d-ṣ-ṣūf*
kzn zit	Olive-oil warehouse	*Ḵzīn d-z-zīt*
kzn zra	Grain warehouse	*Ḵzīn d-z-zraᶜ*
iqm	* Mint seller	*Mūl-l-liqāma*
mgn	† Watchmaker	*Mūl l-mwāgen*
mht	† Plowmaker	*Mḥārtī*
mkn dum	Mattress factory[p]	*Makina d-dūm*
mkn sbn	Soap factory	*Makina d-ṣ-ṣābun*
mkn thn	Motor-driven flour mill	*Makina d-ṭ-ṭḥīn*
mkn zit	Motor-driven olive-oil mill	*Makina d-z-zīt*
mns	† Modern carpenter, sawmill owner	*Menīsiwī*
mshrb	* Soft drink seller	*Mūl l-mešrūb*
mul khb	* Electrical supplies, appliances	*Mūl l-'ālāt l-kehrabā*
mzn	† Weigher/measurer	*Mūl l-mizān, ᶜabbār*
Nhs	* Seller of tea equipment, trays, etc.	*Mūl n-nḥās*
Njr	† Carpenter	*Nejjār*
pmp	† Gasoline station man	*Pumpīst*
Gds	† Traditional plumber	*Qwādsī*

Abbreviation	Approximate English gloss	Arabic term
qhw	† Cafe keeper	*Qeḥwājī*
qsdr	† Tinsmith	*Qṣādrī*
rha	Water-driven grain mill	*Rḥd b-l-mā*
sdf	† Button maker[a]	*Ṣedaīf*
Sfz	† Fried doughnut seller	*Šfāž* (see tyb)
shik	† Singer/musician	*Sīk̲, ġiyyāt, ṭebbāl*
shrb	* Barkeep, liquor seller	*Mūl š-šrāb*
shrt	Cord maker	*Šerrāṭ*
ska	* Tobacconist	*Ṣaka*
ski	† Bicycle seller/repairman	*Sīklist*
smr	† Horseshoer	*Semmār* (see brd)
snm	Movie house owner	*Mūl s-sinima*
suf	* Wool/hide trader	*Mūl ṣ-ṣūf*
swr	† Photographer	*Ṣuwwūr*
syg	† Goldsmith/jeweler	*Ṣiyyāġ, d̲eḥḥāb*
tbl	† Drummer	*Ṭebbāl*
tbn	* Fodder seller	*Mūl t-tbin*
thn	* Flour seller	*Mūl ṭ-ṭḥīn*
tks	† Taxi owner/driver	*Mūl ṭ-ṭāksi*
trf	† Shoemaker	*Ṭerrāf* (see big, krz)
tsbn mkn	† Machine launderer	*Teṣbln b-l-makina*
tub	* Cloth seller[j]	*Mūl t-tūb* (see ktn)
twj	* Pottery seller	*Mūl ṭ-ṭwājen*
tyb	† Prepared food seller[s]	*Ṭiyyāb*
tyr	† Western-style tailor	*Ṭaīyūr*
Utl	† Innkeeper	*Mūl l-uṭīl*
zaj	† Glazier	*Zajjāj*
zra	* Grain seller	*Mūl z-zraʿ*
zrb	* Rug seller	*Mūl z-zrābī*
zrz[t]	† Porter	*Zerzaī, ḥammāl*
zyt	* Olive oil dealer	*Ziyyāt*

* Commercial trader (*biyyāʿ/šerrāī*), see text Figure 6.

† Artisan (*ṣnayʿī*), see text Figure 6.

[a] Herbalists sell various medicinal herbs as well as diagnosing the illness for which the herbs are appropriate. They are a combination of traditional doctor and pharmacist. Nowadays, some sell various cooking spices as well, but most of the permanent market spice trade (herbalists are even more prominent in the periodic market) remains in the hands of the hardware/spice sellers. See note *h*.

[b c] *Aṭṭār*, which derives from the word "perfume," was traditionally used in Morocco for someone who sold sugar, tea, candles, soap, scent, etc., particularly wandering peddlers; now it has come to mean any very small grocer, as opposed to *beqqāl*, by now the overwhelmingly most common name for grocer.

[c] *Awwūḍ*, which comes from a root meaning "to restore," "come back," "revive," and in noun form "the normal, customary, usual state of affairs" is the most common word for a traditional curer, as opposed to a Western doctor, *ṭabīb*. In Sefrou, the most common types of curers are people who suck illness from a patient's throat and those who irritate his skin at appropriate points with burning cotton wadding.

[d] *Blaḡī* make traditional slippers, called *belḡa*, a once flourishing Jewish trade now almost wholly disappeared. Almost all shoemakers are now called *ṭerrāf*, a word that also means, in Morocco, "a faithless friend," "an untrustworthy person," and "a habitual thief."

[e] *Beqqāl* strictly means, in Morocco, "someone who sells butter, oil, or milk," but has come to be the standard term for a grocer of any sort (except greengrocer, as it means in some other parts of the Arabic world), with *ʿaṭṭār* being reserved for particularly small grocers (see note *b*) and *mūl l-herī* for particularly large ones (see note *k*), though both these are frequently merely referred to as *beqqāl* as well. For some representative inventories (not from Sefrou) of traditional grocers, see Troin, *op. cit.*, p. 150. Another form of grocer, selling only tea and sugar, called *skākrī*, and important in many places in Morocco, is apparently not found in Sefrou, where tea and sugar are sold by regular beqqals.

[f] "Saddlemaker" is a poor gloss, because these men make, not leather riding saddles but cloth pack-saddle bags for mules and donkeys. Although once separate trades, and much larger than now, saddlemakers and horse (mule) shoers have now essentially fused into a single occupation.

[g] A *fqīh* teaches young children, for a fee, to chant the Quran in a special school, called a *msid*. Not all are listed in the survey, for many of the msids are in residential areas.

[h] For reasons not wholly clear, hardware (knives, tools, nails) and cooking spices are fused into a single trade in Sefrou. Each *hadīd* has a special trade-secret mixture of seasoning spices called *rās l-ḥanut* ("head of the shop"), which Moroccans use in cooking and upon which his reputation as a spice seller mainly rests, though the actual variation in the mixtures does not seem very great.

[i] Traditional barbers in Morocco are all also cuppers (i.e., they drain blood, usually from the back of the neck, for curative purposes). Many are also circumcision experts.

[j] Most bathhouses are habus-owned (see text) and rented to the keepers.

[k] *Mūl l-herī* are large grocers (*herī* means "warehouse," "granary"). They are discussed in the text. See also note *e*.

[l] A *jellāba* is a long cloak, with a hood, worn as traditional male dress. A jellaba seller sells very cheap or secondhand cloaks only to very poor people. A man with any means at all buys the cloth from a cloth seller and has his jellaba made by a tailor specializing in their manufacture. A *selhām*, also traditional male dress, is a light satin overrobe with a hood and no sleeves.

[m] Bread sellers serve only the very poor. Almost everyone else makes the dough at home and sends it, usually via a child who carries it on a board on his or her head, to the baker to be baked. In the main the clientele of the bread sellers was, like that of the jellaba sellers (see note *l*) and the blaghi (see note *d*), the rural Berbers, unused to town facilities. But nowadays these persons too have their bread baked, and the bread-selling trade has contracted, like jellaba selling and blaghi selling, virtually to disappearance.

[n] The tailoring trade is highly subspecialized – even more than is indicated here. Yet all form a single trade in their own eyes, even if certain specialties (e.g., kaftan tailoring) are considered more prestigious than others.

[o] Almost anything may be stored in a *kzln*. Only the major sorts, connected with important trades, are indicated here.

[p] Palmetto (*düm*) and esparto grass (*ḥelfa*) are used to stuff mattresses, pillows, saddlebags, etc. The gathering of these materials, which grow wild, is a valuable income adjunct for the rural poor, and there are a couple of such factories in the countryside as well as the one in Sefrou town proper.

[q] A *ṣedaīf*, of which there are hardly any left in Sefrou and never seem to have been very many, makes and/or trades in shell, mother-of-pearl, and plastic buttons, as opposed to the thread made by silk merchants through the putting-out system (see text).

[r] *Tūb* is used mainly for sellers of traditional hand-woven fabrics, *kettān* for those of manufactured textiles, but the distinction is not clear-cut and many cloth sellers sell both.

[s] Prepared-food sellers, include sellers of soup (*ḥrīra*), fried doughnuts (*sfinž*), ground meat (*kifta*), and broiled mutton (*mešwī*), often all together. They are sharply distinguished, however, from café keepers.

[t] In Fez (see Le Tourneau, *Fès avant*, p. 385), a distinction between *zerzaī* as Berber porters and *hāmmāla* as Arab porters seems to have existed, but it does not in Sefrou. *Hāmmal* also sometimes meant a mule skinner, and so is a synonym for *ḥammār*.

General Note: A few trade abbreviations are listed but not represented in the figures because no permanent establishments of them were found, though representatives of them exist in Sefrou. They are included for the sake of completeness. For an assuredly incomplete (it totals but forty-three) list of trades in Sefrou in 1924, see Massignon, *Enquête*, Appendix III. His lists also give the following number of trades for other towns at that time: Fez, 164; Marrakech, 89; Sale, 93, Meknes, 106; Casablanca, 64; Mogador, 39; Mazagan, 23; Wezzan, 36; Taza, 10 (an impossible figure); Boujad, 18; Taroudant, 19. The method by which the data were gathered makes these figures not strictly comparable, but in rank-size terms, the high position for Sefrou among the smaller towns is probably about right.

Table A. 3 *Nisba class of owners and masters of Sefrou bazaar enterprises*

Abbreviation	Gloss and explanation	Number	Percent of total
SA	Sefrou Arabs. Nisbas indicating long-time, Arabic-speaking residence in Sefrou town (including the Qla^ca). There is a list of the more eminent of such families in the city records, and the others are relatively easily determined by questioning informants.	435	44
SRA	Sefrou rural Arabs. Nisbas indicating membership in Arabic-speaking tribes within the Sefrou Cercle. The main ones are a large confederation to the east of town, called the Beni Yazgha, and a group gathered into a large-village/small-town north of it called Bhalil. But various Arabic-speaking groups are scattered in villages, even sections of villages, all along the piedmont from Sefrou to El Menzel.	150	15
SB	Sefrou Berber speakers. Nisbas of old urban Berber-speaking (though, like all towndwelling Berber men and most women, bilingual in Arabic) families. There are very few of these, most of them descendants of the people around Qaid Umar, the Berber chief of the town ca. 1900 (see text).	14	1
SRB	Sefrou rural Berber speakers. The two main confederations in the area are the Ait Yusi and the Ait Seghoushen, but there are several minor groups as well.	102	10 .
F	Fassis. Nisbas from the city of Fez.	22	2

Abbreviation	Gloss and explanation	Number	Percent of total
UA	Urban Arabs. Nisbas of Arab speakers from other towns (except Fez). They are scattered, Marrakech, Meknes, and Taza being among the leading sources.	16	2
J	Jews. Virtually all Jews are old Sefrou families.	29	3
Ss	Sussis. Nisbas of rural Berbers from southwest Morocco.	26	3
RA	Rural Arabs. Nisbas of Arabic speakers from outside the Cercle of Sefrou. Most are from the Jebel area northwest of Fez, a fair number from the pre-Sahara (i.e., the extreme South and Southeast), and some from the Fez-Meknes plain, the Sais.	126	13
RB	Rural Berbers. Nisbas of Berber speakers (except Sussis) from outside the Cercle of Sefrou. Most are from the Rif, the mountainous area north of Fez, but some are from the Marrakech region.	52	10
E	Europeans. Almost all French, save for a couple of Spaniards.	9	1
X	Nisba unknown. These are mostly either very recent newcomers at the time of the survey or very marginal figures.	10	1
Total		991	

Table A.4. *Public ovens and public baths in Sefrou market area*

Identification	Nisba class of baker or bathhouse keeper	Description	Location
Modern oven (o)[a]			
1	Owned since 1961 by Sefrou Arab; managed for him by Spaniard; originally French-owned	Once electrified; this proved uneconomic and use of wood fuel was resumed	Fig. A.2
2	Owned by rural Arab from northwest Morocco		Fig. A.5
3	Owned since 1960 by rural Arab from south of Fez; originally Jewish-owned		Fig. A.6
Traditional ovens in medina (□)[b]			
1	Managed by Sefrou rural Arab	The original oven for the Qla^ca	Fig. A.12
2	Managed by two Sefrou Arabs from the Qla^ca	Established in 1954, after factional fight in Qla^ca, just outside walls	Fig. A.12
3	Managed cooperatively by several Sefrou Arabs	Originally built by Qaid Umar	Fig. A.13
4	Managed by Sefrou Arab		Fig. A.13
5	Managed by Sefrou rural Arab		Fig. A.13
6	Managed by Sefrou Arab	Supposedly oldest of medina ovens; referred to as Ferran l-Habus	Fig. A.19
7	Managed by Sefrou Arab		Fig. A.19
8	Managed by Sefrou rural Arab; formerly Jewish-owned, sold ca. 1960		Fig A.18

Identification	Nisba class of baker or bathhouse keeper	Description	Location
9	Heqdesh-owned, Jewish-managed	Original Jewish oven	Fig A.18
Traditional ovens in new quarters (□)[c]			
10	Owned and run by Sefrou Arab	Built ca. 1960	Fig. A.7
11	Owned and run by Sefrou Arab	Built shortly after oven number 10	Fig. A.7
12	Owned by two Sefrou Arabs (brothers); leased to Sefrou rural Arab	Built ca. 1963	Fig. A.7
13	Owned by Sefrou Arab family habus; leased to Sefrou rural Arab	Built in 1967	Fig. A.10
14	Owned by Sefrou Arab family habus; leased to family member	Built ca. 1965	Fig. A.10
15	Built and run by urban Arab from Marrakech		Fig. A.11
16	Built and run by Fassi	Built in 1968	Fig. A.11
17	Owned by Sefrou family habus; leased to family member	Despite extramural location (in the olive gardens), oven is quite old	Fig. A.8
Public baths (▲)[d]			
1	Habus-owned; leased to Sefrou Arab	Called the "lower" bath	Fig. A.19
2	Originally habus-owned; now family habus and leased to family member, a Sefrou Arab	Called the "upper" bath	Fig. A.13
3	Owned by two Sefrou Arabs; leased to Sefrou rural Arab	Built (as private [enterprise] ca. 1920 for Jews in mellah by former pasha	Fig. A.13

Identification	Nisba class of baker or bathhouse keeper	Description	Location
4	Owned by partnership of six Sefrou Arabs from Qla^ca; run by one of them	Built in 1940s to replace original Qla^ca bath, which collapsed	Fig. A.12
5	Built by Sefrou Arab; run by his son	Built ca. 1912, first building in new quarters	Fig. A.6
6	Built by habus; leased to Sefrou Arab	Built in 1968, in modern style, with separate buildings for men and women[e]	Fig. A.9

[a] These ovens – all of which date from after World War II – make both French-style long loaves and flat, round Moroccan loaves. The bakers sell the bread to modern grocers and to peddlers, who then retail it. The modern ovens buy flour, have a staff of workers, and are larger than the traditional ovens. All are privately owned.

[b] These ovens (except the formerly Jewish ones) are habus-owned and auctioned by the nadir to the bakers who run them. In addition to the nine ovens listed, two others in the medina (in Shebbak and Nas Adlun) were destroyed in the 1950 flood.

[c] These ovens are all privately owned.

[d] There were originally two baths, called "upper" and "lower," in the medina. Later, after the Protectorate, the Moroccan pasha of Sefrou built a bath in the mellah, which had not before been permitted to have one.

[e] At the other baths men and women use the same facilities at different times.

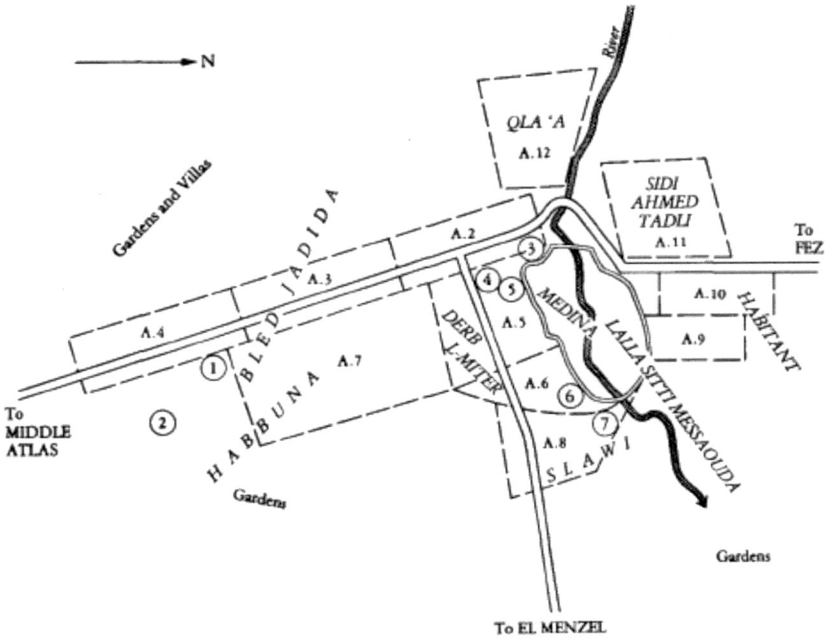

Figure A.1. Locality key to figures (A.2–A.12) charting the extramedina areas. Circled numbers indicate Thursday markets: *1*, animals; *2*, vegetables; *3*, baskets; *4*, wheat and beans; *5*, wool; 6, flea market (jutia); 7, rugs.

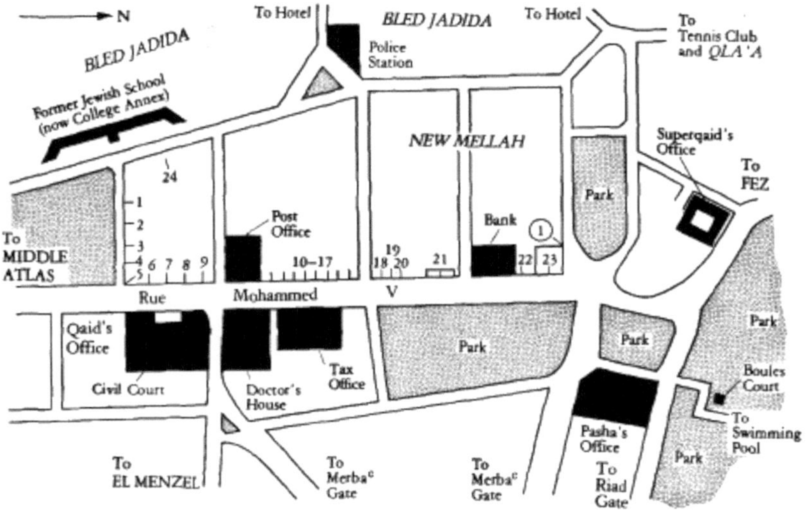

Figure A.2. Bled Jadida and Rue Mohammed V.
Key: nisba class of owner and type of trade practiced

1	SA kyt	7	SA qhw	13	J qhw (and shrb)	19	SRB hlb
2	SA tyr	8	SS epc	14	SA grj	20	E shrb
3	SA (two partners) hdid	9	SS pmp	15	SA kwf	21	SA snm
4	SA swr	10	J ska	16	J mul khb	22	E epc
5	SA bql	11	SA epc	17	SA mns	23	E utl
6	SRB qhw	12	Vacant	18	J epc	24	J shrb

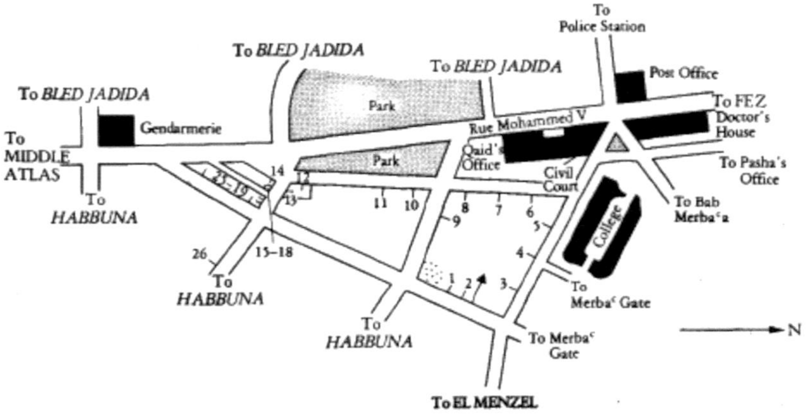

Figure A.3. New cinema area.
Key: nisba class of owner and type of trade practiced

1	SA hdid	12	SA qhw
2	RA bql	13	SA snm
3	SA grj	14	SA hlw
4	SA grj	15–18	Vacant
5	Government youth and sports bureau	19	RA bql
6	SA mns	20	SS grj
7	SRB kzn zra	21	RA fqh
8	Government transport office	22	SA grj
9	SA grj	23	SA bql
10	SA grj	24–25	Vacant
11	SA ski	26	SA grj

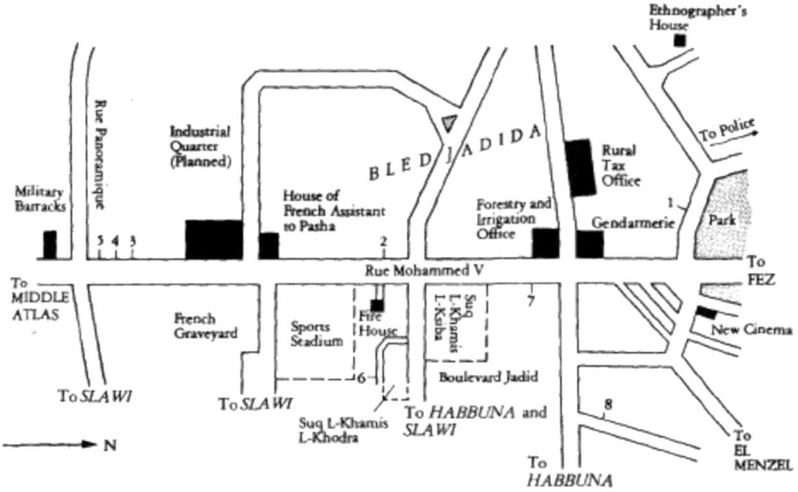

Figure A.4. Rue Mohammed V, southern end.

Key: nisba class of owner and type of trade practiced

1 SA pmp
2 SA pmp
3 SA mns
4 E mkn dum
5 J mkn zit
6 E small canning factory for olives
7 SS mkn zit
8 RA grj (also skl)

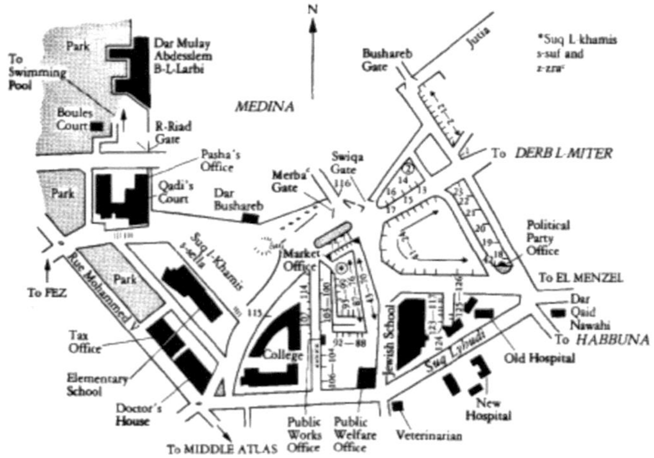

Figure A.5. Rue Mohammed V to upper Derb l-Miter.

Key: nisba class of owner and type of trade practiced

1	SA bql	41	SRA grj	84	SA zra
2	RA bql	42	RA qds	85	SA zra
3	RA bql	43–45	Vacant	86	J zra
4	SA ska	46	RA trf	87	SRB zra
5	J kyt mkn	47, 48	Vacant	88	RA zra
6	SR A kyt mkn	49	RA trf	89–92	Vacant
7	SA njr	50	SRA trf	93	SA zra
8	SA hjm	51	SRA trf	94	J zra
9	SA njr	52	Vacant	95	SA kzn zra
10	SA kyt jib	53	SRA trf	96	SRB zra
11	SA kyt mkn	54	Vacant	97	J zra
12	SA njr	55	SA trf	98	SRB zra
13	SA ktn	56	Vacant	99	RB zra
14	SA swr	57	RA trf	100	RA kdr
15	SA mns	58	SRA trf	101	SA kdr
16	E kar	59	RA trf	102	UA kmn
17	SA qhw	60	SRA hjm	103	SA khb
18	SA hdid	61	SA trf	104	RA kdr
19	SA hdid	62	J trf	105	SRA ktb
20	SA kwf	63	RB trf	106	J mns

21	SRA qhw	64	SA trf	107	SRB mkn thn	116–126 are all part of the *heqdes*, Jewish public property, and known generally as *suq l-yhudi* ("Jewish market"), which until recently (and after the Jewish exodus from the Mellah) it was.
22	SA mgn	65	SRA trf	108	SRB grj	
23	SA bql	66	SA trf	109	SRB kdr	
24	Vacant	67	RB trf	110	SRA grj	
25	J mgn	68	SA trf	111	SRB bql	
26	SRA ski	69	SRB trf	112	SA kwf	
27	SRA hwj	70	SRB qhw	113	SB dwa	
28	Vacant	71	SS ska	114	SS hri	
29	SS hri	72	SA bql	115	J pmp	
30	SS hri	73	Fhlb	116	SA kar	
31	SS kar	74	SS hri	117	RA zra	
32	RA tyb	75	J grj	118	SA drz	
33	SA kar (also kmn)	76	SA mkn thn	119	SA drz	
34	J zra	77	RB fkr	120	SA drz	
35	J kzn zra	78	SRA fkr	121	J zra	
36	J zra	79	SA mkn thn	122	SA drz	
37	SS hri	80	SA mkn thn	123	SA drz	
38	SA fkr	81	SRB mkn thn	124	RA kzn suf	
39	RA grj	82	SA mkn thn	125	J zra	
40	SA grj	83	SRB kzn zra	126	Storage place for Jewish ritual equipment:	

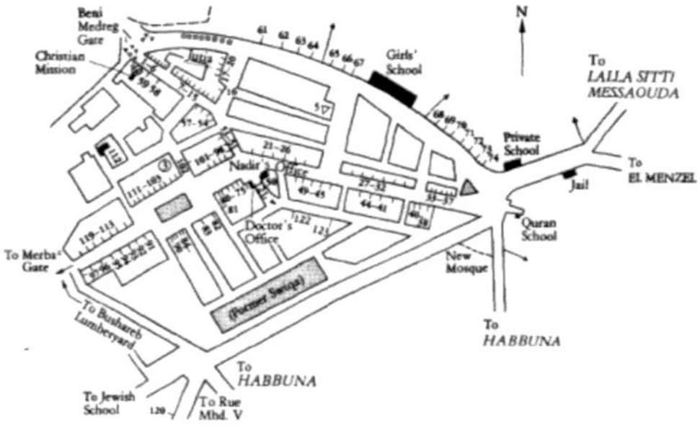

Figure A.6. Lower Derb l-Miter.

Key: nisba class of owner and type of trade practiced

1	SRA hjm	42	SA bql	83	SA qhw
2	RA khb	43	SA bql	84	SRB ktn
3	RA khb	44	RB bql	85	SA ktn
4	RA khb	45	SRB bql	86	SA ktn
5	RA ashb	46	SS zra	87	SA ktn
6	RA hjm	47	SRA bql	88	SA ktn
7	RB bql	48	SRA bql	89	STA ktn
8	Vacant	49	RA kyt	90	SA ktn
9	SA hjm	50	Office of religious properties	91	F kyt jlb
10	RA hjm	51	RA ska (habus)	92	SRA ktn
11	Vacant	52	RA bql	93	SA kzn zra
12	RA bql	53	RB bql	94	Vacant
13	Vacant	54	Vacant	95	SRA hwj
14	SA mul khb	55	SA mns	96	SA kyt jlb
15	SA hwj	56	SA hwj	97	SS hri
16	SA njr	57	RA skl	98	RA ska
17	Vacant	58	SA mns	99	SA swr
18	SA drz	59	RA ski	100	SA skl
19	SA hdid	60	SA bql	101	SA bql
20	SA hdid	61	RA krd	102	SS hri
21	Vacant	62	SA fkr	103	SA hwj
22	SA tyb (sfz)	63	SRA krd	104	J hwj
23	SRB kyt mkn	64	SA krd	105	UA kwf
24	SRA bql	65	SA fkr	106	SA ktn
25	RA bql	66	SA grj	107	SA khb

26	SRB bql	67	SA njr	108	SA kyt mkn
27	SA bql	68	SA njr	109	SRA qhw
28	RB bql	69	SRA ska	110	SA kwf
29	SRB bql	70	Vacant	111	SA kwf
30	SA kyt mkn	71	SRA bql	112	SA, SA, SA (3 partners) mns
31	UA tyb (sfz)	72	SRB bql	113	SA ktn
32	SRB hjm	73	SRA bql	114	SA hjm
33	RB bql	74	SRA bql	115	SA njr
34	SRA bql	75	SRB kwf	116	RA ktn
35	SA qhw	76	SA trf	117	Vacant
36	F tsbn mkn	77	SRA skl	118	Vacant
37	SA bql	78	RA hlb	119	J hdid
38	SA ktb mkn	79	SA mns	120	SA pmp
39	SA ktb mkn	80	SA zaj	121	SA hdid
40	UA bql	81	RA skl	122	SA njr
41	SAgzr	82	J mns	123	SRA drz

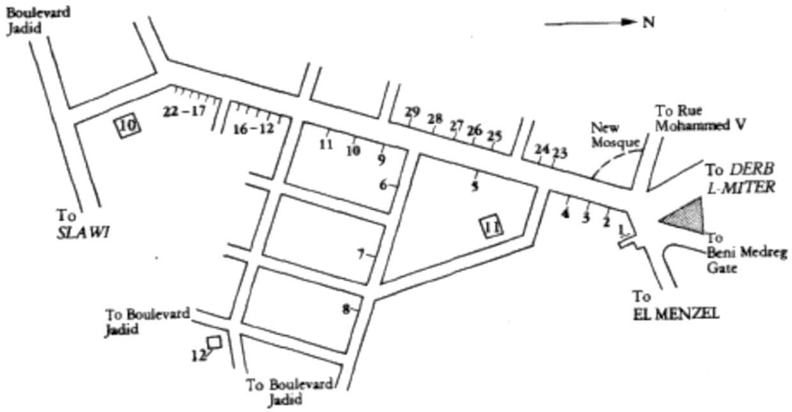

Figure A.7. Habbuna.

Key: nisba class of owner and type of trade practiced

1	SRB fqh	9	E hlb (French farm owner; his agent sells milk here)	19	RB bql
2	SRA bql	10	SRA kdr	20–22	Vacant
3	RB bql	11	Vacant	23	SA grj
4	RA bql	12	SA bql	24	SA grj
5	RB grj	13–16	Vacant	25	SRB bql
6	SRA bql	17	RB bql	26–28	Vacant
7	SA bql	18	RB bql	29	RA fqh
8	SRB tks				

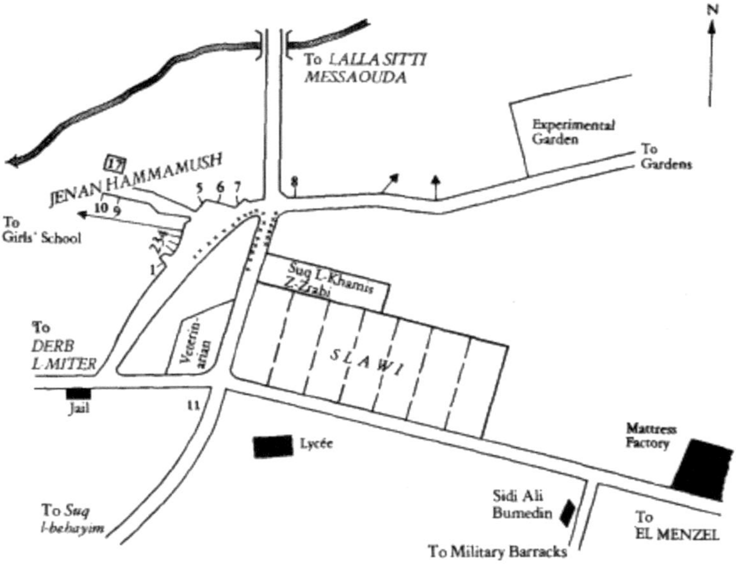

Figure A.8. Slawi.

Key: nisba class of owner and type of trade practiced

1 SA tbn
2 RB kzn zit
3 SA bgr
4 SA ska
5 RA bql
6 SRB bql
7 SA grj
8 SA grj
9 SA bql
10 SA kzn zit
11 RB pmp

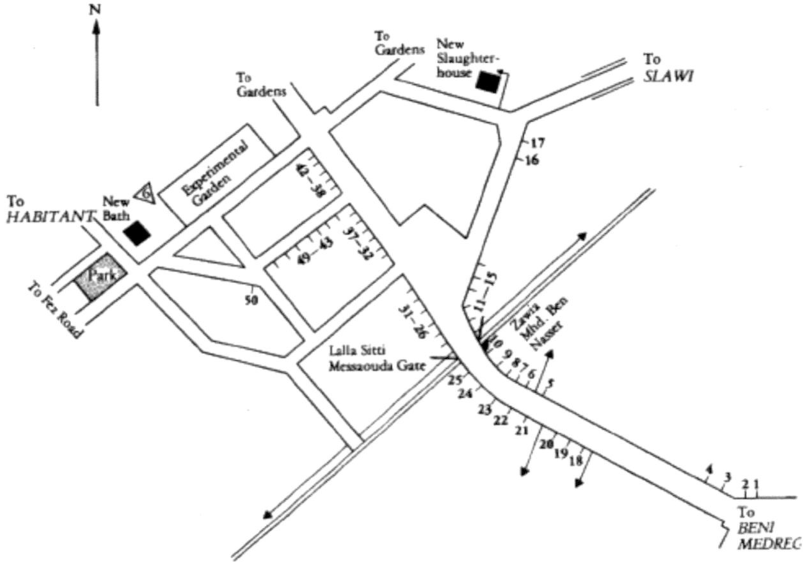

Figure A.9. Lalla Sitti Messaouda.

Key: nisba class of owner and type of trade practiced

1	SA bql	16	SRB bql	31	RA bql
2	Labor union/political party office	17	SA bql	32	SRA bql
3	Government clinic	18	SA bql	33	SS bql
4	SRA drz	19	SA bql	34	Vacant
5	SRA bql	20	SA bql	35	UA bql
6	SA drz	21	SA trf	36–40	Vacant
7	RA bql	22	RB bql	41	SB fkr
8	RA bql	23	Vacant	42	SB fkr
9	RB bql	24	SA bql	43	SA drz
10	Vacant	25	SA bql	44, 45	Vacant
11	RA tyb (sfz)	26	SA bql	46	SA drz
12	SA bql	27	SA ska	47	SA drz
13	Vacant	28	SRB bql	48	SA bql
14	Vacant	29	UA bql	49	Vacant
15	SRB grj	30	SRA bql	50	SRB att

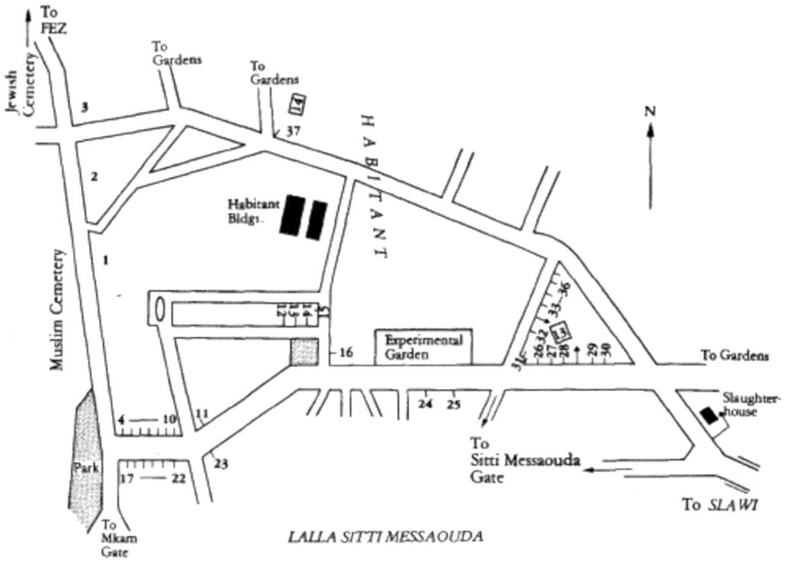

Figure A.10. Habitant.

Key: nisba class of owner and type of trade practiced

1	E utl (shrb)	12, 13	Vacant	23	SRA zra
2	SA, F, E (partners) mkn zit	14	SRB bql	24	SA fkr
3	SA pmp	15	SA bql	25	SA tbn
4	SA pmp	16	SA hmm	26	X kyt
5	Vacant	17	SB grj	27	X bql
6	SA njr	18	Vacant	28–30	Vacant
7–9	Vacant	19	RA fkr	31	SA frn
10	SRA bql	20, 21	Vacant	32	SA grj
11	SRB bql	22	SA hlb	33–36	Vacant
				37	SA frn

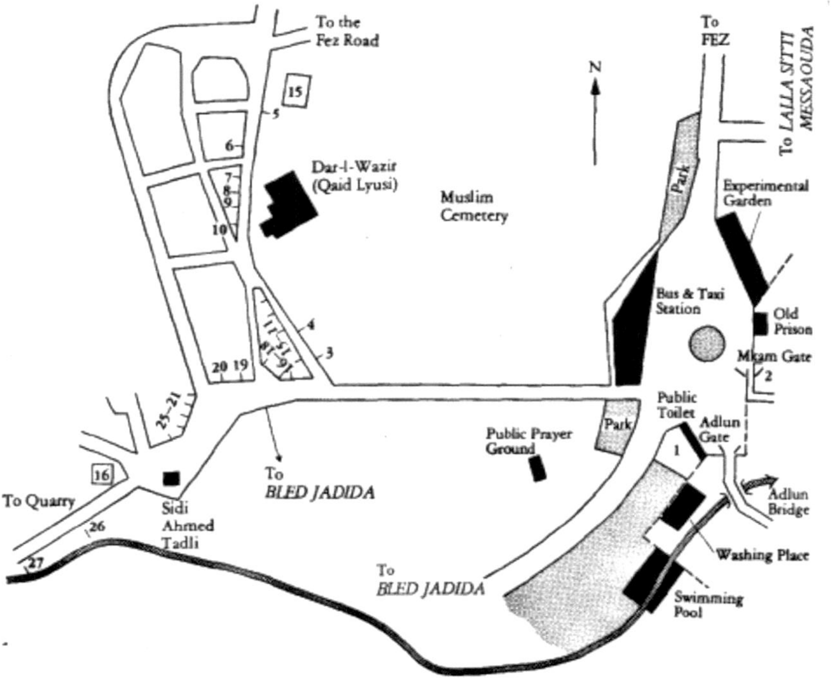

Figure A.11. Sidi Ahmed Tadli.

Key: nisba class of owner and type of trade practiced

1	SA qhw	6	SA bql	16	SA bql	21–23	Vacant
2	SRA ska	7–10	Vacant	17	RB ska	24	SA bql
3	Closed	11	SRB grj	18	SA bql	25	SA drz
4	SA bql	12	SRB grj	19	RB bql	26	SRA rha
5	SRA frn	13–15	Vacant	20	RA njr	27	SRA rha

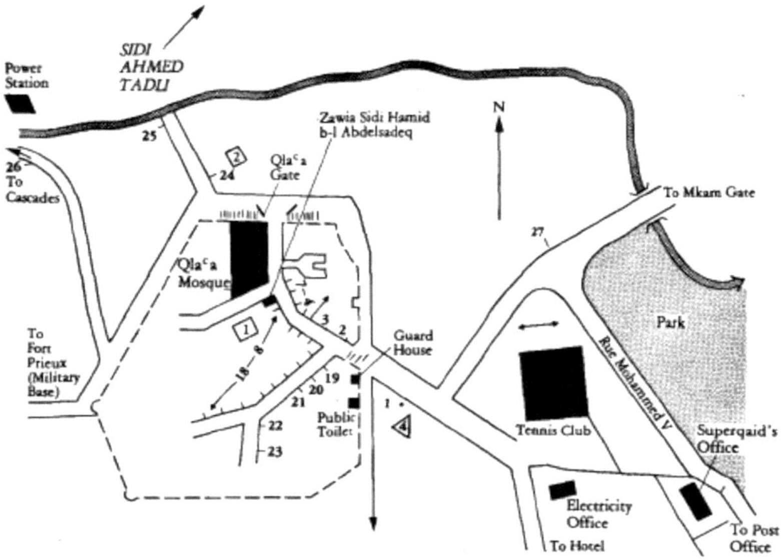

Figure A.12. L-Qlaᶜa.

Key: nisba class of owner and type of trade practiced

1	SA hmm	8	SA krd	15	SA bql	22	SA bql
2	SA bql	9	SA bql	16	SA bql	23	RA bql
3	SRA bql	10	SA bql	17	SA bql	24	SA fm
4	SRA bql	11	SA ska	18	SRA bql	25	SA rha
5	SRA bql	12	SA bql	19	SA asa	26	J utl
6	F bql	13	SA bql	20	SA bql	27	SA grj
7	Vacant	14	SA bql	21	SA bql		

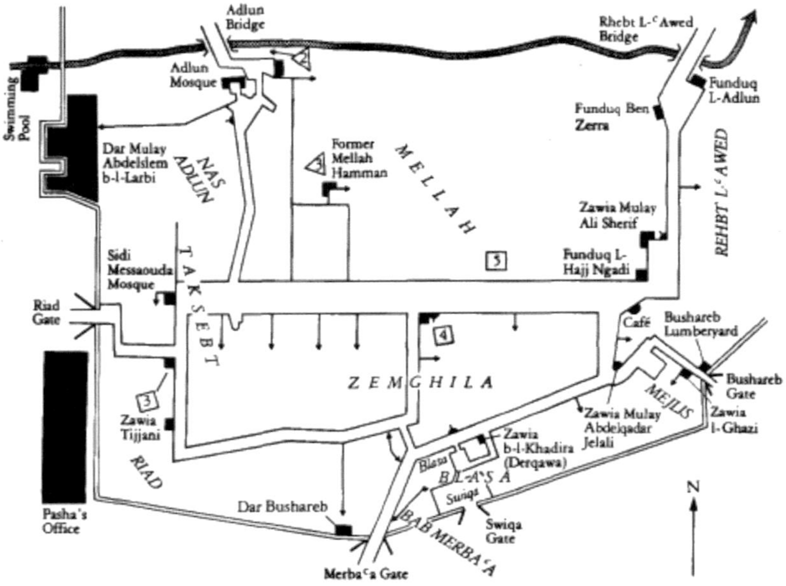

Figure A.13. General layout of southern half (right bank) of the medina.

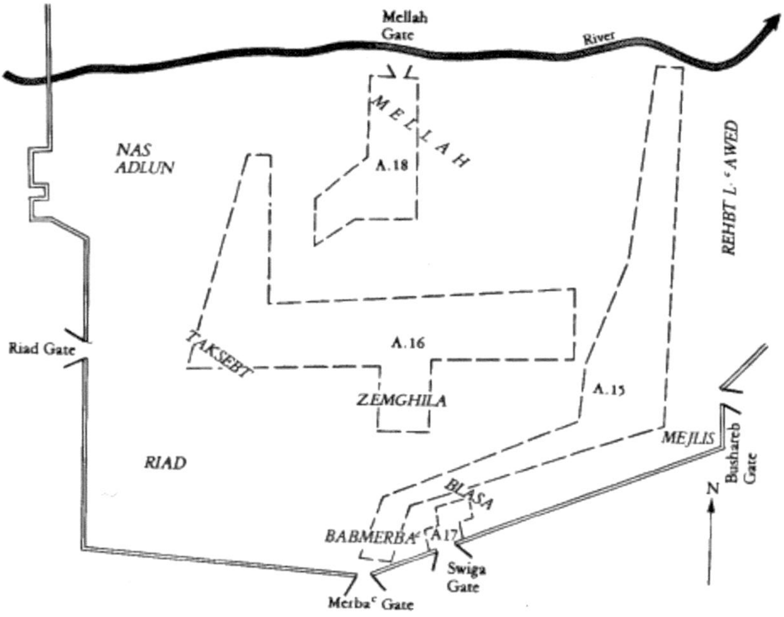

Figure A.14. Locality key to figures (A.15–A.18) charting the right bank of the medina.

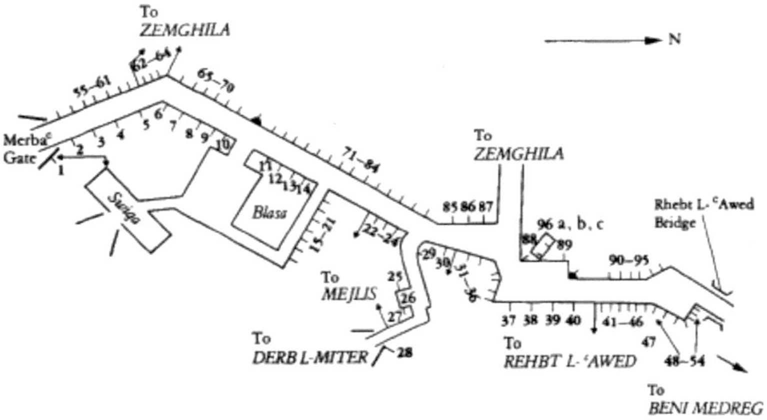

Figure A.15. Merba^{c} gate to Rehbt l-^{c}Awed bridge.

Key: nisba class of owner and type of trade practiced

1	SA tyb (kft)	34	SA mshrb	67	RB bql
2	SA qhw	35	SA, SA (partners) qhw	68	Vacant
3	SA gzr	36	F bql	69	RB bql
4	SRB bql	37	SA gzr	70	SA ska
5	SA gzr	38	Vacant	71	SA mul khb
6	RB bql	39	RA bql	72	SRB bql
7	SRB hwj	40	RB fkkr	73	SA bql
8	RB hwj	41	SS bql	74	SA bql
9	RB hwj	42	RA gzr	75	F hwj
10	RB hwj	43	SA kdr	76	SA hwj
11	SA gzr	44	SS bql	77	SS hwj
12	RA mgn	45	RA gzr	78	SS bql
13	X bql	46	SAgbl	79	RA att
14	Derqawa zawia (B-l-Khedira)	47	SA jld	80	Vacant
15	SA gzr	48	Vacant	81	SA hwj
16	SA gzr	49	SRA bql	82	SA hwj
17	X bql	50	SRA bql	83	SRA hwj
18	SA gzr	51	SA fndq	84	SRA drz
19	SA gzr	52	SA rha	85	RA att

20	RA gzr	53	X tyb (sfz)	86	J hwj
21	Vacant	54	SRB kbz	87	J hwj
22	SRA hwj	55	RB kdr	88	SA fndq (see 96a,b,c)
23	SRB hwj	56	SS ashb	89	Zawia Mulay Ali Sherif
24	SA hwj	57	SRA bql	90	RA zyt
25	RA bql	58	SA bql	91	F bql
26	SRA hwj	59	Vacant	92	SA fndq
27	SRB hjtn	60	RA bql	93	RB zyt
28	SA mns	61	SRB bql	94	SRA att
29	Mulay Abdel Qader Jillali zawia	62	SA gzr	95	SA ktb
30	SRA bql	63	SA qhw (tyb)	96	Second floor of 88
31	SA njr	64	SA bql		a. SA drz
32	SA hwj	65	SS hri		b. SA drz
33	SRA qhw	66	SA gzr		c. SA drz

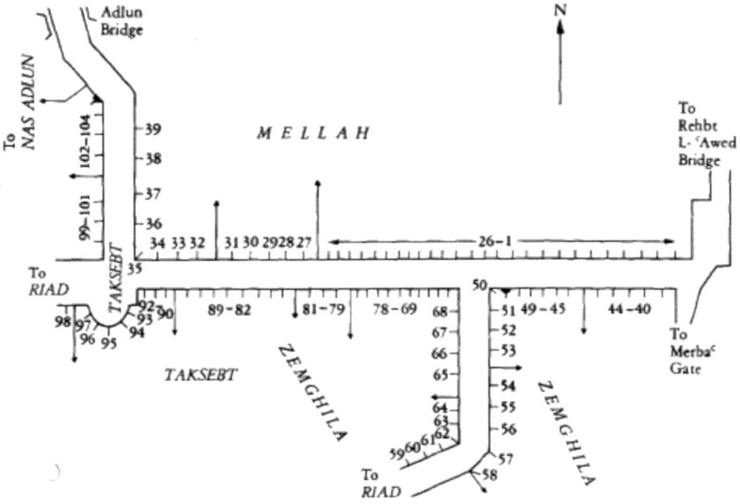

Figure A.16. Zemghila-Taksebt.
Key: nisba class of owner and type of trade practiced

1	SS bql	36	RA bql	71	SRB kyt mkn
2	J ktn	37	SRA att	72	Vacant
3	SS hwj	38	SRB att	73	SRA kyt mkn
4	SA hjm	39	SRB hrr	74	RA hjm
5	SRB hjm	40	SRA kyt qft	75	RA att
6	SRA hjm	41	RB ska	76	SA kyt jib
7	SRA kyt jib	42	UA kyt hwj	77	RA bql
8	RA bql	43	SRA kyt hwj	78	SRB kyt mkn
9	SA kyt jib	44	SA kyt hwj	79	Vacant
10	SRA frn	45	RA kyt qft	80	SRA kyt mkn
11	SRA kyt qft	46	RA kyt qft	81, 82	Vacant
12	Vacant	47	RA kyt qft	83	SA hrr
13	RA kyt mkn	48	RA kyt qft	84	SA kyt mkn
14	SRA sdf	49	Vacant	85	RA kyt mkn
15	Vacant	50	SA frn	86	Vacant
16	SRA kyt mkn	51	SA trf	87	SA hrr
17	SRA kyt mkn	52	Fblg	88	SRB bql
18	SRA kyt jib	53	SA kyt jib	89, 90	Vacant

19	SRA kyt qft	54–56	Closed	91	SA big
20	UA khb	57	SA thn	92	SA bql
21, 22	Vacant	58	RA bql	93	Vacant
23	SRB suf	59	SA bql	94	SRA kyt jib
24, 25	Vacant	60	SRA att	95	SRA bql
26	SRA hrr	61	SRB fkr	96	RA bql
27	SA kyt jib	62	SRB att	97	SRA bql
28	SA bql	63	SA bql	98	SA kyt jib
29	SA kyt jib	64	RB att	99	RA bql
30	SA kyt jib	65	SRA kyt mkn	100	SRA bql
31	SA kyt jib	66	SRA kyt mkn	101	SRB hrr
32	Ffkr	67	SA, SA (partners) kyt jib	102	SRA kyt jib
33	RA kyt jib	68	RA kyt mkn	103	SRA bql
34	Vacant	69	RA kyt mkn	104	SRA bql
35	SRB hlb	70	RA kyt mkn		

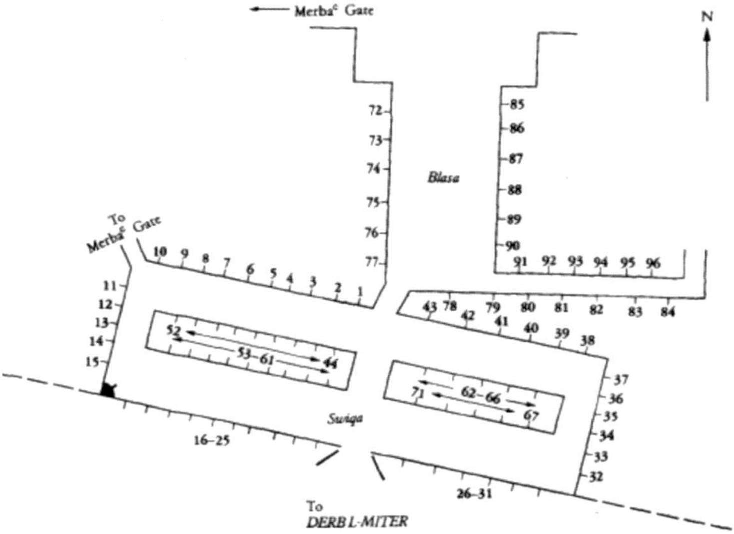

Figure A.17. Swiga and Blasa.

Key: nisba class of owner and type of trade practiced

1	SRA kdr	33	SRB kdr	64	RB kdr
2	SRB kdr	34	SRB kdr	65	SRB kdr
3	SRA kdr	35	RB kdr	66	SRA kdr
4	SA kdr	36	RA kdr	67	RA kdr
5	SRB kdr	37	SRB kdr	68	SA kdr
6	RB kdr	38	SRB kdr	69	SRB kdr
7	SRA kdr	39	RA kdr	70	RB kdr
8	RB kdr	40	SB kdr	71	RB kdr
9	UA kdr	41	SB kdr	72	SRA gzr
10	SRB kdr	42	SRA kdr	73	SA kdr
11	RB kdr	43	SRA kdr	74	SA kdr
12	SA kdr	44	SB kdr	75	SA kdr
13	SRB kdr	45	SB kdr	76	SA kdr
14	RB kdr	46	SRB kdr	77	SRA gzr
15	SRB kdr	47	SA kdr	78	SA gzr
16	RA kdr	48	SA kdr	79	SA kdr
17	SA kdr	49	SRB kdr	80	SRA Iqm
18	SRA kdr	50	SRB kdr	81	RB kdr

19	RA kdr
20	SA kdr
21	SRB kdr
22	SRA kdr
23	RA kdr
24	SA kdr
25	SRA kdr
26	SA kdr
27	SRA kdr
28	SRA kdr
29	SRB kdr
30	SA kdr
31	SRB (partner of 30) kdr
32	SRB kdr
51	SRB kdr
52	SRB kdr
53	SRB kdr
54	SRB kdr
55	RA kdr
56	RA kdr
57	SRB kdr
58	SRB kdr
59	SB kdr
60	RA kdr
61	SA kdr
62	SRB kdr
63	SRA kdr
82	SRB kdr
83	SA kdr
84	Vacant
85	SA gzr
86	SA gzr
87	SA gzr
88	SA gzr
89	SRA kdr
90	SA hut
91	SRA Iqm
92	SRA kdr
93	RB kdr
94–96	Vacant

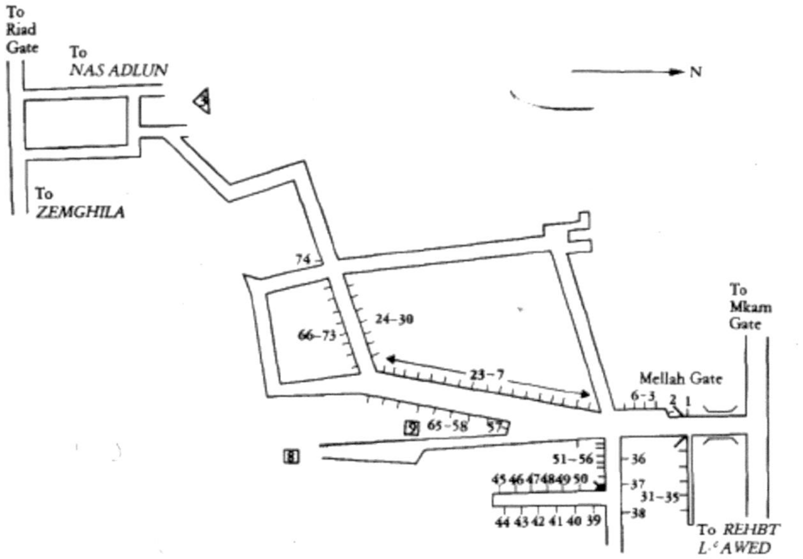

Figure A.18. Mellah.

Key: nisba class of owner and type of trade practiced

1	SA asa	28	RA zrz	50	F bql
2	V acant	29	Vacant	51	RB kdr
3	UA ska	30	J bql.	52	SRB kdr
4	SRB kdr	31	Meeting place for quarter chiefs	53	SA att
5	SRB kdr	32	RA hlf	54	SRB kdr
6	RA kdr	33	SA kyt mkn	55, 56	Vacant
7	RB att	34	Vacant	57	RA bql
8	RA kdr	35	SA hrr	58	RA fkr
9	RB att	36	RB bql	59	RA fkr
10	RB bql	37	RA fkr	60	RA fkr
11	RA ashb	38	RA bql	61,62	V acant
12	RB fkr	39	SA qsdr	63	SS big
13	RA krd	40–44	Vacant	64	Vacant
14	RA qsdr	45	SRB awd	65	RA bql
15	SA ashb	46	SRA big	66	RA bql
16, 17	Vacant	47	SRA big	67–72	Vacant
18	RA trf	48	J gzr	73	RB big
19–27	Vacant	49	RA hut	74	RA big

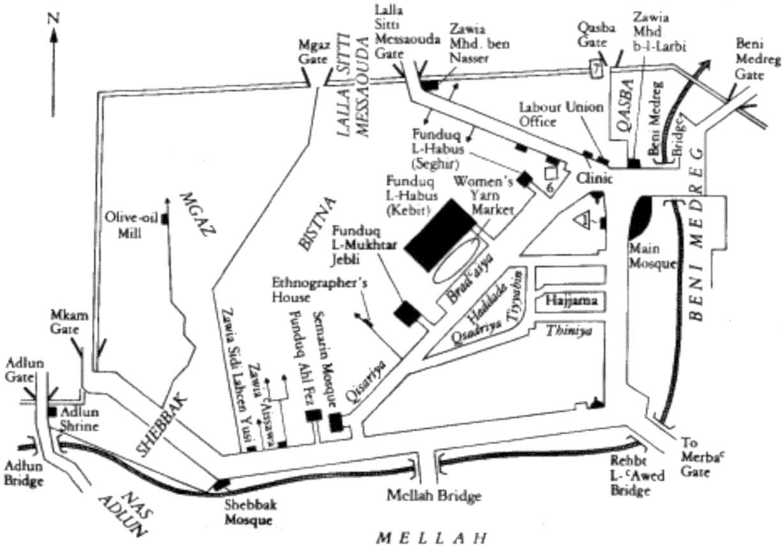

Figure A.19. General layout of northern half (left bank) of the medina.

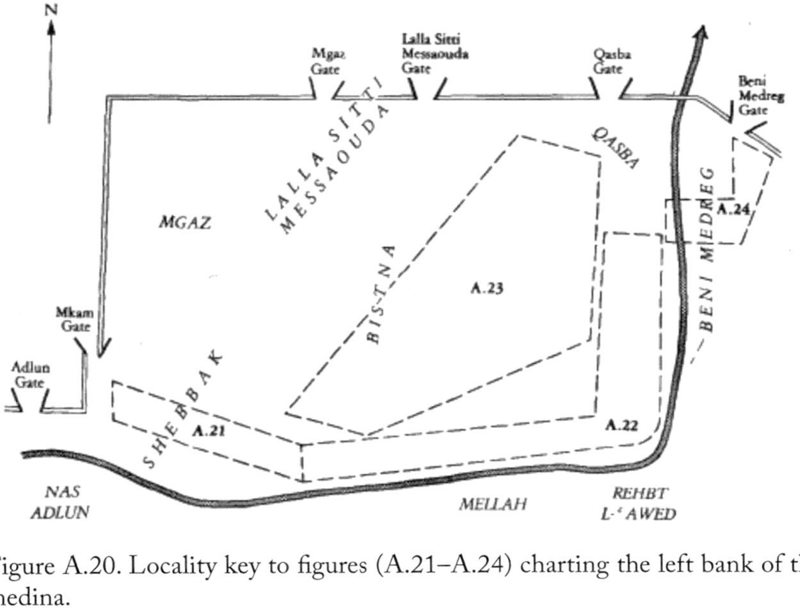

Figure A.20. Locality key to figures (A.21–A.24) charting the left bank of the medina.

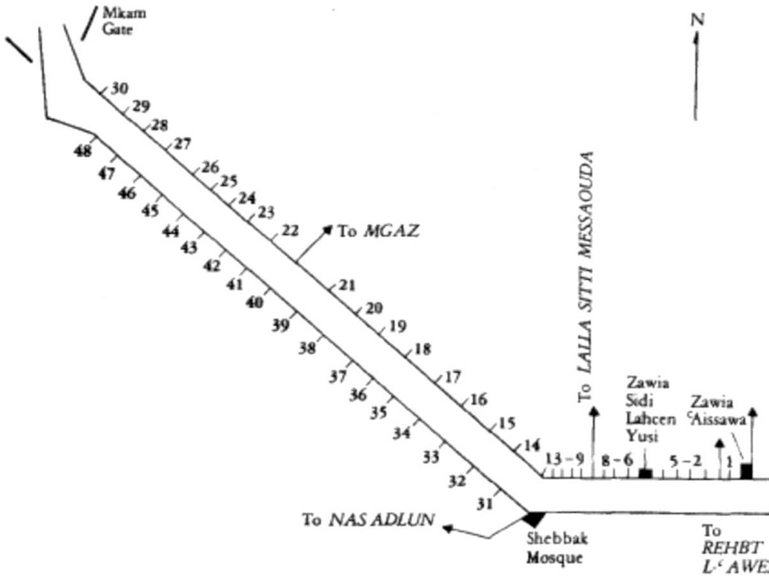

Figure A.21. Shebbak

Key: nisba class of owner and type of trade practiced

1	SA hlb	13	SA hrr	25	SRA hrr	37	SA bql
2	SRA hrr	14	RA bql	26	SA bql	38	Vacant
3	SRA hrr	15	SRA hwj	27	SRA hrr	39	SS tyb
4	SA hrr	16	SA bql	28	SA hrr	40	SA bql
5	SRB bql	17	Vacant	29	RA fkr	41	SA bql
6	SA hjm	18	SRA bql	30	SRA hrr	42	SA hjm
7	SRB bql	19	SRA qsdr	31	SB hwj	43	SA kyt jib
8	RA qhw	20	F hrr	32	SA kdr	44	SA hjm
9	SRA mul khb	21	SRA awwd	33	SA hrr	45	SRA mul khb
10	SA bql	22	SRA hrr	34	Vacant	46	SA hjm
11	RA bql	23	SA bql	35	SRB hwj	47	SRA utl
12	SA hrr	24	SA kdr	36	F bql	48	Political party office

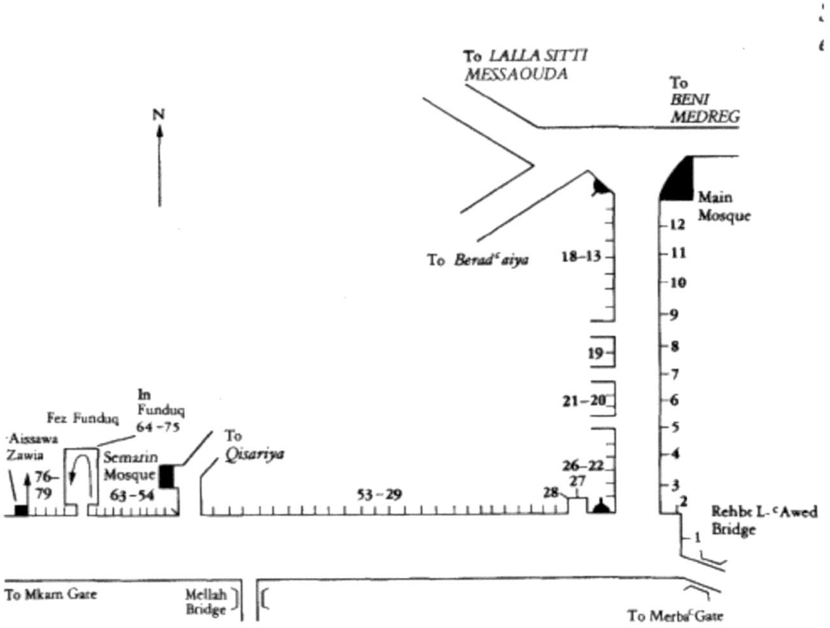

Figure A.22. Main mosque to ᶜAissawa Zaura.
Key: nisba class of owner and type of trade practiced

1	SA hdid	28	RA big	54	SA bql
2	SRA qhw	29	X tyb (sfz)	55	SRB bql
3	SA ska	30	RA hlf	56	SRB bql
4	SB kbz	31	SA hlf	57	SA bql
5	SRA kbz	32	SA hjm	58	SRA bql
6	SA kbz	33	J ktn	59	SA bql
7	SRB suf	34	SRA hwj	60	SRA bql
8	SA bql	35	SRA hwj	61	SA bql
9	SA bql	36	SRB bql	62	UA bql
10	RA bql	37	RA bql	63	SRA bql
11	F hdid	38	SA hdid	64	RA Iqm
12	SA hwj	39	SA hdid	65	SRA kyt mkn
13	SA hrr	40	RA hwj	66	SRB kyt mkn
14	RB hjm	41	SA hrr	67	SRA kyt mkn
15	SA hmm	42	SRA kyt mkn	68	Vacant
16	SA bql	43	J ktn	69	SRA hlf

17	SRA bql	44	RA ktn	70	SA thn
18	SRA hwj	45	RA ktn	71	Vacant
19	SA bql	46	RB jib	72	SRA kyt mkn
20	RB hwj	47	SA kyt	73	RA kyt mkn
21	SA bql	48	J ktn	74	SA kyt mkn
22	SA hdid	49	X ktn	75	SRA kyt mkn
23	SRA bql	50	UA ktn	76	SA bql
24	SRB kbz	51	SRA ktn	77	SA bql
25	SA kdr	52	SRA ktn	78	SA bql
26	SRA bql	53	SA ska	79	SA bql
27	SRA zrb				

Note: Establishments 64–75 are in the funduq, indicated by arrow. The funduq is owned by the heirs of its original owners; there are a dozen or more of them and they all live in Fez.

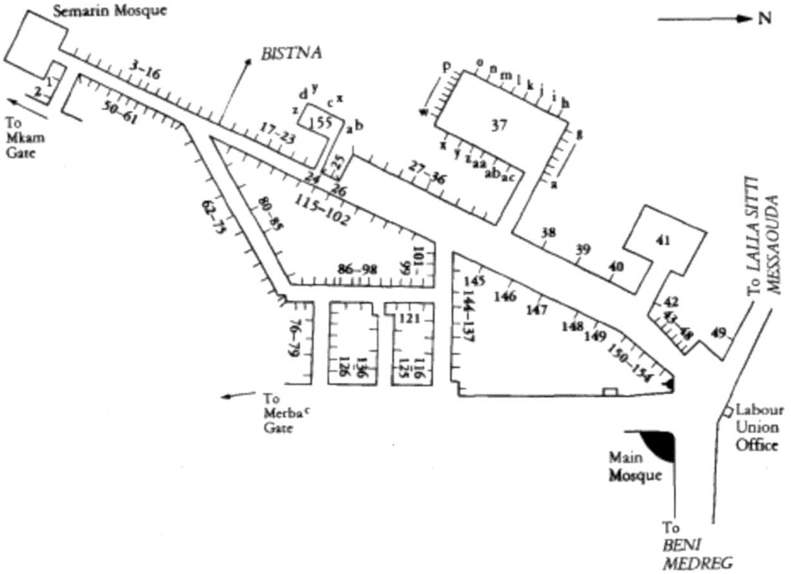

Figure A.23. Semarin mosque to main mosque area.
Key: nisba class of owner and type of trade practiced

1	SA hlb	16	J ktn	31	SA smr
2	Public washroom	17	RB kyt (also ktn)	32	SA hdd
3	Entrance area, for ablutions, to Semarin mosque	18	SA tub	33	SAbrd
4	SRA kyt mkn	19	Jsyg	34	SA smr
5	RA tub	20	Vacant	35	SA smr
6	J tub	21	SRA hjm	36	SA tyb
7	SA tub	22	F syg	37	Funduq l-habus kebir
8	SRB kyt mkn	23	SA hjm		a SA kzn
9	SA ktn	24	RA fndq		b SA kyt jib
10	RA tub	25	SA hjm		c SAkrd
11	SA tub	26	SA brd		d SRAkrd
12	RA kyt mkn	27	SA smr		e SA drz
13	SA ktn	28	SA hdd		f SA drz
14	SRB tub	29	SA smr		g Storage place for mosque equipment
15	SA tub	30	SA qhw		h SAhrr

37	i SA kyt jib	47	SA hjm	78	RA hjm
	j SA kyt jib	48	SA hjm	79	SA hjm
	k SA zrb	49	SA frn	80	SA kyt mkn
	1 SRB krd	50	RA kyt mkn	81	SA hrr
	m F hrr	51	SA kyt mkn	82	RA qsdr
	n–p Vacant	52	RA tub	83	SA qsdr
	q F krd	53	RA tub	84	SA qsdr
	r F krd	54	RA tub	85	UA qsdr
	s SAkrd	55	RB tub	86	SA kyt jib
	t SA krd	56	SRB tub	87	SA hjm
	u, v Vacant	57, 58	Vacant	88	SA hjm
	w SA big	59	RA tub	89	SA thn
	x Vacant	60	Vacant	90	SA twj
	y SA krd	61	SRB kyt mkn	91	SRB bql
	z SRB krd	62	J ktn	92	SRB hjm
	aa F zrb	63	RA kyt mkn	93	SA hjm
	ab J big	64	SRB kyt mkn	94	SA tyb
	ac SA asa	65	SA awd	95	RA tyb
38	SA brd	66	SRA kyt mkn	96	SA tyb
39	SA brd	67	SA hjm	97	SRA tyb (kft)
40	SA brd	68	SA hjm	95	RA tyb
41	SA fndq	69	SRA bql	96	SA tyb
42	Vacant	70	RA tyb (sfz)	97	SRA tyb (kft)
43	SB trf	71	UA qsdr	98	SA tbn
44	SA hrr	72	RA hjm	99	Vacant
45	SA dll	73	SA qhw	100	SA bql
46	SA hrr	74	SA qhw	101	SA hdd
39	SA brd	75	SA hrr	102	RA hdd
40	SA brd	76	SRA hjm	103	Vacant
41	SA fndq	72	RA hjm	104	SA hjm
42	Vacant	73	SA qhw	105	SA qhw
43	SB trf	74	SA qhw	106	SA smr
44	SA hrr	75	SA hrr	107	SA hdd
45	SA dll	76	SRA hjm	108	SA ghw
46	SA hrr	77	Vacant	109	SA hdd

110 SA awd
111 SA qsdr
112, 113 Vacant
114 J syg
115 SRB kyt mkn
116 SA bql
117 SA bql
118 UA bql
119 SRA tyb
120 SA bql
121 SRA tyb (kft)
122 SRA tyb (kft)
114 J syg
115 SRB kyt mkn
116 SA bql
117 SA bql
118 UA bql
119 SRA tyb
120 SA bql
121 SRA tyb (kft)
122 SRA tyb (kft)
123 SRA tyb
•124 SRA krd
125 UA awd
126 SA bql
127 SA bqlz
128 SA bql:
129, 130 Vacant
131 SA tyb (kft)
132 Vacant
133 SA tyb
134 SRA tyb
135 SA krd
136 SA nhs
137 SA bql
138 Closed
139 SS bql
140 SRA hjm
141 SS ful
142 SA tyb (kft)
143 SA tyb (kft)
144 SA tyb (sfz)
145 SA hdd
146 SA brd
147 Vacant
148 SA njr
149 SA njr
150 SA bql
151 RA qsdr
152 SS bql
153 SA bql
154 Public toilet
155 Funduq l-Mukhtar Jebli
First floor:
a SA hdd
b SA drz
c SA drz
d SA dr
Second floor
x Vacant
y SA drz
z SA drz

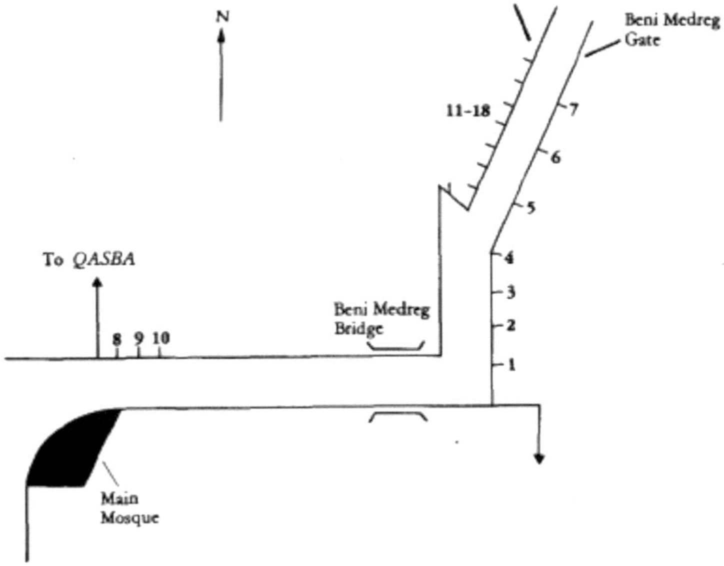

Figure A.24. Beni Medreg.

Key: nisba class of owner and type of trade practiced

1	SA krd	4	SRA mgn	7	SA hjm	10	RA att	13	SA att	16	RA kyt jlb
2	SA krd	5	SRA swr	8	SA bql	11	SA qhw	14	SA ska	17	SRB att
3	RA hlf	6	Vacant	9	RA att	12	Vacant	15	F blg	18	Vacant

Annex B: The markets of Sefrou around 1910

The market area of Sefrou was somewhat differently arranged around 1910 than at the time of the bazaar survey described in Annex A. The layout shown in Figure B.1 is based on information obtained during 1964–6 from extended interviews with aged informants. The locations of the various enterprises are, therefore, only approximate.

This is especially true of the nine olive-oil mills and thirteen flour mills stretched along the river. None of these is now in existence. In 1910 all were habus-owned and rented to private entrepreneurs. In the 1930s they began to be replaced by motor-driven mills, and the 1950 flood wiped out all that remained in operation.

In 1910 kosher butchers, grocers, shoemakers, and tinsmiths (enterprises 9, 18, and 19 on Figure B.1) were largely (in the kosher cases, exclusively) Jewish. Now (1968) both tinsmithing and shoemaking are largely Muslim, though a few Jews remain in these trades.

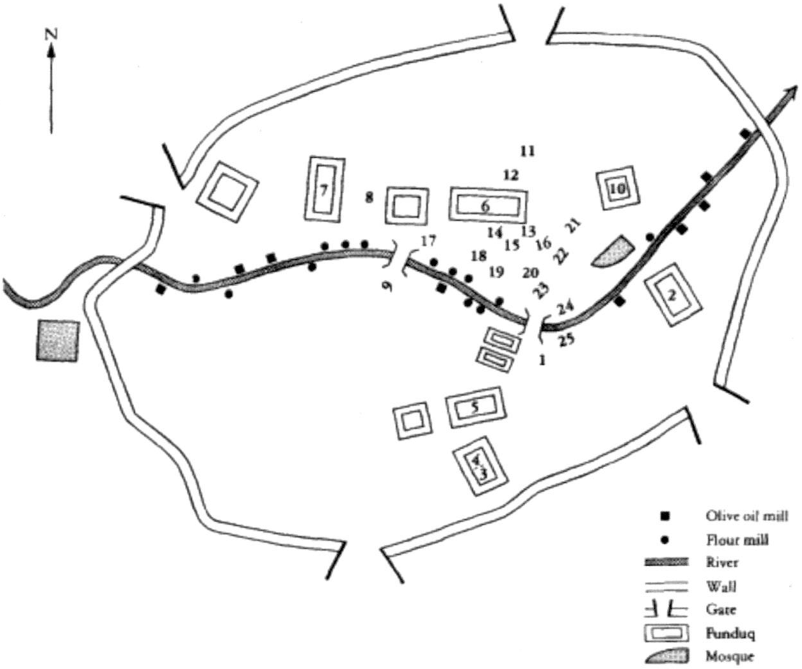

Figure B.1. Location of markets in Sefrou, ca. 1910.

1 Wood sellers, medicine sellers, rug merchants
2 Grain
3 Wool
4 Lumber
5 Hides, leather
6 Tea, sugar, spices, packaged groceries
7 Olives, olive oil
8 Vegetables, fruit
9 Kosher butchers, grocers
10 Animals: cattle, sheep, goats
11 Animals: donkeys, horses, mules
12 Hay, fodder
13 Saddlemakers
14 Horseshoers
15 Blacksmiths
16 Carpenters
17 Cloth sellers
18 Shoemakers
19 Tinsmiths
20 Cooked food
21 Barbers, cuppers
22 Bread sellers
23 Flea market
24 Butchers
25 Slaughterhouse

Annex C: The Tuesday locality-focusing market, 1967, at Aioun Senam

The market opens about seven in the morning and is largely closed by the early afternoon, a typical pattern for periodic suqs, including that of Sefrou town. It is served by a bus from Sefrou town, which can carry about thirty people with merchandise on top. Also, anywhere from one or two to ten or so trucks and autos, depending on the season, travel from the town to the market. This suq has been at its present location (see Figure 1 of text) only three years, having moved (or more accurately having been moved, under government stimulation) from another, less suitable site at Annonceur, 4 or 5 kilometers away. Rural markets frequently, indeed almost characteristically, show such minor spatial instability, changing sites to adjust to minor local changes in residence patterns, transport routes, water supply, and so on.

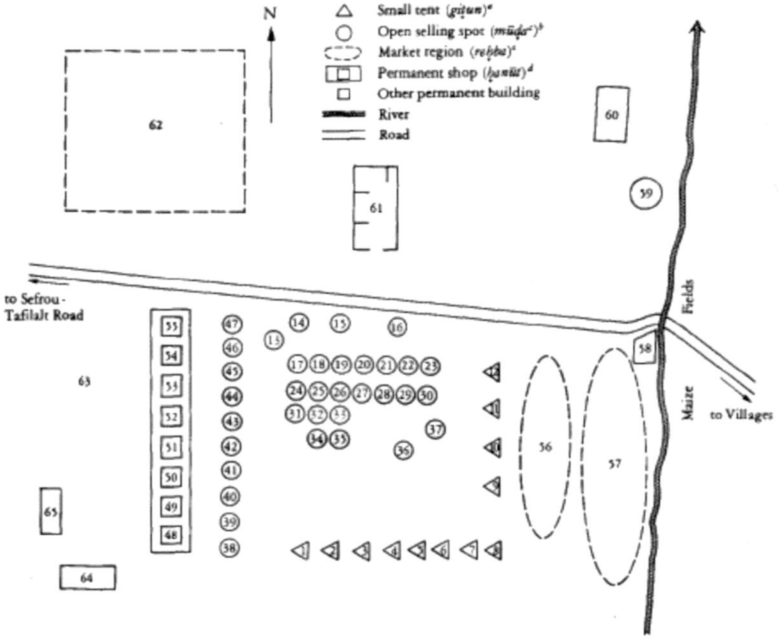

Figure C.1. The Tuesday locality-focusing market at Aioun Senam, 1967.

Key: Inside the market (*dakel ṣ-ṣūq*)

1–8	Small grocer (*beqqāl*)[a]
9	Fried fritter seller (*seffāj*)
10	Small grocer
11	Cooked-food seller (*ṭiyyāb*)
12	Small grocer
13, 14	Bread seller (*mūl l-kubz*)
15	Pottery seller (*fekkar*)
16	Olive-oil seller (*mūl z-zit*)
17–20	Fruit seller (*ğellāl*)
21–30	Vegetable seller (*keḍḍār*)
31–35	Ready-made-clothes seller (*mūl l-ḥwāyj*)
36	Salt seller (*mūi l-mleḥ*)
37	Dish seller (*mūl ṭ-ṭwājen*)
38–47	Butcher (*gezzār*)
48–51	Small grocer
52, 53	Hardware seller (*mūl l-ḥadīd*)
54	Coffee shop (*qeḥwa*)
55	Unoccupied

Outside the market (*berra min ṣ-ṣūq*)

56	Grain market (*reḥbt z-zraᶜ*)[e]
57	Animal market (*reḥbt l-beḥāyim*)[e]
58	Office of market inspector (*š-šaik ṣ-ṣūq*)[f]
59	Spring
60	Religious shrine
61	Slaughterhouse (*gūrna*)[g]
62	Corral (*ksiba*)[h]
63	Parking place for motor vehicles
64	School

The border of the market (*ṭarf ṣ-ṣūq*) 65 Commune council house

[a] These are small, lean-to type canvas tents, hardly more than 20–25 square meters.

[b] The "place" usually consists of a rug or cloth spread on the ground, plus sometimes a small table or two and various display boxes. Butchers have hanging racks and cutting blocks. The same "place" tends to be occupied by the same person each week so that quasi-property rights are acquired, at least by the more regular traders.

[c] Any specialized region of the market may be called a rehba; sometimes muda is extended to such a use: *mūḍaᶜ dyal l-gezzāra* ("place of the butchers"). When the space involved is a trading area, the word suq itself is frequently used: *ṣ-ṣuq z-zraᶜ* ("the grain market").

[d] These are built of wood and concrete, owned by the commune (as are the school, the commune meeting house, and the suq as a whole).

[e] The grain and animal markets vary extremely widely in size week to week, by season, temporary economic conditions, etc. The qaidal office in Sefrou estimates that about 3,000 sheep and 4,000 goats are sold during the year; 1,000 quintals of barley, 250 of maize, and 50 of wheat.

[f] The main function of the sheikh is to sell tickets to vendors and collect rents. (Two or three policemen sent out from the Sefrou qaidal office maintain order.) A tent location cost about 75 cents in 1966; a spot, 30 cents. To sell a goat or sheep cost 50 cents; a chicken, 10 cents; a donkey load of grain 20 cents; a mule load, 30 cents. (Animals and grain brought to market but not sold are untaxed.) The permanent stores rented for $5 a month, the ksiba corral for $100 a year. A butcher paid $1 to slaughter a sheep or goat in the slaughterhouse. These taxes go to the treasury of the communal council, but the market is generally regulated by the qaid's office in Sefrou, the local sheikh being as much his representative as the council's – given Morroccan political realities, far more so.

[g] The slaughterhouse is owned by the commune; the butchers do their own slaughtering there.

[h] Strictly, ksiba means animal market, but in the Sefrou area it is used for the place where the donkeys and mules of suq attenders are "parked," on the model of the urban funduqs, a term also sometimes used for these corrals. Occasionally a donkey or mule will be sold there, and there is a blacksmith (*ḥaddād*) in residence, but basically it is merely a pen.

Annex D: The song of the baker

Oral recitation of poetry remains a live art in the Moroccan countryside. Such recitations are given by local folk poets, who sing either their own compositions or those of others in a metallic falsetto, usually accompanied by a chorus, tambourines, and lines of male dancers. Most of the poems (for some other examples, see Geertz, C., "Art as a Cultural System," *MLN* 91:1473–99 [1976]) express popular concerns in a popular idiom, and indeed the individuals to whom they refer are often present. "The Song of the Baker," which was collected in Sefrou, depicts a criticism addressed to the amin of that trade concerning a particular baker by an aggrieved client. It exemplifies the complex of moral expectations (*ᶜurf*) surrounding an important bazaar trade, as well as the seriousness with which those expectations are taken. The translation makes no attempt to reproduce the poetic devices of the original and is quite free.

Chorus:

O God! O bakers! I come to you[1] to complain about the baker.
My bread is always treated as his enemy in his bakery.
O God! O bakers! I come to you to complain about the baker.
My bread is always treated as his enemy in his bakery.

Verses:

He said [the man who is complaining about the baker]:
    O by God, O bakers, what shall I do?
Our baker came to our quarter and swore never to serve us first.

He doesn't want our tips and he is always contrary with us.
And the dough that we have kneaded always makes him angry, la! la! la!
And I am tired of pleading with him, and I am tired of urging him to a good job.
And I give him his pay promptly every week.
And I bring him any news or gossip I hear quickly.
Yet he has sworn not to give my bread its due.

[Chorus]

And the plaintiff said: O sir! Sometimes the baker lets my bread get hard.[2]
Sometimes he puts it in too soon; sometimes he loses it.[3]
He doesn't put the cloth[4] back on the bread; anything that comes near him he takes.
I try to be patient with him so that he will deign to look for my bread tray.
May God bring some relief from this faithless one, this man of little religion.
He has even lost our covering cloth and he makes us go without our dinner.
Our bread is cooked too fast and it becomes hard and is black with smoke.
And yet my sugar is never absent from his bakery.[5]

[Chorus]

And the plaintiff said: O we have had a birth feast.[6]
A new little baby was born.
And the women of the family decided to have a small party.
They have made a few little butter cookies and almond crescents.
I took the cookies to the baker myself.[7]
So that, God willing, he would see my face and do me a kindness.
And the baker said to me: O kinsman, take care of me on the holiday.
Give me my share of the dry meat, and bring me my share of the eve-of-Ramadhan gifts.[8]

[Chorus]

And prepare for me the soup of Ramadhan.[9]

And if you bring cookies to be baked bring the money for them too.
The plaintiff said: O sirs! We made cookies on the day of the end of the fast.
My mother's sister made them and my neighbor counted them
And I took them to the baker myself.
In hopes that when he saw my face he would do me a kindness
That he would bake them carefully in the best part of the oven
And they would come out with the right texture.

[Chorus]

And that he would put them into the oven gently
And that all my household would be happy
And that the baker would be our friend by heart and by completeness.[10]
But despite all that we still quarreled in his bakery.
The plaintiff said: O sirs! We made cookies on the Day of the Sacrifice.
My mother's sister made them, and my neighbor counted them.
And Marjana [a young girl of the house] took them to the baker's oven
And she found the baker annoyed and troubled, la! la! la!

[Chorus]

The baker's mind was empty due to hashish
And he was confused by the cookies and lost track of them.
She [Marjana] told the baker: "I am in a hurry, do it quickly for us."
Upon hearing this the baker chased her from the bakery and swore after her, the bad and irreligious man.
The plaintiff said: O sirs! I say only good things about bakers.[11]
There are capable ones among them
There are brave and noble men
Bakers do good on the earth.

[Chorus]

And their profession is a good one.
In all respects its dignity is great, la! la! la!
And I am ashamed to speak badly of one of them.
Some of them I keep company with as a friend.[12]

Notes

1. The amin of the bakers.
2. If the baker doesn't let the bread sit for a certain amount of time before putting it in the oven, so that it has a chance to rise, it becomes hard upon baking.
3. That is, he gives it to someone else out of carelessness.
4. A piece of toweling or tablecloth covers the bread when it is brought to the oven. If it is left off afterward, the soot of the oven and other dirt will collect on the finished loaf.
5. Usually people give a gift of sugar to the baker as a gesture of goodwill and so that he will cook their bread well.
6. *Sbu'*, a naming celebration held by the family on the seventh day after the birth of a child.
7. That is, he didn't just send a small girl from the family, as people normally do, but went himself so as to shame the baker into doing a good job.
8. Meat salted and dried during the fast month (Ramadhan, *Ramdan*) is distributed to various people – friends, neighbors, clients – on the holiday ending that month. Immediately preceding the fast month other gifts – wheat and so on-are similarly distributed.
9. During Ramadhan the fast is broken in the evening by sipping a soup called *hrira*.
10. That is, he would complete the family; the family would not be complete without him. This is a reference to the fact that the baker's activity, like the bathhouse keeper's, is ideally viewed as part of domestic life, and thus he is, so to speak, an honorary family member.
11. That is, about bakers in general. He doesn't slander the whole profession, just this one member.
12. This "some of my best friends are bakers" plaint ends the body of the poem. Several versus follow praising poets and their ability to put men in the balance and judge between them. The poet protests that he has told the story of the errant baker only so that other bakers will act differently and not in order to slander the trade. He also calls on the bakers to give gifts to the poets and to honor the sultan.

Annex E: The integrated Thursday market, 1976

Beginning in the mid-1970s the Moroccan government began construction of a marketplace for all the Thursday markets, previously scattered at various points in the new quarters of the town. By 1976 this market, though still unfinished was in full operation, and the scattered marketplaces had all been absorbed into it. The grain mills remained in the old grain market, but housing for them was in process of construction at the new site.

The new market is located at the extreme southern edge of town and thus is even more clearly separated from the permanent medina market, about 1.5 kilometers to the north, than were the earlier scattered markets. The new market consists of a large walled area divided into three main sections: a general market and two animal markets, one of which is not yet in operation. Hanuts are being constructed in the general market, but are not yet occupied. A covered market area in the central part of the general market is also as yet incomplete, though the space is filled with traders.

The construction of the integrated market completes the differentiation of the periodic market from the permanent market traced in the text. This differentiation has occurred in three main stages:

1. Around 1900–25: both periodic and permanent markets inside the medina with only partial separation of the two (see Annex B).
2. Around 1925–75: movement of the periodic elements to various sites immediately outside the walls of the medina, the animal market (ca. 1935) and the vegetable market (1970) eventually moving to more peripheral locations southward (see Annex A).

3. 1975–present: concentration of the periodic markets at a single site at the extreme southern edge of town.

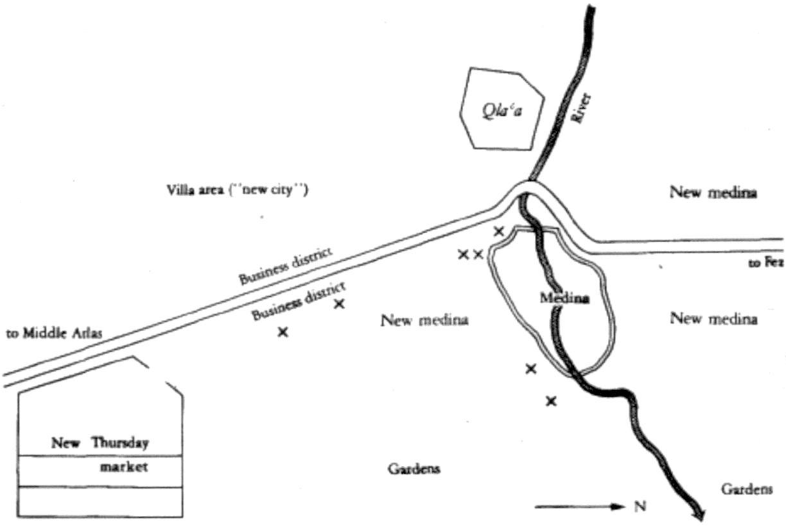

Figure E.1. Location of new (1976) integrated periodic market (*suq l-k̲emīs*). *X*, former scattered market locations.

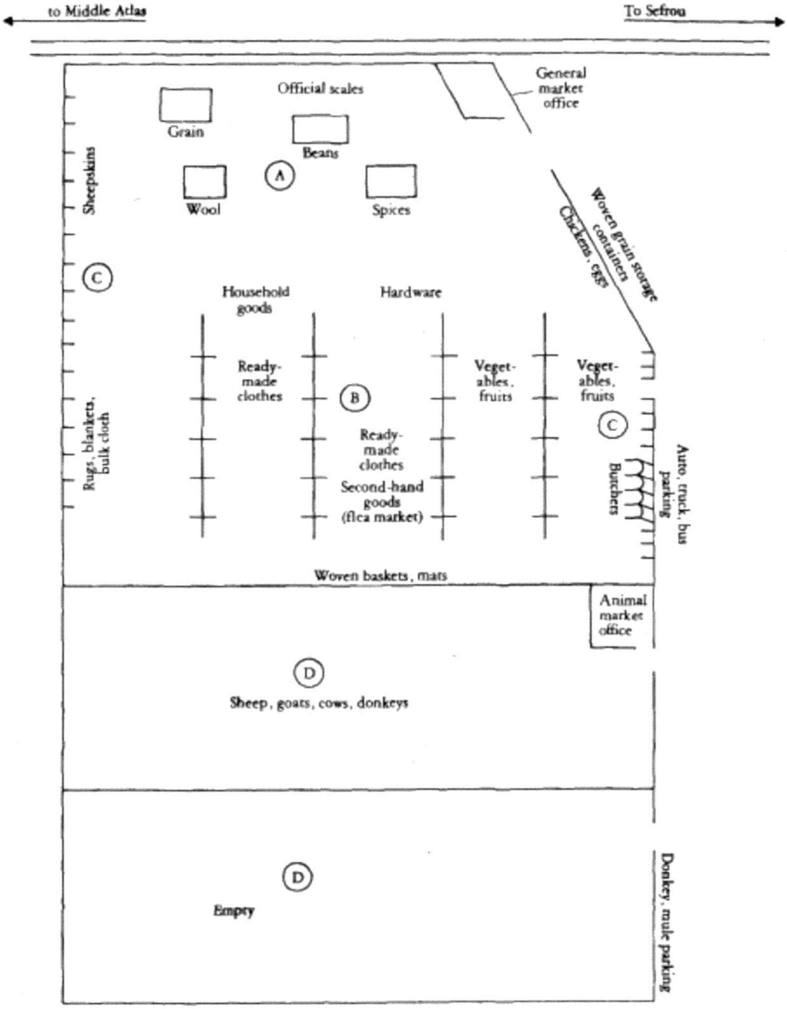

Figure E.2. Layout of integrated Thursday market (*sūq l-ḵemīs*). *A*, open plaza with low concrete platforms for grain, beans, etc. Housing for mills is in process of construction. *B*, covered market (incomplete). *C*, shops (incomplete and unoccupied). *D*, animal markets (only one as yet operative).

Index*

* Adapted from the index for *Meaning and Order in Moroccan Society.*